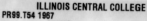

ESSAYS
IN
CRITICISM AND RESEARCH

ESSAYS
IN
CRITICISM AND RESEARCH

by

GEOFFREY TILLOTSON

He falls to such perusal of my face
As a' woud draw it.

WITH A NEW PREFACE BY THE AUTHOR

ARCHON BOOKS
1967

FIRST PUBLISHED 1942
CAMBRIDGE UNIVERSITY PRESS

REPRINTED 1967 WITH PERMISSION

LIBRARY OF CONGRESS CATALOG CARD NUMBER: 67–11476
PRINTED IN THE UNITED STATES OF AMERICA

To K.

Where the heart lies, let the brain lie also.

Verdigris bites the fiery loins of feudal lions
Brazen in blazon on manor gates and tombs: on raven
Gloss of goddesses in devoted gardens pigeons
Settle, on the metal dribble and stipple the stains.

The living defraud the dead of their dear-bought honour insured:
Limber bones kick, quick finger-bones knit, grey jaw-bones spit
On top of the bones unknit, whose individual tablets
Are ranged like folded chairs against the secular wall.

Bones, never vivid as blood, longer resist the sucking
Of mould and worms; but poets' words, their written breath,
Fix faster than chalk of bones, their lips of ink intact,
And look, to a lover's eye, the dew of the breath still blooms.

PREFACE TO THE 1967 EDITION

THE opportunity afforded by the reprinting of my book enables me to make an apology which I can make less self-consciously now than I could have in 1941. The essays in it were brought together, revised and prefaced during the evenings when London was being bombed round and about me. The book was prepared, as it were, half-posthumously! I really thought it might serve as an epitaph—a pretty one, because it was to be the last book printed by the Cambridge University Press before the dingy wartime restrictions of paper and lay-out came into force. That is the reason I put so many different sorts of things into it.

The review of it that interested me most was the long one in the *Times Literary Supplement.* The reviewer found the unity of most of its items to consist in my concern with time and its changes. He prompted me to see that since the age at which I first became aware that things have more than a present to them I have been interested not only in my own natural response to them, but also in the modification of it by my sense of the date of what I am responding to. Plainly everybody responds to things for themselves (though they do not always allow themselves to respond to *literary* things without anxiously consulting the response of others!). But it is equally plain that many people take what offers without seeing that as often as not it is old. Certainly many critics of past literature ignore its age. And so, to my way of thinking, they do not see it as its author left it. What they see is a thing made once by a human being and then re-made by the accident of its having survived. For me, therefore, what they say about it will have interest only when it is said about things in it that have survived without change. But having written that last phrase I see that no surviving piece of writing can have survived without having been changed wholly, more or less and except for the purport of words like 'the' and 'is . With that exception the sense borne by all its words cannot but have undergone some degree of modification, for at the least they will have come to denote something that is not now rated just as it was at the time of writing. When Hamlet says 'The rest is silence,' he is saying something which if it meant only that the remainder could not be spoken would mean it still, though it would be weighted for any reader by the personage who spoke it, and for any present-day reader by that personage can now be fully and fairly understood only as we enter into Shakespeare's view of him, which was that of a man alive four hundred years ago. If those words also mean, as I think they must do*, that 'The rest in music is a duration of silence', then to receive that second meaning as Shakespeare meant us to, we should have to recover the Elizabethan sophistication that saw puns as delightful. Again, when Keats wrote: 'A thing of beauty is a joy for ever', it meant in 1817 even more than it means now, for in the early nineteenth century some poets were tending to turn away from men, the topic most valued by their eighteenth-century predecessors. There is no defiance in that line for us because we have had 150 years in which to benefit from the discovery that Keats expressed in it. But there was a defiance in it originally, which is now lost. The words used by Keats may still be defined by our present-day dictionaries as they were defined for Keats, but the aura they had for him is now discernible only by the scholar.

In writing this I am aware that I shall be surprising some of my readers, as I tried to surprise the first readers of my book. There are even fewer signs now than there were then that the growth of the historical sense is recognised as being what the English Departments of our universities exist first of all to encourage. And yet without its acquisition the critic, I maintain, never sees the work he thinks he is criticising. Perhaps when he finds Robert

*Shakespeare made Hamlet the most intellectual and university-sophisticated of all his personages.

Preface to the 1967 Edition

Harrison, the Elizabethan translator of Lavater's book on spirits, telling us that

> Authors write that Lions are not feared with
> any bugs: for they are full of stomache and
> deuiode of feare;

and when he finds Sir Christopher Wren describing St. Paul's as 'very awful and artificial', he may guess that the one-volume dictionary on his shelves will give definitions that do not help. But any less startling change in the meaning (including the 'colour') of words he will not recognise as having happened. Let him keep off, I say, what he lacks the means of seeing truly.

The moral—to use the good old word—of my work, in this book and others, is that all students of literature (as of all writings whatever) should discover as far as they can what the words of any written thing meant to its writer and its first readers. In proportion as that is achieved they will gain mental possession of the piece and so have a sound basis for criticising it. When we increase our historical knowledge many literary problems disappear. But in any event the critic who is armed with the necessary knowledge will be able to show us all his brilliance, knowing it is not irrelevant.

Since the first publication of my book some of its items (with some verbal revision) have appeared in anthologies or have been reprinted in company with other writings of mine.

On the present occasion a few misprints call for correction:
p. xx, 1.17: *for* Lady Anne Winchelsea *read* Lady Winchelsea
p. xx, 11.24, 29 and 34 (and p. xxi, 1.1): *for* Lady Anne *read* Lady Winchelsea
p. xxv, 1.27: *for* seeing *read* see

G. T.

London, June, 1966

CONTENTS

PREFACE

THE essays here collected divide themselves into several categories: I intend to describe what the essays in one or two of these categories are attempting.

I

Certain essays are engaged in attacking received opinions on literary figures and periods, in attacking opinions received as true by the textbooks and by the incurious generally. Such attacks are usually made by fanatics,[1] whose propaganda is considered to demand of its readers too sweeping a conversion: textbooks and general opinion do not get an author as wrong as all that. What has been needed most, however, at certain points on the curve of a literary reputation, is not a wise and final statement but rather a horn blown in an unexpected key. Only such a blast will shiver the smug Doric pillars between which so many earnest students plod in and out of the airless sanctuary. The essay on Bacon and the former essay on Pope attempt to shake the uprights of dull estimates. As final summaries of Bacon and Pope they are inadequate. But it is hoped that they let a fresher air into the temple.

In some essays I have attempted to be more comprehensive.

II

There are other things, too, which some of these essays are attempting. They are attempting to see the full value of the material manifestation of literature, its embodiment in words. They are written on the assumption that the face of literature is also its spirit. To study the configurations of the flesh is, I claim,

---

1 Mr Hugh de Sélincourt in the 'Sunday Times' referred to the anonymous author of the essay on Pope (pp. 86–98 below) as 'one enthusiast', and Mr G. W. Stonier, reviewing my book on Pope in the 'New Statesman and Nation', headed his remarks 'A Panegyric on Pope'.

Preface

to study the very 'message' of the work. Elizabethan decoration is no accident in the literature of the time; it is the tell-tale finger-print, individually whorled and sharp, left by an age voluble and also pedantically precise. The controlled variety of Pope's couplets is evidence of a moral control: Lytton Strachey, neglecting all Pope's direct moral and satiric statement, went so far as to say that Pope's criticism of life *was* the heroic couplet. And 'the reasons why the eighteenth-century poets use [poetic] diction share in the central reasons why they write poetry at all'.

If the face of the work is also its spirit, that face will be worth considering intently. It has not always been a printed page, of course. An English author before Caxton worked towards manu-script publication or towards publication through recital. Chaucer, for example, never forgot his public of listeners, and the empty tags which have often been remarked in his lines—*parde* and *ywis* and so on—are seen as polite graces when we remember this.[1] Moreover, dramatists and writers of songs and sermons have written first, and sometimes (as they thought) last, for the ears of a crowd or circle, and for a publisher or publishers whose par-ticular tones and gestures they could count on. The authentic face of such works is difficult indeed for a historian to get at, and the task need not, fortunately, be attempted here, since most of the authors treated of in the present book wrote in the hope or the expectation of print, accepting and probably welcoming the printer's metamorphosis into ship-shape. So far as they were concerned, the face of the work was the printed page and it is what exists there, in statement, in symbol, or between the lines, that will claim our attention as sacrosanct. But sacrosanct for what it originally was: not for what it may accidentally have become by the time that it is our turn to examine it. What is sacrosanct is not the appearance of the work at any point on its curve of fame, but the work as it lay complete before that curve began its rise, the work as it lay complete under the sabbath eye of its author. It is his look, his eyeful, that we must try to share, a

1 Contrast William Morris, pp. 142-3 below.

Preface

look which perhaps faded quickly for the author as he turned aside to other work, but which was his once and superlatively (I am assuming that the poem is a good one, that the author resting saw that his work was good). The only means of our getting near to sharing his look is by centring on the poem a historical and critical clairvoyance, a clairvoyance which, being partly historical, is possible only for the scholar, but which not all scholars have been able to apply. Those who have lacked its aid have not always wanted to possess it: the literature of the past provides so much of interest that a variety of pensioners have always been found doing themselves well on its margins; happy as beetles, they examine the fascinating corpse of literature; like bibliographers, they show no preference for a good book over a bad so long as a book is old. But he who seeks to be a critic of past literature must start with a sympathy towards literature as literature. He must start with it, or, since youth is an arrow rather than a net, he must start with a capacity to acquire it. He must like literature, or come to like it, in whatever form, new or old, classic or vulgar, it is embodied. If these are necessary qualifications for a critic, it follows that it is by accident that Milton is for him an old author living in a different century, writing an English which is as foreign as Cockney is to a boy from Ickornshaw. The critic of Milton who will be worthy of his hire will have been drawn to the poet, not drawn to the seventeenth-century figure, nor even to the seventeenth-century poet. He will lack the true critical salt if he could not as readily have chosen to write on Auden. But having said that, I can go on to say more. A critic of Auden needs nothing but his critical sense, since the contemporary world is common environment for both subject and student: the history in the poems, their twentieth-century content, exists concurrently in the consciousness of the student. But the history in Milton's poems has to be learned from scratch before criticism can begin, or before it can begin with authority. The student who has acquired the historical knowledge but has nothing else to show is, of course, no critic: we call him a scholar.

But if the scholar has acquired the historical knowledge in the hopes of finding the whole poet in Milton, then there is a chance that he will become a critic of Milton's poetry. Mark Pattison's belief that an appreciation of Milton was the last reward of consummated scholarship sets a high standard on the historical side. And though Pattison knew much, he did not know as well as we how numerous are the elements which go to make up that scholarship. When the scholar arises who fulfils our amplified condition and who is also critic to match, we shall have, at last, the adequate interpreter of Milton. He will be Milton's best critic whose reconstruction of the work as it lay completed under Milton's eye revitalizes the bones and tissues which have puzzled us with their dryness, lying as they do among bones and tissues which, even to the least historical eye, have survived unmistakably alive. (It is because of the life in some of the old bones yet that he seeks to resuscitate the marrow of those from which the life seems drained.) The organism which functions after the witchdoctoring of the historical critic will be a strange organism, but its functioning will show that it is alive, and its strangeness that its life is not at least a reflection of our own—the first condition, at any rate, for the attaining of that positive critical ideal, its life as it was originally.

III

If the face of the poem has the importance I claim for it, it follows that the historical critic will be interested in the form in which the textual critic presents the poem to him. To some extent the work of the textual critic overlaps his own. For if the textual critic is to establish the words of the poem according to the intentions of the author, he must understand the poem as the author understood it. Or, if this is exactly what the problems of the text forbiddingly invite of everybody, he must understand the author generally so that his guess at clearing any particular obscurity will have the more authority. Only by such understanding can he hope to adjudicate between those readings which are not ranked for him by the machinery of textual method. The historical critic will welcome the findings of the textual critic and will use them as basis for his own work.

I will take two examples.

A textually competent editor will reproduce the original text of a poem in such a way as to make clear the metrical intentions of the poet. This is the twenty-second Amour of Drayton's 'Ideas Mirrour' as it was first printed in 1594:

> My hart imprisoned in a hopeles Ile,
>   Peopled with Armies of pale iealous eyes,
>   The shores beset with thousand secret spyes,
>   Must passe by ayre, or else dye in exile.
>
> He framd him wings with feathers of his thought,
>   Which by theyr nature learn'd to mount the skye,
>   And with the same he practised to flye,
>   Till he himselfe thys Eagles art had taught.
>
> Thus soring still, not looking once below,
>   So neere thyne eyes celestiall sunne aspyred,
>   That with the rayes his wafting pyneons fired.
>   Thus was the wanton cause of hys owne woe.
> Downe fell he in thy Beauties Ocean drenched,
> Yet there he burnes, in fire thats neuer quenched.

If a textually competent editor were preparing a text of this sonnet, he would print the first line as follows (I take it that he would preserve the original spelling since it helps a modern reader to improve his historical mood, and, in this instance, helps him to suspect a pun on *heart*):

> My hart imprisond in a hopeles Ile.

The 'imprisoned' of the original is a misprint. It is a syllable too long. The verbal termination *-ed* was syllabic till the late seventeenth century (it survives even now in Anglican liturgy). As authority for his correction, the editor might cite the second line of Amour 33:

> My wofull hart imprisond in my breast.

Preface

His correction would point the reader to the correct understanding of the metre of the poem, pointing him to understand
that Drayton intended an *-ed* to be syllabic. Which is especially
important when it comes to four of the rime-words of the sestet:
aspyred, fired, drenched and *quenched* are planned as feminine rimes.
And those four feminine rimes are, obviously, part of the spirit
of the piece. Pick up any modern reprint of, say, Shakespeare's
works and, unless you are lucky, observe that the editor had no
idea that the syllabic *-ed* existed in rime-positions (only those who
should not be reading verse at all can miss it in medial positions)
and accordingly punctured the proud full sail of the metre.[1]

My second example is almost comic in the economy of its
accomplishment. For generations critics were to be observed
'pinnacled dim in the intense inane', interpreting the close of
Keat's 'Ode on a Grecian Urn'. I quote the last stanza from
'Poems' 1820:

> O Attic shape! Fair attitude! with brede
> Of marble men and maidens overwrought,
> With forest branches and the trodden weed;
> Thou, silent form, dost tease us out of thought
> As doth eternity: Cold Pastoral!
> When old age shall this generation waste,
> Thou shalt remain, in midst of other woe
> Than ours, a friend to man, to whom thou say'st,
> "Beauty is truth, truth beauty,"—that is all
> Ye know on earth, and all ye need to know.

The critics have spun beautiful cobwebs 'without substance or
profit' out of those last two lines. In 1938, however, Mr G. St

---

1 The Elizabethan poets used the enriching feminine rimes freely. Contrast
the couplet writers of the Waller-Dryden-Pope-Johnson series. The
masculine rimes of the 'eighteenth-century' couplet marked it off strongly
from the dramatic blank verse of the time, the fifth stressed syllable of
which is usually followed by an unstressed one. In Beaumont and
Fletcher this feminine ending was added to a loosely stressed line, but
later tragic poets are virtually writing in a pentametric Hiawatha metre.

Preface

Quintin robbed them of much of their imaginary weft. He interpreted the obscurity as follows:

> Keats...says that the Urn will always remain 'a friend to man' because it will always give the message, 'Beauty is Truth, Truth Beauty'; and the following words...are interpreted as being addressed to all who are capable of hearing and understanding it....Even allowing for the fact that Keats was not writing a philosophical treatise and may be vague in his use of terms, it is difficult to believe that he really meant this...as a significant message to humanity at large.
>
> An alternative suggestion is to assume that the 'ye' of the last line is addressed to the figures on the Urn. For them Beauty *is* Truth because their experience is limited to the beautiful as depicted on the Urn....This interpretation, of course, requires that only the words 'Beauty is Truth, Truth Beauty' be printed in inverted commas, as in Professor de Sélincourt's edition.[1]

Mr St Quintin's 'alternative suggestion' must be given its place in any discussion of the text of the poem. This is not the occasion for any such discussion, but it is already clear that Mr St Quintin's discovery helps to confirm the authority of the text of 'Poems' 1820. Unfortunately the latest edition prints the text as it appeared in 'The Annals of the Fine Arts', a text which does not employ any quotation marks. If Keats were responsible for the text in the 'Annals', it seems that he deliberately revised the pointing for 'Poems' 1820 in the hope, unfulfilled for over a century, that quotation marks would make his meaning clear. Mr St Quintin's understanding of the pointing, and therefore his discriminating of the choice of meanings for 'ye', and therefore his choice of the better one—this chain of deduction has relieved Keats of a charge of pretentiousness which everything else he wrote renders him unlikely to have deserved. If the Ode cannot be allowed to end as well as it began and continued—the grammar of the close is not self-evident enough to be happy—Keats is at least found writing an admirable sense.

1 Letter in 'Times Literary Supplement', 5 Feb. 1938.

IV

If a critic has a textual critic's respect for the words of a poem, he will run fewer risks, when quoting them, of committing mutilation. Our hurried journalistic age has many sins of textual travesty on its doorstep—or in its shop window. One Professor of English has written as follows:

it is not altogether idle to ponder why Ben Jonson should have written:

> 'What beckoning ghost besprent with April dew
> Hails me so solemnly to yonder yew....'

while Pope should have preferred:

> 'What beckoning ghost athwart the moonlit glade
> Invites my steps, and points to yonder shade.'

But Jonson wrote (I, too, modernize the text):

> What gentle ghost, besprent with April dew,
> Hails me, so solemnly, to yonder yew?
> And beck'ning woos me...?

and Pope:

> What beck'ning ghost, along the moonlight shade
> Invites my step, and points to yonder glade?

And again the same critic has written:

we have...to soak ourselves so deeply in all that words meant for Pope, that even such a line as

> 'The dying gales that pant upon the breeze'

does not strike us as ridiculous.

Why not? we ask; Pope wrote 'trees'.

And there is Mr Empson, who, examining ambiguities in poetry, appeared only half interested in examining them as the poets made them. Sometimes, of course, he may have examined correct texts but printed them incorrectly, in which event the commentary stands if the text is restored. But much as we admire the intelligence at work—or at play?—our faith is not improved when the genuine pioneer in subtlety fails to detect the flies which

have crawled off himself into the exquisite ointment. One recalls
the 'Dunciad':

> Let standard-authors, thus, like trophies borne,
> Appear more glorious as more hack'd and torn.
> And you, my Critics! in the chequer'd shade,
> Admire new light thro' holes yourselves have made.

(There were, of course, other reasons for finding Mr Empson's
analyses unsatisfactory, and reasons pertinent for the present essay:
he often treats past poetry as if it were contemporary, sometimes
as if it mixed past and contemporary.)

Misquotation matters less when no critical comment is focused
on the product. No one minds much that Mr Eliot's 'Gerontion'
continues to appear with the motto from 'Measure for Measure'
weakened by 'dreaming of both' instead of 'dreaming on both'.
No one minds much when an essay of Mrs Woolf's croons lines
she is remembering wrongly but which are almost part of her own
prose. But it matters horribly when a deflowered text is followed
by an advertisement of its subtleties. The most scrupulous of
quoters will not succeed in avoiding every error, but modern
carelessness is often wanton.

V

The historical critic will make all reasonable attempts to read and
quote correctly. And he will try to understand the original significance of what his eye sees and holds accurately. He will set
great store by what is briefly summarized in the two shelf-fulls
of the 'Oxford English Dictionary'.[1] No one wrestles often with
these volumes (the verb is literally applicable) without growing
suspicious of the mum faces of old words. He soon sees that many
of the words of an old poem are blotted with fickle mercury
which gives him back the reflection of his own usage. He becomes conscious that language has a history, that it develops

1 This great work, of course, does not claim to be final. It is not difficult
to find earlier instances than some of those cited. But, if not a solid, it is
a solid framework, and every student is free to help fill in the spaces
between its girders or to build on additional accommodation.

Preface

through a course of changes; and that, for the discussion of a work
of literature, only those changes are relevant which have preceded
it, and so have produced the contemporary state of language,
or which had produced those earlier states of language that con-
ditioned the writings of earlier authors to whom the author of
the work in question owes an eclectic debt of words or syntax.

On p. 80 below, I have referred to Dr Johnson's dissatisfaction
with that famous speech of Macbeth which, because it employed
the 'low' words *blanket, dun* and *knife*, struck him as ludicrous.
In our turn we see Johnson as ludicrous. When we discover the
reasons for Johnson's laugh, ours changes to regret that a critic
should have allowed such merely contemporary reasons, however
forceful, to throw away anything of 'Macbeth' for him. But
there is need to turn our laughter and regret back on ourselves,
since language has played its silent pranks on us, too. Indeed it
has played more pranks on us than on Johnson, since it has had
two hundred more years to play them in. We may respond to
Shakespeare's free use of words more 'naturally' than could
Johnson, for the reason that, in our own age, words are free again.
But if we accept Shakespeare whole in a way that was impossible
two hundred years ago, our very freedom tends to make the usage
of a more constricted age irksome and unintelligible. Our laugh
at Johnson's laugh comes badly when, with reasons of equal
cogency, we laugh with equal irrelevance at such things as:

> and the voice of the turtle is heard in our land;[1]

> The Nymphs forsaking ev'ry cave and spring,
> Their early fruit, and milk-white turtles bring;[2]

> ...the fair Hesperian Tree
> Laden with blooming gold;[3]

> And blast the blooming Promise of the Year.[4]

> ...some calm and blooming cove.[5]

1 'Song of Songs', II. 12; Lewis Carroll, of course, availed himself of the
dilemma into which time had placed this phrase.
2 Pope, 'Pastorals', II, 51 f.   3 Milton, 'Comus', 393 f.
4 Gray, 'Alliance of Education and Government', 21
5 Shelley, 'Lines Written among the Euganean Hills', 342.

Preface

We have, I grant, a perfect right to laugh once: these words have
suffered a Bergsonian collapse. But to laugh once only; and after
that once, to lift the unfortunates out of the gutter. Otherwise we
are still at the mental stage of schoolboys who have a vested
interest in laughing as long as possible.

We can see more clearly our duties towards fallen words if we
imagine deterioration overtaking good words of our own. We
should be both angry and sorry if any critic of A.D. 2000 carelessly
dismissed the poet who wrote

> The force that through the green fuse drives the flower,

because, in the intervening years, *fuse* had become a slang word
for, say, *nose*. We should have no patience for foolishness which
exposed people so completely to the mercy of what time did to
words when the price was the missing of the strong fancy we see
in that line and the remedy a glance back into the past, a glance at
our harmless selves. And yet the same unreasonableness often
stultifies our enjoyment and proper evaluation of, say, eighteenth-
century poetry, or the dialogue of Scott's or Dickens's heroes.
It is time that it was laid down boldly that no critic should be
allowed a hearing on Milton or eighteenth-century poetry till he
has washed his mind historically clean to receive *blooming promise*,
fleecy care and the rest with the delight that was once novelly their
due and which, to the historical eye, appears their due still.

VI

And there is a more elusive cause for irrelevant emotions.
When the serious student encounters *blooming promise*, he works
back to the original meaning of *blooming*.[1] Gray meant something

[1] I originally intended to run Milton's *blooming gold* as my instance, but
became aware that it did not make its point well, and this for an interesting reason. *Gold* is a word which, in an age of banknotes, we use so
infrequently that its strangeness acts on *blooming* and preserves it from the
slang sense which is fairly strong in *blooming promise*. But there are signs
that this slang sense is waning. The word is ceasing to provide adequate
relief for casually blasphemous emotion. In a year or two I might have
to choose another word altogether for my instance, eighteenth-century
poetry recovering accordingly.

better than we mean by that word and so we restore to dignity a context obviously let down. But if a word has changed its meaning without this drop in rank, there may be nothing or little in the context to advertise the change, and accordingly we need more than mere willing commonsense to guide us. We need knowledge, or, instead, that fine suspiciousness of flawed surface meaning which leads us to get knowledge, leads us, that is, to turn again to the 'O.E.D.'

And here again is room for boldness—the bold assertion that the original meaning of a word in a great poem is the only one worth attending to. However delightful the meaning arising out of new verbal connotations, such meaning is irrelevant to the author's poem. He must stand by his poem as he meant it. If it is not fair to hold him responsible for the degradation of *blooming*, he should not be accredited with incidental gains which may have befallen other words of his.

When Lady Anne Winchelsea wrote

> Nor will in fading silks compose
> Faintly the inimitable rose,

she meant that she disliked the common feminine pastime of embroidery since it can produce only a poor 'imitation' of an actual rose. But following on after the romantic poets and all the talk about pure poetry, those lines have accidentally taken on a beauty which did not exist for their author. (Lady Anne did not express her meaning with complete scrupulousness: if all that is against silks is their fadingness, they still last much longer than a rose, or even than a season of roses. But because the word used unscrupulously is a pretty word, that is no reason for supposing that Lady Anne was attempting pure poetry.) The beauty of those lines is historically fictitious but it is only active when their almost humdrum sense is ignored as only our own century and the last can ignore it. It is one of the bits of earlier poetry which, after Keats, have been attracted to the further side of magic casements. These casements and the perilous foam did not exist for Lady

Preface

Anne, and 'The Spleen' is spoiled as a poem if we lavish a romantic emotion on one humble delicate scrap of it. To read later emotions here and there into a poem is a tedious error in criticism and worthy only of the insipidly fickle florilegist. One may state it as a rule that if accidental time, acting on a good poem, has improved one of its lines or passages in itself, it will have proportionately impaired that line or passage in relation to its neighbours, since any good poem is a web of language, a web of mood or moods, each thread of which was chosen consciously. Or, at least, approved consciously. 'Kubla Khan' may have been scribbled by a hand still sodden with dreams, but Coleridge published the poem because he approved it in full daylight soberness.

Anybody can detect his own errors. Here are two of mine. In 1932 as part of article XIX below, I wrote:

Look at the expression from 'Antony and Cleopatra', 'downy windows' (a periphrasis, if one dare cool it with a textbook term, for *eyes*). 'Windows' by itself is the wrong image. Cleopatra's eyes were nothing like windows. But by the addition of that boldest of epithets the stark rectangle of window dissolves and trembles into a human eye:

> 'Downy windows, close;
> And golden Phoebus never be beheld
> Of eyes again so royal....'

If one compares 'downy windows' with Matthew Arnold's expression 'jasmine-muffled lattices', one gets a fair idea of the gamut between the Elizabethan and the Victorian poets. Arnold's phrase is not an image. Shakespeare's is. But that discrepancy, a significance which is unfair though suggestive, must here be set aside. Arnold's expression tries hard to be beautiful: jasmine is a flower and therefore beautiful, as sound it is almost jammy, muffled is soft and deep in wool, lattices are the most picturesque and diamonded of windows. And yet the words fail hopelessly, in the same way that the artists fail who paint for calendars and chocolate-box lids. Shakespeare's 'downy windows' has no sense of effort behind it, of course. But it is its boldness which contrasts so immediately with Arnold's studious selection of his samites. Boldness of poetic purpose is not enough of itself. It is better to grab than to select, but one must grab the right things. For all his picking fingers, Arnold

xxv

Preface

chose the wrong ones, mistaking sateen for satin in the half-light of his inspiration.

This passage, for what it is worth, deals fairly by Arnold except in so far as lattices had a purer beauty in 1861 than in 1932: so much nearer was he than ourselves to the silver springs of the 'Gothic Revival'. But the remarks on Shakespeare looked sheepish when it became clear that for Shakespeare *windows* meant *shutters*.[1] Another instance. After swallowing the line whole at the age of thirteen, I continued for many years to admire

> Sleep that knits up the ravell'd sleeve of care.

But the image I responded to was one prompted by time not by Shakespeare, one prompted by the sum of human usage which has conferred on *sleeve* the denotation of the arm-covering part of clothes and deprived it of the denotation of *skein*: a tangle of wool or silk was what the word meant for Shakespeare.[2]

In accepting the wrong meaning for *windows* and *sleeve*, I stand convicted of having accepted the poetry loosely. If I had read with proper attention, I might have suspected, since textual corruption seems unlikely, that nonsense in Shakespeare, even though nonsense with a Shakespearean glory about it, was fungus raised by time. What was the point of death's closing windows when eyes can still see through closed windows? And if sleep knits up care's ravelled sleeve, will not care be all the brisker for it?[3]

VII

Since words behave oddly of themselves, so to speak, there is no justification for a modern critic who incites them to behave oddly on his own account. One recent instance occurs to mind:

> 'The expense of spirit in a waste of shame.' (Shakespeare.)

---

[1] See Appendix I, pp. 204–7 below.
[2] Cf. Drayton, 'The Quest of Cynthia' (in the 'Battaile of Agincourt'):
> 'The Banck with Daffadillies dight
> With grasse like Sleave was matted.'
[3] Not all scholars can possess the 'O.E.D.', but a convenient substitute so far as Shakespeare goes exists in Dr C. T. Onions' 'Shakespeare Glossary'.

xxvi

Preface

The line contains two submerged puns. 'Expense' suggests 'expanse' and prepares the way for 'waste'; 'waste' suggests 'waist', which reinforces the sexual implications of the sonnet.

We know that Shakespeare and the Elizabethans liked puns. But if their sense of the pun was so strong as to make 'expense' suggest 'expanse', then their literature puns on every other word. For I can put forward my own suggestions: I can say that 'waste' suggests 'waifs' and 'shame' 'sham', both of which words can be made out to reinforce the general meaning of the sonnet. But to make suggestions such as these is to throw language back to Babel. In the hands of people who have something to say, language is always attempting precision. Even when the effect aimed at is an effect of vagueness, it is a peculiar effect of vagueness that is aimed at, not any or every effect of vagueness. And the language required to achieve any effect that is peculiar will be precise language; as, for example, in the lines

yet from those flames
No light, but rather darkness visible.

However much a poet may aim at suggestiveness and 'atmosphere', he wants only the right suggestiveness and the right 'atmosphere'; and we do not help him if we let words free themselves from their contexts, crawl about as they like in our minds and mate promiscuously. Shakespeare, I think, did not expect us to confuse *expense* with *expanse*: *expense* is too powerful to brook a rival in our attention. He may well have hoped, however, that we should see the *waist* in *waste*. And the reason for my thinking this is that there is another and earlier pun staring from the line: *spirit* is the Elizabethan word for the seminal fluid as well as for the 'soul'. Both these puns make the line complex, but they do not make it confused, as expense-expanse make it confused. There is enough precise complexity in poetry to engage all our attention without our making more for ourselves.

VIII

The face of literature is also its spirit, and the historical and critical functions of the historical critic might seem to fall apart nicely, one adhering to face, one to spirit. But to separate the twin functions is impossible in practice. It is partly by his working on historical reconstruction that the critic proper has time to form an opinion of the face that he sees in the slow process of growing vital, to form it and to improve on it. It is by participating in the reconstruction that he earns the right to see and to say what he sees. Historical reconstruction takes time. It is indeed never satisfactorily at an end. It is always needing the help of the other specialists—textual critics, bibliographers, biographers, psychologists, social historians, all the dogged compilers of theses. But accompanying the historical labours and finally standing out on top of them is the more purely critical function. The critic at the end of it all is left to describe and communicate the face, now that it can be looked at for what it was, and to assess its beauty or its peculiar strength.

IX

I have said that the critic gets help from biographers. It has been recently argued by Mr C. S. Lewis, however, that biographers do not serve the business of literary criticism. Dr Tillyard, who replied on the positive side, was surely right when he remarked that Mr Lewis 'presses the distinction between art and life too far'.[1] Dr Tillyard sees poems as more intimately related to their makers, but even he does not allow the potential relevance, for reader and critic, of 'literary gossip' about the 'quotidian personality' of the poet. He agrees with Mr Lewis that if it were known that Keats first read of senators (which, to put it bluntly, he used as a metaphor for trees in 'Hyperion') 'in a little brown book, in a room smelling of boiled beef, the same day that he pulled out a loose tooth', that scrap of biography would have no value for the reader of 'Hyperion'. But surely such an instance,

1 'The Personal Heresy' (1939), p. 78.

Preface

simply because it is invented, has no place in the argument. If such a fact had survived, it would presumably have survived through the agency of Keats. If so, it would tell us something about Keats's mind and senses, about the way he experienced his life and, when all is said and done, it is out of that mind that the poems spring, or crawl. If Keats had come to the point of recording this fact, he might not have been the poet to see trees as senators at all. What is preserved is preserved because someone, perhaps the poet, perhaps a friend, thinks it worth preserving. If the poet preserves it, the thing preserved has obvious importance; if the friend, its importance depends on the quality of the friend as a witness (Aubrey's gossip often tells us more about Aubrey than about its subject). But because the value of the fact is difficult to assess, this does not mean that the reader and critic are free to despise it. If they lack the key to its significance for the poet, and so for his poem, they may have their own imperfect perception to blame; or, alternately, the fact itself, which may be too fragmentary to suggest a whole or a context. The reader and critic can afford to neglect nothing (not even bibliography!). When they learn, for instance, that for Keats as a boy fighting was 'meat and drink', they are ready to notice, perhaps for the first time, some quality in the bone and flesh of the poems themselves. A poem addresses itself to the best readers at their best. Literary 'gossip' can play a part in helping readers to achieve their best.

X

My criticism cannot be called modern, except by empty courtesy of its being that of one still alive. A wish to see the past with sympathy and humility, to seeing it, as far as possible, as it was, has ceased long ago to earn one the coveted title of 'modern critic' since critics nowadays are seldom historians in any serious sense. The Universities, if they breed critics of past literature at all, seem, unwillingly or otherwise, to breed the kind who brightly decorate the pages of the journals. What these critics say about the past is of small value as such, but between their lines shines or

Preface

sputters the spirit of our own age; and the historian of twentieth-century criticism will, therefore, need to give them more attention than their historical instinct for their historical themes would in itself warrant. When the modern critic masquerades as a historically-minded critic, he discloses, more completely perhaps than he is always aware of, the modern attitude to the past. For it is surely true that never since the sixteenth century has there been less desire to see the past as it was. All that usually happens in modern historical criticism is that a hand preoccupied with modern sensation reaches out lazily and plucks here and there a faded but still vivid flower, a voice exclaiming that a mind is charmed. We might compare our modern critics to the more romantic Protestants of the seventeenth century who preferred the maggots and butterflies in heads then alive to right thinking in heads alive no longer—a preference which constitutes the last treachery against past ages while spiritedly asserting the claims of the present. The maggots and butterflies led these Protestants to write some charming prose: they thought themselves theologians, but at bottom they were essayists, dilettanti. In the same way many critics of to-day are small literary men, small creative essayists, prose poets snatching up morsels of past literature to nourish their own talents, gaily advertising their own discoveries in past ages—their discoveries fragmentary, enthusiastic, idiosyncratic, uninstructed, titillating, inaccurate.[1]

The weakness of the historical sense is perhaps a sign of the chaos of our times, for the historical critic sees order not chaos, human responsibility (even though an author draws on language which is accidentally accumulated) not acquiescence, justice not carelessness. He undertakes the business of historical criticism because he believes that a good author is worth understanding in the sense he intended rather than in the sense that has been foisted on him simply by his having been tough enough to go on

---

[1] Some of my essays may seem to come in for some of my own satire: since the 'modern' element in them decreases on the whole as the decade in which they were written advances, I have affixed dates.

Preface

existing. Like the Deists, he believes that the author approved his creation, whatever haphazard fortune has overtaken it since he turned away. He believes that since we look at the past at all—and to those jealous for the past it is a hopeful sign that the moderns look at it so often—it is up to us to be its guardians. The historical critic does not feel that he is playing truant from his own times, for he has this advantage over the critic who confounds all times into one: he can include his own times in the historical field. He will read old authors in their own light, and the moderns in the light that he salutes as new.

G. T.

as from UNIVERSITY COLLEGE, LONDON
MARCH 1941

ACKNOWLEDGEMENTS

I, II, IV, V, VII (1), VIII (1), IX, X, XI, XII and XVII are reprinted by permission of the editor of the 'Times Literary Supplement'; VII (2) from 'Essays and Studies 1939', and VIII (2) from 'Fifteen Poets', by permission of the Clarendon Press; XIII and a paragraph of the Preface by permission of the editors of the 'Modern Language Review'; XVI and XXII by permission of the editor of the 'Fortnightly'; XVIII by permission of the editor of 'English'; XIV appeared originally in the 'London Mercury' and XIX in the 'Bookman'. Paragraphs of two of them were incorporated into my book on Pope and are printed here because that book has for some time been out of print.

The help of Kathleen Tillotson in 'Elizabethan Decoration' amounted to collaboration, and it is to her permission and that of the editor of the 'Review of English Studies' that I owe the appendix on windows. '"Othello" and "The Alchemist"' received the benefit of Professor C. J. Sisson's suggestions.

G. T.

I. THE 'FABLES' OF ROBERT HENRYSON

HENRYSON'S fame as a poet depends, like Chaucer's, on his ability to tell a story and to pack it with human reference. There is something distinctive in the way a Chaucerian tells a story; and this is most noticeable when the story is a fable, when its characters are animals. The poet, of course, makes the animals act as men act. But more than this, he makes them act as men act when they are at their most human, their most worldly. The human beings which the animals resemble are not the great ones of the earth. They are ordinary folk, often the shabby-genteel, the genteel who have a touch of shabbiness in mind or circumstances. There is always something vulgar about them. Only the vulgar speak their thoughts with quite that relish, that pained or perky abandon.

One can see this anywhere. Henryson's telling of the Aesopian fable of the town and country mouse will serve as example. The story begins almost soberly. The mice are set up in benefits and deprivations which are those of men. Then the town mouse visits her poor sister, and the human resemblance is suddenly entire:

> Throw mosse and mure, throw bankis, busk & breir,
> Scho ran cryand, quhill scho came to a balk:
> 'Cum furth to me, my awin Sister deir,
> Cry peip anis!'...
> ...and furth scho come hir to.
>
> The hartlie joy, God! geve ye had sene,
> Beis kith quhen that thir Sisteris met;
> And grit kyndnes wes schawin thame betwene,
> For quhylis thay leuch, and quhylis for joy thay gret,
> Quhyle(s) kissit sweit, quhylis in armis plet;
> And thus thay fure quhill soberit wes thair mude,
> Syne ffute ffor ffute unto the chalmer yude.

The 'Fables' of Robert Henryson

The country mouse 'glides' into her buttery and prepares the best meal it can afford. But

> The Burges Mous prompit forth in pryde,
> And said, 'sister, is this your dayly fude?'
> 'Quhy not,' quod scho, 'is not this meit rycht gude?'

Then the town mouse has to speak out—one can see her contracting her offended body within her dress, rising in considered rejection:

> 'My fair sister' (quod scho), 'have me excusit.
> This rude dyat and I can not accord.
> To tender meit my stomok is ay usit,
> For quhylis I fair alsweill as ony Lord.
> Thir wydderit peis, and nuttis, or thay be bord,
> Wil brek my teith, and mak my wame fful sklender,
> Quhilk wes before usit to meitis tender.'

And so the story progresses, scarcely less centrally human than the Wife of Bath's Prologue.

The detail of crying 'peep' reappears in the next century, when Wyat tells the same story in his second epistle to John Poyns:

> At last she asked softly who was there.
> And in her langage, as well as she cowd,
> 'Pepe,' quod the othr, 'syster, I ame here.'

But apart from this survival, the intimate human quality of the Chaucerian manner has gone by the time it is Wyat's turn to tell the tale. Wyat is, of course, as sage and serious a poet as Spenser, and he is, moreover, thinking of satire rather than of fable. One would not expect Wyat to write what Henryson calls 'jolly verse'. And yet Henryson was himself three parts sage and serious too, and, living in that age, could combine with high seriousness the fun of the fair. That particular human element was offered to adult readers in the fourteenth century, and offered as poetry. It only exists nowadays in children's books. The spirit of Chaucer and Henryson lives on as fresh as ever, and sometimes almost as strong, in the prose of children's books written in the nineteenth and twentieth centuries.

The 'Fables' of Robert Henryson

Henryson was sage and serious. It was part of his Scottishness. The Scots seem to have a capacity for finding sap in what to more southern minds is dry tare. (One recalls Dr Johnson's definition of oats.) The Scots find in a high sentence, in a *moralitas*, a nutriment which they can sustain themselves on richly. This may have been a more widely spread capacity in the middle ages than now. What was then the taste of Christendom may since have shrunk to Scotland. But even then Chaucer had less of it than Henryson. In the tales of the Parson and Monk, Chaucer can be sufficiently dramatic to deal out *moralitas* generously as porridge in Scotland, but his view of life demands some formula less simple. To Henryson the world and its people are controlled by firm and uncomplicated moral machinery. Human life for him is thoroughly governable, both in theory and practice.

> 'Lo...thus it happinnis mony syis
> On thame that will not tak counsall nor reid
> Off Prudent men, or Clerkis that ar wyis....

But among Chaucer's prudent men and clerks that are wise there are alarming discrepancies. His friar is a devil: Chaucer's irony is for once plain as a pikestaff. And yet—

> ...certainly he hadde a murye note;

and

> His eyen twynkled in his heed aright,
> As doon the sterres in the frosty nyght.

His monk is even more of a puzzle: 'And I seyde, his opinioun was good.'

There is nothing in Henryson to confuse the moral issue as the Prologue confuses it, or as the whole Canterbury pilgrimage confuses it—a pilgrimage on which the tales of Hugh of Lincoln and of the miller meet and kiss each other. Chaucer sees to it that he keeps the issue confused. He advances beyond an accepted morality into a morality which is finer and more difficult, rather of the New Testament than of the Old. Chaucer, who appreciated the complex cross-purposes of human minds, has no place for a

3   1-2

moral. Henryson has plenty of place for a moral. The real difference between his 'Cock and the Fox' and Chaucer's is that Henryson is seen to be working towards his *moralitas*. It is during three stanzas only of his twenty-seven that Henryson wanders (the three stanzas which air the views of the widowed hens). His telling of the fable of how the swallow preached to the other birds and preached in vain is moralist let loose. Here there are three sermons, two of which are long ones, and a moral elegy. But this does not suffice. In his own person he introduces the story with thirteen stanzas of theological argument, stately as Boethius. To balance this he concludes with a *moralitas* of nine stanzas. And what a *moralitas* it is: the fable

> ...at this tyme may weill be applicate
> To guid morall edificatioun,
> Haifand ane sentence, according to ressoun.

This capacity for loaded-up edification has remained strong in Scotland. The marvel is, in Henryson as in Scottish preachers generally, that the *moralitas* can be so vigorous, its images so rampant:

> Allace! quhat cair, quhat weiping is and wo,
> Quhen Saull and bodie departit ar in twane!
> The bodie to the wormis Keitching go,
> The Saull to Fyre, to everlestand pane.
> Quhat helpis than this calf, thir gudis vane,
> Quhen thow art put in Luceferis bag,
> And brocht to hell, and hangit be the crag?

The Scots' humour can sweeten any porridge.

1933

II. ELIZABETHAN DECORATION

I

THE Elizabethans do not seem to have made much distinction between decoration in an object and what would now be called its functional quality, the quality by virtue of which it does the work for which it exists. At no other time was there more interest in functional efficacy, in knowing how everything was best to be made or done. This interest in making and doing things was seldom specialized to one craft. Everybody was interested in every craft. And there is no distinction between an art and a craft. Writers like Gervase Markham and Sir Hugh Platt, for instance, show familiarity with an encyclopaedic range of practical methods. Much of the poetic imagery of the Elizabethans in prose and verse (and the ready use of original material for images is a sure sign of intimacy)[1] is drawn from the technical means of a score of different arts—music (execution and composition), building, bookbinding, dressmaking, farriery, tennis, archery, hunting and so on. Their interest in means was strong but did not stop when the practical end had been attained. While that practical end was no more than roughly attained, they were already considering it as the opportunity for a further value, that of ornament, already imagining how they should both improve the practical efficacy and at the same time provide the requisite aesthetic quality.

1 If certain kinds of imagery become fashionable, use of those kinds is a sure sign only of intimacy with fashionable literature. The Elizabethan use of imagery may be said never to have reached the restrictiveness implied in 'certain kinds'. It was fashionable to use imagery, but the sources of the imagery used were universal. Moreover, though any writer could copy an expression like 'as clear as crystal', only one possessing the adequate technical knowledge could reapply an image drawn from, say, counterpoint.

Elizabethan Decoration

2

Few people in any age seem capable of resting content for long with the beauty of perfected function, and, among Englishmen, the Elizabethans least of all. They demanded that function should show spirit, exclaim, cut capers over and above what was practically necessary. Indeed in taking images from the technicalities of the crafts the Elizabethans are caught using the functional itself as decoration. It is art that delights them most in all material things. They see external nature in terms of art. Art is more valued than nature. Nature is valued as it resembles art. This, for example, in 1595, is Drayton's description of a 'stately grove', made up of trees

> Which Nature in such order had disposed,
> And there-withall these goodly walkes inclosed,
> As serv'd for hangings and rich Tapestry,
> To beautifie this stately Gallery:
> Imbraudring these in curious trailes along,
> The clustred Grapes, the golden Citrons hung,
> More glorious then the precious fruite were these,
> Kept by the Dragon in *Hesperides*;
> Or gorgious Arras in rich colours wrought,
> With silk from Affrick, or from Indie brought:
> Out of thys soyle sweet bubling Fountains crept,
> As though for joy the sencelesse stones had wept;
> With straying channels dauncing sundry wayes,
> With often turnes, like to a curious Maze:
> Which breaking forth, the tender grasse bedewed,
> Whose silver sand with orient Pearle was strewed,
> Shadowed with Roses and sweet Eglantine,
> Dipping theyr sprayes into this christalline:
> From which the byrds the purple berries pruned,
> And to theyr loves their small recorders tuned....

The transition from nature to art bends back on itself. Man weaves tapestry copying 'curious trailes' from nature ('trailes' was a technical term for arabesque). These trails satisfy the contemporary sense of beauty more completely than their originals.

When therefore the Elizabethan wants to commend a vine he says it is as beautiful as a picture of it. The new word 'landscape' is interesting in this connexion. It is borrowed from the Dutch and its first meaning is the appearance of the land when represented in a picture. While the land remained unrepresented there was no need of the word. The Elizabethans are pleased if things are 'curious', which meant, for example, 'made with care or art, skilfully, elaborately, or beautifully wrought' ('O.E.D.'). An epithet of praise is 'artificial'.

3

Every item in the daily life of the Elizabethans is decorated as much as possible. J. Alfred Gotch in his 'Architecture of the Renaissance in England' (1894) sees Elizabethan architecture as another instance of their fancy:

Longford Castle, in Wiltshire, is a triangular house, still inhabited, though modernized. At Lyvedon are the remains of a house fashioned like a Greek cross. Some houses were E-shaped, presumably out of compliment to the queen, while extravagant in this respect is John Thorpe's design for his own house, formed of his initials I T. Nor were practical designers singular in this respect; they had the countenance of the poets, for Spenser makes at least one of the castles of the 'Faerie Queene' bow to arbitrary rules, and fashions it partly circular, partly triangular, and partly on a quadrate 'proportioned equally by seven and nine'.

The decoration is in the detail as well as the structure. There were ceilings of plaster 'elaborately decorated with mouldings or bands, which bent themselves in and out in a regular pattern over the whole surface, and frequently enclosed as they went various forms of the family arms or crest or cognisance'. Walter Gedde in 1615 published about a hundred elaborate designs 'Principaly serving for Glasiers: And not Impertinent for Plasterers, and Gardiners....' Gervase Markham can stand for the many designers of gardens. The principles of his 'Country Farm' (1615) are summarized by Sir Reginald Blomfield in that excellent book 'The Formal Garden in England':

> The noticeable point in Markham's account of the gardens is the emphasis with which he insists on the necessity of ordered design, not only for all kinds of gardens, but for the orchards and fishponds as well. Everything is to be laid out in comely order. The kitchen garden is not to be a dreary wilderness of vegetables, but should have its broad, trim paths, its borders of lavender or roses, its well or fountain, and even its arbours or 'turrets of lattice fashion', as in the garden of pleasure.

It is the same with their dress. Lytton Strachey's prose became almost stanzaic in enumerating the 'serried complexities of Queen Elizabeth's raiment':

> the huge hoop, the stiff ruff, the swollen sleeves, the powdered pearls, the spreading, gilded gauzes.

Their music was almost all contrapuntal. Their food was prepared 'curiously'. Their horses danced rather than moved naturally—they were required to learn the gestures of the manage. The pageant and, later, the masque supplied themselves with all the kinds of decoration together. Most completely of all, the pageants and masques were decoration *in excelsis*.

Decoration is so ubiquitous and fundamental that it is not surprising to find cross-references between the arts of embroidery and confectionery and the 'finer' arts. Bacon, who recoiled from excess of decoration, could not bear 'the Making of *Knots*, or *Figures*, with *Diuers Coloured Earths*...they be but Toyes: one may see as good Sights, many times, in Tarts'. (The chill cloud passes, however, a moment later when he counsels 'some other little *Figure*, with Broad Plates of *Round Coloured Glasse*, gilt, for the *Sunne*, to Play upon'.) Sir Hugh Platt makes a similar cross-reference. He will not trouble to give rules for the shaping or fashioning of an orchard—'every Drawer or embroiderer, nay, almost each Dancing-master may pretend to such niceties'. Two of the popular technical terms for gardens are 'knot' and 'embroidered'.

8

Elizabethan Decoration

4

It follows from all this that the decoration in Elizabethan literature is part of an ubiquitous and fundamental system. It was because he did not allow for this system that Mr F. W. Bateson in his provocative book 'English Poetry and the English Language' (1934) got the Elizabethan poet wrong. The style adopted by the poets, he writes,

was designed, it would seem, to *counterbalance* the tendencies of the language [there are complaints of the unsettled state of vocabulary].

So far so good. But Mr Bateson goes on:

They had an uneasy feeling all the time that their vocabulary was slipping from under them, and suspecting and distrusting it, they did not dare to confide the whole of their meaning to a single word or phrase. (That word or phrase might be obsolete before the year was out.) And so they reinforced their primary meanings with repetitions, glosses, and amplifications.

Spenser's 'Amoretti' LIX is then quoted as 'typical, in its diffuseness and repetitions, of the Elizabethan style'. But Elizabethan poetry, outside some of Spenser perhaps, is not diffuse. It is, indeed, often too definite, hard as nails. The Elizabethan poetic style was not 'facile, fluent'. 'The non-committal tautologies' did not 'result in a verbal smudge.' Mr Bateson is thinking of Swinburne, not of the Elizabethan poets. Nor can one agree that 'in a last resort [the Elizabethan poet] would always rather have written his poem without words', for no poets could be further from Mallarmé. Tennyson had his jewels five words long, but his jewellery was languid in comparison with the sharp bright patterning of the Elizabethan poet. The Elizabethan poet saw words as jewels, or rather perhaps as bits of '*Coloured Glasse*, gilt', inviting him to relate them in geometrical patterns. There may be talk of the change of language, but the old words remained firm, and it was more with the old words than with the new that the poet patterned his page. Nor was he timid about the new words. In the later dramatic poetry especially, he rode the chaos like a surf-rider. The meaning of an Elizabethan poem may be thin, but it is, always, hard—'gold to ayery thinnesse beate'. It is never diffuse as Swinburne is. And it is seldom unpatterned.

5

The Elizabethans are as literary as Ovid or Pope. They think of literature as an art. The art of speech and literature must be learned like any other art, like playing on the virginals, for example. That art was taught by the books of rhetoric. If M. Jourdain had been born a generation earlier and in England, he would have been made to realize from boyhood that what he spoke was prose, and that prose was rules, figures. When the Elizabethans have written without observing the current rules for art, they feel the need for an apology. Campion's first lyrics (1601) are offered only as 'ear-pleasing rhymes without art'. (Campion is more confident in his next preface some twelve years later:

short airs, if they be skilfully framed and naturally expressed, are like quick and good epigrams in poesy, many of them showing as much artifice, and breeding as great difficulty as a larger poem.)

In his manuscript dedication of the 1612 collection of essays to Prince Henry, Bacon remarks that his 'certaine brief notes' are 'sette downe rather significantlye, then curiously'. Polonius forgoes his art with elaborate pain:

> Madam, I swear I use no art at all.
> That he is mad, 'tis true: 'tis true 'tis pity;
> And pity 'tis 'tis true: a foolish figure;
> But farewell it, for I will use no art.

The gravedigger in the same play indicates that Polonius was not alone in his taste for the figures. As early as 1587, indeed, Abraham Fraunce had said that every cobbler could crack a syllogism.

The literary decoration scarcely needs example. But one cannot note much of it before one becomes conscious of development. The history of this development may some day be written. John

Elizabethan Decoration

Hoskins's 'Directions for Speech and Style', which was printed in full for the first time by Professor Hoyt H. Hudson in 1935, indicates how quickly fashions changed. This is Hoskins's summary of the development of spoken English in the 1590's:

> ...For now there are such schisms of eloquence that it is enough for any ten years that all the bravest wits do imitate some one figure which a critic hath taught some great personage.... It is true that we study according to the predominancy of courtly inclinations: whilst mathematics were in requests, all our similitudes came from lines, circles, and angles [this has important bearing on the metaphysical style in poetry]; whilst moral philosophy is now a while spoken of, it is rudeness not to be sententious. And for my part, I'll make one. I have used and outworn six several styles since I was first Fellow of New College, and am yet able to bear the fashion of [the] writing company.

Parody and revision show how the wind veers. Kyd's fine formula

> O eyes! no eyes, but fountains fraught with tears,

and the notorious 'Revenge' passage in the 'True Tragedy' are both parodied by 1600. Drayton's heavily adorned poems of the 1590's are revised line by line ten years later and most of their decorations destroyed. Some of the 'nectared sweets' seem to have gone sour as the century closed. The satirists are mocking at excess. The drama is turning from the vivid, academic, verbal elaboration to freer effects—still as much an art, though a less rigid one. The sonnet craze is ending (or, rather, leaving England for its St Martin's summer in Scotland). But perhaps there is not so much a change as a division. While some men choose another style of decoration, others develop the old one; or, perhaps, while some things become less ornate, others madly enrich themselves. Costume gets more florid while the Puritans grow dowdier. Women are painting 'an inch thick', and many gorges rise besides Hamlet's. Masques become so elaborate that Ben Jonson exclaims bitterly:

> Painting and carpentry are the soul of masque.

Elizabethan Decoration

For Ascham 'a faire stone requireth to be sette in the finest gold, with the best workmanship'. But for Bacon 'Vertue is like a Rich Stone, best plaine set'. (This contrast is noted in Mr K. O. Myrick's recent book on Sidney.) Launcelot Gobbo and the gravedigger are already imitating their betters of a few years back. Samuel Rowlands in his 'Letting of Humours Blood in the Head Vaine' (1600) gives examples of how the cloth of country fellows' speech 'now compares with velvet breech'. Osric shows how aristocratic speech is already off on another tack. This is not the place, however, for anything more than indications of how ornament developed.

6

Two kinds may be distinguished as permanent in Elizabethan decoration. There is the kind that is formal, numerical, geometrical, and there is the kind that is rich, profuse, sometimes luxuriously meandering. The formal is the more common and the rich is seldom without a stiffening of it. The formal should be distinguished from the simple. The Elizabethan mansion and garden are both called simple by Gotch and Sir R. Blomfield respectively. But the Elizabethan formal design is only simple if the face of a clock is simple. It is better to think of it as complicated but candid. The square and the circle are the bases of this kind of ornament. John Thorpe left a plan of a small house and garden—a square building with courts back and front, with a garden at the side subdivided into smaller knots and squares. On the back court he writes 'nothing out of square'. Bacon says that the garden is best square. William Lawson in 'A New Orchard and Garden' (1617–18) writes:

> The forme that men like in generall is a square...yet if any man be rather delighted with some other forme, or if the ground will not beare a square, I discommend not any form, so it be formall.

Lawson gives ten designs for filling in the squares. All of them are formed from simple geometrical bases—ovals, circles, triangles, etc.—but all are complicated by multiplicity.

Elizabethan Decoration

This formal principle is found working in the literature. A few examples may be given. There are the early examples of Berners's tripartite phrases in the pompous preface to his Froissart. Sidney demonstrates the exactitude of a tripartite scheme by means of numbers:

1   2   3   1   2   3

Vertue, Bewty and Speeche, did stryke, wounde, Charme,

1   2   3   1   2   3

My Hart, Eyes, Eares with wonder, Love, Delighte. . . .

Shakespeare (Sonnet CIV) has the phrase 'when first your eye I ey'd'. 'Euphues' is all formal pattern. Acrostics, shaped poems and echo poems are popular. Many poets write in the sestina form, a form in which the fixed words at the end of the lines revolve as if by clockwork. William Browne writes a devotional poem which contains three quotations from the Bible running through it a few letters at a time in three vertical columns.

Decoration by enrichment may be illustrated from Spenser and the longer amorous poems of Marlowe, Shakespeare, Drayton, and later by the couplets of Browne and Wither; or from Marlowe's plays and the later drama and masque; or from Drummond's 'Cypress Grove'. An interesting example from painting is Nicholas Hilliard's miniature (in the Victoria and Albert Museum) of a youth leaning against a tree. The youth and his background are made to appear through a free tracery of rose 'trails' painted at close quarters.

7

Often both kinds of decoration are found in the same author, and some of the finest things in Elizabethan literature result from a simultaneous combination of both kinds. The pattern is sometimes drowned in colour or feeling. The bead-frame sometimes catches fire. Among small instances there is the vowel-patterned and moving line which opens an anonymous poem in 'The Gorgeous Gallery of Gallant Inventions' (1578):

Ay mee, ay mee, I sighe to see, the Sythe afield;

13

or this refrain from no. xxiii of William Byrd's 'Songs of Sundrie Natures' (1589):

> Adieu love, adieu love, untrue love,
> Your mind is light, soon lost for new love;

or this from the 'Passionate Pilgrim':

> Good night, good rest, ah neither be my share:
> She bad good night, that kept my rest away,
> And daft me to a cabben hangde with care:
> To descant on the doubts of my decay.
> Farewell (quoth she) and come againe to morrow:
> Fare well I could not, for I supt with sorrow;

or this from 'Richard II':

> I wasted Time, and now doth Time waste me;

or this in 'Timon of Athens' (v, iv):

> And by the hazard of the spotted dye [dice]
> Let dye the spotted,

or some of Shakespeare's and other poets' sonnets. Or this speech:

> If it were done, when 'tis done, then 'twer well,
> It were done quickly: If th' Assassination
> Could trammell vp the Consequence, and catch
> With his surcease, Successe: that but this blow
> Might be the be all, and the end all. Heere,
> But heere, vpon this Banke and Shoal of time,
> Wee'ld iumpe the life to come....

A climax in Leontes's mad jealousy is closely patterned:

> Is whispering nothing?
> Is leaning Cheeke to Cheeke? is meating Noses?
> ...Is this nothing?
> Why then the world, and all that's in't, is nothing,
> The couering Skie is nothing, *Bohemia* nothing,
> My Wife is nothing, nor Nothing have these Nothings,
> If this be nothing.

Shakespeare's later plays as a whole combine the two kinds of decoration. All their rich elements are planned, consciously or otherwise, from a centre. The passion of Donne's poems is not only drawn 'through rime's vexations', but is set in tight patterns, sometimes in patterns too tight. In prose, there is Sidney's 'Arcadia'; John Hoskins culls from it his examples of the figures, yet its figures are not merely academic good form: they are drawn in a royal crimson. Hooker's voluminous sentences are marked off like a ruler, yet billow like sails. Donne's sermons become more closely patterned the more they become passionate. The famous 'Let me wither' passage from Sermon XLVI is composed of two huge sentences, the second ending:

When it comes to this height, that the fever is not in the humors, but in the spirits, that mine enemy is not an imaginary enemy, fortune, nor a transitory enemy, malice in great persons, but a reall, and an irresistible, and an inexorable, and an everlasting enemy, The Lord of Hosts himselfe, The Almighty God himselfe, the Almighty God himself only knowes the waight of this affliction, and except hee put in that *pondus gloriae*, that exceeding waight of an eternall glory, with his owne hand, into the other scale, we are waighed downe, we are swallowed up, irreparably, irrevocably, irrecoverably, irremediably.

Andrewes's style is almost as excited as Donne's, though in a very different way. The neater, smaller patterning of his sermons is usually the outward sign of a precision and completeness of thought. But it exists partly for its own sake. Its filling in of small squares goes on when there is no particular purpose in thought's being precise. His prose is mechanized sometimes more by the thought than the pattern, sometimes more by the pattern than the thought. He is different from all the other Elizabethans and yet is a kind of algebraic fulfilment of their dream. This is a paragraph from the sermon on John xx, 19:

To stand then: But, to stand, in a certain place. Every where to stand, will not serve the turne. *Stetit in medio*, that standing place is assigned for it, thus guiding our feet into the way of Peace. And, the Place, is materiall, for peace. All bodies naturall never leave moving, are never quiet, till they recover their proper places; and, there, they find peace. The midst is Christ's place, by Nature. He, is the second person *in divinis*; and so, the middle-most of the other two. And, on earth, follow Him

Elizabethan Decoration

(if you will) you shall not (lightly) find Him out of it: Not, according to the letter, speaking of the materiall place. At His birth; *In medio animalium*, in the Stable. After (a child) *In medio Doctorum*, in the Temple. After (a man) *Medius vestrûm stetit* (saith Iohn Baptist) in the midst of the people; saith He of Himselfe, *Ecce Ego in medio vestri*, in the midst of His Apostles. At His death, it fell to His turne likewise, that place; even then, he was in the midst. And now (rising) there He is (we see). They, in the midst of the Iewes: and He, in the midst of them. After this, in Patmos, Saint Iohn saw Him in heaven, in the middst of the throne: in earth, walking in the middst of the Candlesticks. And, at the last day, He shalbe in the midst, too, of the sheepe on His right hand, and the goates on His left. All which shew, the place and He, sort very well.

Among other prose, there is Nashe's abuse of Gabriel Harvey which explodes its fireworks from an elaborate architecture of wire. In the 'Carde of Fancie' Greene reproduces the jewellery of 'Euphues' in outrageously tawdry glass. In music, among all the other examples, there is the holy desolation and smarting ecstasy of Byrd working in the confines of counterpoint. The Elizabethans would have understood Coleridge's profound discovery that the great poet provides 'a more than usual state of emotion with more than usual order'. At the commonest moments they had a 'more than usual order', and when in 'a more than usual state of emotion' saw to it that method outpaced madness. In the very torrent, tempest and whirlwind of their passion they acquired and begot a temperance, an order, a pattern.

1937

III. THE PROSE OF LYLY'S COMEDIES

1

THE importance of Lyly in Elizabethan drama is obvious for several reasons, but the chief reason is not that he is the first English dramatist to produce the first completely original play in English prose. The great step, the step from verse to prose, had been taken some dozen years earlier when George Gascoigne translated into English prose Ariosto's rimed play, 'I Suppositi': Gascoigne's 'Supposes' was acted at Gray's Inn in 1566 and Lyly's 'Endimion' belongs, probably, to 1579. Comedy before Gascoigne exhibited what Marlowe called the jigging veins of riming mother wits and the change from this to prose is as vital a change as could have come over Elizabethan comedy, since it affected the kind and quality of both the content and surface of the play. Lyly used the medium which Gascoigne had used before him, and used it for original work. His example may have made it easier for later poets to use prose for their comedies, but an innovation that is taken up so readily and generally would presumably have come anyhow. The important thing about Lyly is the kind of prose that he uses. Lyly's prose is of major importance to Elizabethan drama both for its influence and for itself. Lyly contributes to the art of his successors, particularly to that of Shakespeare, but to judge him as a mere forerunner is to misjudge him. He stands alone, in his own right. His prose, considered as dramatic prose, is often perfect—that is, it convinces you that the effect gained is the effect aimed at—and though Lyly's principles are re-applied by later dramatists, his plays are never imitated as wholes.

2

Before writing any of his comedies Lyly had written 'Euphues'. No one would deny that 'Euphues' is perfect in small doses. What makes it unreadable in anything more than small doses is that its perfection is too easy, its repetitions, once the trick is known, mechanical. And, if we substitute an annual for an horal clock so as to allow the contemporary reader time to outgrow its spell-binding novelty, this must have been the contemporary reaction to the book. Certainly the craze for 'Euphues' did not last long. And the reason for this is no doubt related to the reason why the book is unreadable now. There is the further evidence of parody: something must be wrong with a work of art when it meets with early and consummate parody. But 'Euphues' was valuable to Lyly in something like the same way as 'Endymion' was valuable to Keats. Both writers, having plunged into the sea, came out sobered. It would have been possible for Lyly to have gone on writing the prose of 'Euphues' in his comedies, pointing determinedly to 'Gorboduc' as proof that something far more monotonous than recited 'Euphues' could be played before the Queen: he had no rivals, there were no comparisons. But he did not choose to do this: partly, no doubt, because his instinct for drama forbade it, but partly also because, like Keats, he felt that he could do better things. Better things, apart from the kind of those things. His sense of language, for whatever end, had been purified in the fantastic prim debauch of his novel.

In his comedies Lyly took love centrally for his theme because his comedies, to use the title of the collected edition of 1632, were Court Comedies. In the prologue to 'Midas' (circa 1590) courtiers are said to call for comedies since 'their subiect is loue'.[1] How complete was their amorousness may be gathered from Spenser's 'Colin Clout's Come Home Againe' (published 1595):

> ...loue most aboundeth there [the court].
> For all the walls and windows there are writ,
> All full of loue, and loue, and loue my deare,
> And all their talke and studie is of it.

Lyly's subject had to be love, but by great good fortune the love that was presentable on the stage—the 'courting' as we might say

[1] My quotations are made from R. Warwick Bond's edition, Oxford, 1902.

—was for courtiers largely a matter of language. The lover was expected to talk away skilfully as if he were playing an instrument. The training in love which, in Lyly's 'Sapho and Phao', the old hag Sybilla gives to Phao is largely a training in language; she reverts again and again to linguistic advice (II, iv). It is love which endows the comic Sir Tophas with words, though mainly with Latin words: 'Loue hath made you very eloquent', says his page Epiton. Cynthia in 'Endimion' tries to forestall, in vain, a continuation of the eloquence of Tellus: 'Well, *Tellus*, proceede, but breeflie, least taking delight in vttering thy loue, thou offende vs with the length of it.' Words and oaths, two of the five things that procure love, are cynically but figuratively defined by the cold maidens of 'Love's Metamorphosis' as 'golden blastes, out of Leaden bellowes'. Lyly repeatedly affirms that the tongues of (court) lovers are 'dipt to the root in amorous words and sweet discourses'. The courtier looked for words and Lyly was the man to show him them. Lyly frequently looks at words as words. Sir Tophas informs Dares that 'There cõmeth no soft syllable within my lips; custome hath made my wordes bloudy, and my hart barbarous: that pelting word loue, how watrish it is in my mouth, it carrieth no sound; hate, horror, death, are speaches that nourish my spirits'. And Tellus, later in the same play, makes a personal criticism involve a criticism of the same word:

I meruaile *Corsites* that you being a Captaine, who should sound nothing but terror, and suck nothing but blood, can finde in your hart to talke such smooth wordes, for that it agreeth not with your calling to vse words so soft as that of loue.

Phao is seen at a moment of small crisis to be watching his words:

Thou doest not flatter thy selfe Phao, thou art faire: faire? I feare mee faire be a word too foule for a face so passing fayre.

(which is an example also of the way Lyly makes the alliteration of 'Euphues' dramatic in the plays). Mileta in the same play says:

I laugh at that you all call loue, and iudge it onely a worde called loue.

The Prose of Lyly's Comedies

The siren in 'Love's Metamorphosis' asks Petulius why he stands 'amazed at the word Loue'. Mellacrites tells Midas that 'In this word Gold are all the powers of the gods...'. Later in the play Eristus and Mellacrites are discussing Midas's low spirits:

> *Erist.* I maruell what *Mydas* meaneth to bee so melancholy since his hunting.
> *Mel.* It is a good word in *Mydas*, otherwise I should tearme it in another blockishnes....

'Melancholy' is again discussed as an item of language when Motto, the barber, lays claim to having it applied to himself:

> *Petulius.* How now, *Motto*, what all a mort?
> *Motto.* I am as melancholy as a cat.
> *Licio.* Melancholy? marie gup, is melancholy a word for a barbar's mouth? Thou shouldst say, heauie, dull and doltish: melancholy is the creast of Courtiers armes, and now euerie base companion, beeing in his muble fubles, sayes he is melancholy.
> *Pet.* *Motto*, thou shouldst say thou art lumpish. If thou encroach vpon our courtly tearmes, weele trounce thee: belike if thou shouldst spit often, thou wouldst call it rewme. *Motto*, in men of reputation & credit it is the rewme; in such mechanicall mushrumpes, it is a catarre, a pose, the water euill. You were best weare a veluet patch on your temples too.
> *Mot.* ...I tell you boyes, it is melancholy that now troubleth me.[1]

In 'Mother Bombie' (IV, ii) Lucio exclaims, 'Verie good words, fitly applyed, brought in the nicke'.

This insistence on the word suggests that language is reverting to magic. Primitive peoples consider words as things. They refrain from saying the word that denotes the thing feared, or they say the word of the thing wished: to name a thing is to energize it for good or ill. The thing feared is kept out of language by being periphrased. Lyly and the Elizabethans, though they no longer fear things named, seem only half freed from superstition. They may be said to respect the old superstition up to a point.

1 It is amusing to find the same social barrier protecting the same distemper in the eighteenth century: in 'Spectator' 53 'a Gentleman' objects to 'Fellows in a Tavern Kitchen' claiming to have the spleen.

The Prose of Lyly's Comedies

Things are no longer feared when they are named, but it is still believed that to name them is to energize them. The first instance of the phrase 'to eat one's words' is, according to the 'O.E.D.', that of Golding in 1571. 'God eateth not his word', said Golding, 'when he hath once spoken'; otherwise, no doubt, God might feel bound to act like Pistol when he eats the leek. When Bacon attacked those who 'hunt more after words than matter' he named as offenders greater men than Lyly—to mention dramatists and novelists among his scholars was below his dignity. But even Bacon allows that words when used properly can be 'alive':

> Here therefore is the first distemper of learning, when men study words and not matter....It seems to me that Pygmalion's frenzy is a good emblem or portraiture of this vanity: for words are but the images of matter; and except they have life of reason and invention, to fall in love with them is all one as to fall in love with a picture.[1]

Lyly and many of the Elizabethans, whether or not Bacon would have cared to allow their claim, did succeed in giving a life of invention to their words. Whatever may be said of 'Euphues', Lyly's plays give this life to words. And one of the means towards vitalization is gay repetition. The Elizabethans name things in order to energize them so that their discussions may be the more vivid and concrete. Words are still things to them.

3

Lyly's explicit discrimination over words, here and elsewhere, is an important indication of what lay behind the finished state of his writings: it is equivalent to a glance at his manuscript. That discrimination led him to perfect a style of writing which his predecessors had often made unwieldy, extravagant and cacophonous, and, moreover, led him to make that style suitable for drama.

The prose of 'Supposes' is as efficient as that of Sheridan or

---

1 'Of the Advancement of Learning', I, iv, 3.

The Prose of Lyly's Comedies

Shaw, which, for Elizabethan prose, is unusual praise. As an example of it one might take the opening of I, ii:

> *Cleander.* Were these dames heere, or did mine eyes dazil?
> *Pasiphilo.* Nay, syr, heere were Polynesta and hir nourse.
> *Cl.* Was my Polynesta heere? Alas, I knewe hir not!...
> *Pas.* Syr, it is no maruell; the ayre is very mistie too-day. I my selfe knew hir better by hir apparell than by hir face.
> *Cl.* In good fayth, and I thanke God, I haue mine eye sighte goode and perfit,—little worse than when I was but twentie yeres olde.
> *Pas.* How can it be otherwise? you are but yong.
> *Cl.* I am fiftie yeres olde.
> *Pas.* [aside] He telles ten lesse than he is.
> *Cl.* What sayst thou of ten lesse?
> *Pas.* I say I woulde haue thoughte you tenne lesse; you looke like one of sixe and thirtie, or seuen and thirtie at the moste.
> *Cl.* I am no lesse than I tell.
> *Pas.* You are like inough too liue fiftie more....

The vocabulary and rhythms here are those of common speech at its most common. This kind of speech is basic English, speech used as the most economical means to an end which is kept simple. Lyly's prose, except in the half realistic 'Mother Bombie', is very seldom the most economical means to a simple end. The end, so far as its prose content goes, is always a simple one, but it becomes elaborate because the means become part of the end. The end for Lyly is a combination of the following elements: his story materialized through his characters; what he has to say, sometimes on politics, always on love (love suffering, happy, selfish with lust, or, in spite of the disclaimer before 'Sapho and Phao', pornographical); and finally the inscribing of patterns on the air, patterns that shall satisfy his developed sense of the English language.

This developed sense of the English language was a sense of the rhythms of words in combination, and of the associations and colours of words when combined in small or large groups, i.e. in phrases or in a play as a whole.

The Prose of Lyly's Comedies

4

Lyly's rhythms may be long or short. The long rhythms are those which cover the play generally, or which cover a scene or part of a scene. The short ones are those which cover a phrase, sentence or paragraph.

To begin with the shortest. Lyly seems to be attempting to bring off in English prose what was only just beginning to be done in English verse, that is, to adapt the line pattern of Latin poetry, in so far as Latin poetry is Ovidian (Lyly, like most Elizabethans, quotes Ovid on occasion). Take this line from Ovid:

> Dicite Io Pæan et Io bis dicite Pæan.[1]

This line exhibits the basic principles of Ovid's versification. It is balanced about a point, *et*. *Dicite Pæan* in the second half of the line is a repetition of two of the three items in the first half of the line and a repetition of those two in their original order:

> Dicite...Pæan...dicite Pæan.

Similarly with

> ...Io Pæan...Io...Pæan.

These may be called instances of 'parallel' balance. But the line also provides 'inverted' balance:

> Dicite Io...Io...dicite....

There are plentiful examples from Lyly of the simpler of these balances, the parallel one. Here are some of them:

Loose not the pleasaunt time of your youth, then the which there is nothing swifter, nothing sweeter.

the most holy in heart, to be most hollow of hart.

Consult, *Bacchus* will consent.

Alcumist:...and all things concurre.

Raffe. Concurre? condogge!

...making euerie trifle a title; and all the territories about me, traitours to me.

[1] 'Artis Amatoriae', II, I.

The Prose of Lyly's Comedies

With this may go Lyly's fondness for 'jingle' words: for instance, the prologue to 'Midas' reads:

> If wee present a mingle-mangle, our fault is to be excused, because the whole worlde is become an Hodge-podge.

In the same play one finds 'topsy-turuy', 'cannot tittle tattle' and 'muble fubles'.

There are many examples in Lyly of the inverted balance:

> Die Phao, Phao die.

(An effect repeated at 'Gallathea', v, ii: 'Die *Hæbe, Hæbe* die!')

> Sing and die, nay die, and neuer sing more.
>
> *Pan* is all, and all is *Pan*; thou art *Pan* and all, all *Pan* and tinkerly.
>
> *Apollo* is angrie: blame not *Apollo*....
>
> ...all her teeth are as sweet as the sweet tooth of a calfe.

The scheme is used for comic effect when the servant Petulus has the toothache:

> O teeth! ô torments!—ô torments! ô teeth!

(which might have warded Thomson off his Sophonisba line). Endimion falls asleep to the tune of both parallel and inverted balances:

> No more *Endimion*! sleepe or dye; nay die, for to sleepe, it is impossible, and yet I know not how it commeth to passe, I feele such a heavines both in mine eyes and hart, that I am sodainly benummed, yea in euery ioint; it may be wearinesse, for when did I rest? it may bee deepe melancholy, for when did I not sigh? *Cynthia*! I so; I say *Cynthia*!
>
> *He falles a sleepe.*

Ovid, or Latin generally, may also be responsible for Lyly's interest in getting a sentence to a point where ellipsis becomes possible:

> ...thou seest that of gold there is sacietie, of loue there cannot.
>
> My pride the gods disdaine; my pollicie men....
>
> That which necessitie maketh me indure, loue reverence, wisdome wonder at.
>
> Your Maiesties wordes haue beene alwaies deedes, and your deedes vertues.

(which shows how much Shakespeare is indebted to Lyly for his manner of compliment). This ellipsis is partly explained by a wish to give English the concision of Latin, to clear out of a sentence whatever may be left to implication. With those elements absent the pattern can be blocked more boldly. (Pope adopts similar aims and methods in his couplet.)

These are the kinds of effects which Lyly contrives in a short compass. But more remarkable are those which cover larger areas. Lyly arranges his plots with a greater technical skill than that which any of his predecessors could command, though he never attempts, of course, anything like the elaborate mechanics of Kyd. Lyly's plots are simple: the connecting of sub-plot with main-plot is adequately carpentered. But the way that Lyly realizes his plot in language shows that he can wield larger quantities of words as skilfully as he can manipulate smaller. He distributes different kinds of prose to provide the simple relief of contrast. For instance, I, i and ii of 'Endimion' are almost entirely leisurely in rhythm, I, iii is almost all in 'short sharp barks', I, iv almost all leisurely, II, i begins with a two-page speech by Endimion and, with the entry of Tellus, becomes quicker until, after a tit-for-tat dialogue, it ends leisurely. And Lyly demonstrates, for other reasons than Shaw's, that a speech need not be undramatic because long. Lyly places his long speeches at points in the play where they are dramatically valuable, where they are demanded by the dramatic life of the play or scene, or by the emotion of the character. Midas, for instance, is not seen after I, i till he reappears at III, i. The interim has been filled with reports of his alchemistic embarrassment. The audience is waiting eagerly to see this embarrassment and its effect on Midas. They are kept waiting for what in print is ten pages. When they do see him he is introduced with a speech of one-and-a-half pages (i.e. 64 long lines of prose). Thus speech is dramatically necessary. The author of 'Euphues' still liked to fill a generous playground with his prose antics, but that is not the first reason why Midas speaks at this length. Midas speaks at this length because to have spoken more briefly would have spoiled the balance of the play, would have baulked the purposely incited expectations of the audience. Diana in 'Gallathea' has a speech of one-and-a-half pages, and moreover that speech is in the manner of 'Euphues'. But she is a goddess speaking *ex cathedra* and her theme is chastity. She speaks stiffly, like the Lady in 'Comus' on a similar occasion. There is a different kind of reason for Eumenides's long speech at 'Endimion', III, iv. Eumenides meets the old priest Geron and tells him that he is on his way to Thessaly to find a remedy to awaken Endimion. Geron informs him that further travel may be unnecessary: whoever can clearly see the bottom of the fountain near which they are standing can have remedy for anything, but the sight is only vouchsafed to those who are faithful lovers. Eumenides is full of nervous questions, but at last, calling upon his love Semele, he looks into the water, where he sees a graven invitation for his question. His instinctive desire to ask for success in his love makes him forget for a moment the cause of his travels. Then slowly he remembers that he is seeking relief for Endimion. His speech is a long one (a page) because the claims of love and friendship seem almost equal and the balance hangs uncertain. At the end of the speech Eumenides is still undecided and asks Geron's advice. Geron's speech runs to half a page, since he is bound to give reasons when so much depends on his preferring friendship to love. Eumenides accepts his conclusions and for half a page hymns the quality of friendship. The scene, having reached its climax of story and philosophy, continues and ends in briefer rhythms.

The long speeches, then, are placed with a scrupulous attention to their dramatic value. And, further, they are made interesting in themselves by Lyly's methods of constructing them. He usually organizes his long speeches around alternating proper nouns, which, in his plays, are almost always euphonious with classic syllables and rich in classic connotation. One of the best examples of this stanzaic treatment is the speech of Phao (II, iv) which repeats the names Phao and Sapho (and Sicily) until they are joined with that of Sybilla, the speech ending with what might almost be part of a line of Ovid:

> ...Phao...Phao...Sapho...Sicily...poore Phao....Die Phao, Phao die....Ah Phao...Sycilyan stone....Howe now Phao....O Sapho! faire Sapho!...But ah! thy bewty Sapho, thy bewty!...blabbe it Phao ...Sybilla....O Sapho! sweete Sapho! Sapho!—Sibilla!

At his best Lyly will design a whole scene with the elaboration of an Elizabethan motet. The best example is the final scene of 'Love's Metamorphosis' in which Cupid, after uniting Protea with Petulius, transforms the three girls back into human shape for the benefit of their three lovers. Again the geometry of the situation is enforced by the continuous use of proper nouns. The way the scene runs is worth summarizing: having united Protea to Petulius, Cupid brings on the girls in their right shape ; the men exclaim with delight but the girls will not hear of marriage—they would prefer to be rock, rose-bush and bird again; but when Cupid informs them that their next metamorphosis will be one into abominable beasts, they begin to listen to reason and are at last persuaded of the worth of their lovers. If the three pairs of lovers are represented by the symbols Aa, Bb, and Cc, where the capital letter represents the man, and the small letter the woman, the progress of the scene from the entry of the girls onward may be represented as follows: A. B. C. Ceres. Cupid. A. B. C. Ceres. a. c. b. Ceres. Cupid. A. B. C. Cupid. a. A. b. B. c. C. Cupid. Ceres. a. A. b. B. c. C. Ceres. a. A. a. A. b. B. b. B. c. C. Cupid. Ceres. Cupid. Ceres. Erisicthon. B. Erisicthon. Ceres. A. Ceres. (The treatment here may be compared to Shakespeare's in 'As You Like It', where at v, ii Rosalind plays a part similar to that of Cupid.) This patterning at its simplest may be seen where Phao meets Sapho, both falling in love at first sight. Sapho and Phao enter (from different sides of the stage) and Phao asks who that gentlewoman is, and is told it is Sapho, and Sapho asks what fair boy that is and is told it is Phao. Lyly is here doing little more than drawing two lines, but those two lines cross. Shakespeare does nothing but elaborate this diagram when, at the first encounter of Romeo and Juliet, he makes them share a sonnet. In the 'Magic Flute' the delayed first meeting of Tamino with Pamina takes the form of a short duet which is contrived so that a tripartite phrase is first divided between them in the order Pamina-Tamino-Pamina, and then repeated with the order, and of course the pitch, inverted. Pamina then sings a phrase of eight notes which is repeated an octave lower by Tamino and they finish by singing simultaneously the same phrase (very slightly varied), beginning at the octave and finishing at the sixth. Both Shakespeare and Mozart are in the middle of a rapid and crowded scene and can only spare a moment for this important climax. Only by the boldest, most geometrical strokes can they give the moment its due prominence as climax. Lyly's climax is not so brilliant, but his method is the same. He gets the maximum effect by the simplest means.

5

The change from 'Euphues' and the plays in this matter of the quality and application of rhythm may be paralleled by the change in the quality and application of the imagery. 'Euphues', a young man's book, was crammed with the junk which Greene parodied to perfection in the 'Carde of Fancie'. But, in the plays, the imagery is of a different order. Lyly saw the difference between dramatic prose and narrative prose, or, since 'Euphues' is never really narrative, between prose heard and prose read. He still writes his Euphues prose in which each idea impales three different instances from mythological or pseudo-scientific lore, but he confines it to his prologues. There is very little mediaeval junk among the images of the plays. Instead, to take two examples from 'Endimion', one finds imagery like the following:

Where others number their yeeres, their houres, their minutes, and steppe to age by staires, thou onely hast thy yeeres and times in a cluster, being olde before thou remembrest thou wast younge.

...Loue is a Lorde of misrule, and keepeth Christmas in my corps.

The Prose of Lyly's Comedies

Imagery is plentiful in the comic scenes and is used to create the effect of neat grotesqueness. For example, Petulius cries 'all my nether teeth are lose, and wag like the keyes of a paire of virginals'. Lyly, like all the Elizabethans, uses imagery from 'man-made' things (e.g. arras), or if not 'man-made', man-improved (e.g. jewels). He is particularly fond of stitchery and weaving as a source for imagery—his patron and employer, the Earl of Oxford, had come back from Italy laden with silks and oriental stuffs which had been used for clothes and hangings. Lyly often mentions stuffs directly in his plays. Tellus, in 'Endimion', is imprisoned, but only at a loom ('Shall she worke stories or poetries?' is the only question her jailor asks). Gallathea who has just disguised herself as a boy comments on the change with 'I will now vse for the distaffe the bowe, and play at quaites abroade, that was wont to sowe in my Sampler at home'. In the same play Rami says:

> Come, Cupid,...you shall weaue Samplers all night....All the stories that are in *Dianaes* Arras, which are of loue, you must picke out with your needle, & in that place sowe *Vesta* with her Nuns, and *Diana* with her Nimphes.

In 'Mother Bombie', I, iii, Livia, 'who hath nothing to her dowrie but her needle', is continuously associated with stitchery. Endimion's 'thoughts...are stitched to the starres', and the phrase is repeated by the astronomer in 'Gallathea'. Midas's 'eyes are stitcht on *Cælias* face'. Rami in 'Love's Metamorphosis' avows that 'truth is wouen into [his] loue, as veines into bodies'. Floscula in 'Endimion' describes 'Affection that is bred by enchauntment' as 'like a flower that is wrought in silke, in colour and forme most like, but nothing at all in substance or sauour'. Diana suspects Cupid of being 'the weauer of these woes'. In 'Mother Bombie' cabbage is a cloak for beef and is 'imbrodered' with pepper.

This use of imagery constitutes one of Lyly's major contributions to Elizabethan drama. There is no imagery in the work of previous dramatists that is worth the name. With later dramatists,

29

as every schoolboy now knows, it is different. Except when writing realistic drama like 'Arden of Feversham', or, to a less extent, when writing revenge plays, later dramatists use imagery with the freedom of Lyly and sometimes in imitation of him. Shakespeare in the comedies frequently makes characters speak as Lyly would have made them—to take a simple instance, the clown in 'Twelfth Night' says: 'the tailor make thy doublet of changeable taffeta, for thy mind is a very opal'. Lyly changes the surface quality of the drama at a touch and with the same completeness with which he changes the subject-matter. The change from Fielding to Sterne (the Sterne of the 'Sentimental Journey' and of 'Tristram Shandy' where it resembles the 'Sentimental Journey') would be a fair parallel in the novel.

Lyly's width of diction is remarkable. He combines the most 'beautiful' words (e.g. 'amorous') with slang words ('muble fubles'), yet he so selects and combines that both kinds of words amalgamate to produce a single complex impression. The 'beautiful' words are given warmth and body by the slang and the slang purified by the 'beautiful' words, so that heavenly and earthly fuse as—to compare smaller things with greatest—they fuse in the 'Tempest'. The effect is one only possible for those who have mastered their sense of language, and Lyly, in this respect, comes closest to the Sterne of the 'Sentimental Journey' in the kind of effect he seeks and obtains. Both of them mix words with an apparently free hand, and both contrive that the dominant element in their effect is one of pleasantness, of prettiness, and of the degree of these qualities which requires a word such as beauty. Whenever their prose touches pitch, it seems only to have brushed against dark finely mixed colours on a palette.

1937

IV. WORDS FOR PRINCES:
BACON'S ESSAYS

I

I⊤ is a brazen head in 'Friar Bacon and Friar Bungay' which utters the three empty crashes of wisdom, 'Time is... Time was... Time is past'. Wisdom is notoriously impersonal, and Francis Bacon, even more than Friar Bacon, was notoriously wise. Writing of him in 1657, Dr Rawley sees his wisdom as supernatural: 'His *Opinions*, and *Assertions*, were, for the most part, *Binding*; And not contradicted, by any; Rather like *Oracles*, then *Discourses*.' He seems to have compiled many of the essays with his brain centred like that of a mathematician. He seems often, indeed, to have written with his head severed and placed cleanly before him on the table, an inch or two beyond the farther edge of his manuscript. It was a 'curious' head, severed bloodlessly, a microcosm indefatigably contrived, an enormous packed head. And peering into it, Bacon would find his wisdom cold, firm, convenient—a wisdom which could be pocketed for use like a bunch of keys. Sidney had striven to look in his heart and write. Bacon, it seems, folded his heart away. And, his eyes sharp with their *lumen siccum*, he stared into the clear perspectives in his brain.

2

Before writing an essay, he might, one feels, have made use of the invocation which Chaucer adapts from Dante for the opening of the third Book of the 'Hous of Fame':

> O god of science and of light,
> Apollo, through thy grete might...
> ...helpe me to shewe now
> That in myn hede y-marked is.

Wisdom such as Bacon's seems marked on the mind of its owner,

31

seems to have material actuality. Bacon is so wise that a sentence quoted from Solomon falls with exquisite rightness into the mosaic prepared to receive it, its aged, far-fetched substance hardly detectable as different. An epigram from Seneca, from a Christian Father, from Montaigne, embeds itself deeply into the little gap which he has provided. Bacon searched books widely, and kept a commonplace book at his elbow ready to take in all the notable wisdom of the world, every dust-encumbered coin of truth, the nobles and angels of other times. One by one, as he pursued his close reading, these *dicta* would be noted, and later arranged for convenience under headings. It was a habit of the age. 'Belvedere' and 'England's Parnassus' in 1600 show, for example, the same method applied to verse.

Bacon's distinction lies in the human worth and encyclopaedic extent of his compilings. This habit of his would almost of itself explain the manner of some of his essays. Even if Bacon did not write the 'Essay of a King', where the several points are actually numbered down the margin, such essays as, 'Of the true Greatnesse of Kingdomes and Estates' and 'Of Ambition' make separate points without recording them numerically. These might almost be pages of ordered *sententiae* torn from a commonplace book of things thought. The posthumously printed 'Short Notes for Civil Conversation' is a numbered sequence of nine aphorisms, some of which were rejected and more of which were employed when Bacon came to assemble 'Of Discourse'. In 'Of Ambition' epigram glows darkly after epigram, wisdom drips steadily from the adjusted burette:

> *Ambition* is like *Choler*; Which is an Humour, that maketh Men Actiue, Earnest, Full of Alacritie, and Stirring, if it be not stopped. But if it be stopped, and cannot haue his Way, it becommeth Adust, and thereby Maligne and Venomous. So *Ambitious Men*, if they finde the way Open for their Rising, and still get forward, they are rather Busie than Dangerous....

It might be Minerva dictating to an Elizabethan secretary, almost an Elizabethan typist.

Words for Princes

3

This impersonality of matter and manner derives partly from Bacon's wish to be of especial use to princes. It was hard for the essay at first to leave the council chamber and buttonhole a fellow in the street. Bacon, unlike Charles Lamb, was often not talking to anybody who cared to listen, but to the chosen great ones of the world, whose ears might be inclined or might not, but who would attend, if at all, only to words of a becoming weight and dignity. Even the cordial, sensitive 'Of Gardens' is intended for those who may attain the 'Royall Ordering of *Gardens*'. When he writes of building, it is a palace which he has in mind, the kind Inigo Jones would have been commissioned for.

And yet, impersonal as these writings may be, they are essays. And when a man writes an essay—in Johnson's words 'a loose sally of the mind'—he must seem sooner or later to lay down his pen and continue with spoken words. He must seem to turn to his reader, draw his chair a little closer, and speak what he would feel to be affectation if merely written down. One thinks of Cowley—'I believe I can tell the particular little chance that filled my head first with such chimes of verse, as have never since left ringing there: For I remember...': of Addison—'When I am in a serious humour, I very often walk by myself in Westminster Abbey...': of Lamb—'I have no repugnances...I can read anything which I call a *book*...': of Max Beerbohm—'I should like everyone to go about doing just what he pleased—short of altering any of the things to which I have grown accustomed...'. And fortunately one can think of Bacon—'I knew two *Noble-men* of the West Part of *England*...'. And, encouraged by such nearer scraping of his chair, one cries imploringly, 'Leave your Princes and High Folks, Sir, to yonder Machiavel. Tell us more about the first sugar-man in the Canaries, more about dancers practising in heavy boots, more about the orange-tawny bonnets of Jews, more about the odours of ointments'. But there is not much need to cry out. Like all the Elizabethans, Bacon had the vivid mind that would not stay official. Even in the high essay 'Of Great Place' the wisdom and argument wreath in such exquisite individual words that passion stirs behind their stillness, a passion in this instance envious and disillusioned. When all is said, we read the essays for the man watching, fidgeting, smiling, stealing behind them.

4

If Bacon, then, stared at the head before him, it was at least his own head. And until he made his first letter on the paper the head was of the usual run of heads, set naturally upon the body and warmly communicating with the other members. Bacon, before he set himself squarely at the table, had been walking up and down in the world, engrossed in every step he was taking, his senses those of a quick animal, his wits ticking delicately and incessantly as a watch, receiving, selecting, interpreting. The words of Dr Rawley provide valuable evidence:

He was no *Plodder* upon *Books*; Though he read much; And that, with great Judgement, and Rejection of Impertinences, incident to many *Authours*: For he would ever interlace a *Moderate Relaxation* of His *Minde*, with his *Studies*; As *Walking*; Or *Taking the Aire abroad* in his *Coach*; or some other befitting *Recreation*: And yet he would *loose* no *Time*, In as much as upon his *First* and *Immediate Return*, he would fall to *Reading* again....

And there is also the record of Aubrey: 'He had a delicate lively hazel eye; Dr Harvey told me it was like the eye of a viper.'

Bacon the man was a product of the Renaissance. Man's glory, generous or tense, his opportunities of mind and body, his eye finely rolling across the subtlety and magnificence of the world, his joy in learning, discovering, weighing, creating—all this as it existed in Bacon's mind sifted through into the essays. 'What a piece of work is a man!' cried Hamlet and in the swelling rhapsody that follows he spreads himself like huge branches through heaven and earth. This Tamburlaine-Faustus spirit may have first reached Bacon as a dry echo through his four book-lined walls, but even that echo excited, and pricked him out into the street. Bacon was

34

concerned with Man and the things Man had made. The human mind convoluted as variously as the human body, the expression of the human mind encrusting the earth—towns, villages, roads, fortifications, ships and a thousand more—these were peered into. And there have not been many men who have peered as intensely into the human mind. Even the sea-mud of the subconscious became transparent as water as he gazed.

5

It would be untrue to say in general that Bacon's eye simplified, that he saw things as diagrams which in reality are tangles. He sees men as mechanized at the centre by a single spring, but by a spring which only the trained and lidless eye can discover. Perhaps on occasion the skill for making this discovery may incline Bacon to think that the discovery, if made at all, is made for ever, that only this one particular spring works the man. Like the writer of a comedy of humours, he may not always allow for the control of other springs in their turn. But Bacon knows enough. One has only to glance at 'Of Discourse' to be set trembling for one's dinner conversation. One has only to glance at 'Of Reuenge' to match La Rochefoucauld. Much as Bacon was devoted to books and studies, it was living man that fascinated him most persistently. It took less than spring at his window to sting him to the cry, 'Farewell my book and my devocioun!' It is the first distemper of learning, he said, when men study words and not matter. 'Abeunt studia in mores' was a favourite sentence of his. His curiosity for life and for the things left where life has been tempts him to exhaust those public treasuries which are built without doors or defences. 'Of Trauaile' shows him calculatingly rapacious for every visible and audible detail of foreign lands. The prose palpitates with lists of them.

Hamlet, hymning Man, exclaimed, 'In apprehension how like a god'. Bacon and others were bolder still and exclaimed, 'How like God!' Like Sir Charles Grandison later, Man was 'an imitator of the Almighty'. Or, perhaps, less affirmatively, he could and should be. And so in some of the essays, Bacon, to his own satisfaction, will prove a point (e.g. the advisability of having counsellors) by citing the awful example of Deity. Even that most famous of openings, 'God *Almightie* first Planted a *Garden*', carries the implied *ergo*, Man is quite right in following suit. Man stood firm.

But there were times when the godlike and Godlike powers in Man dwindled hideously, daemonizing before his eyes. Hamlet, one remembers, would have counted himself king of infinite space were it not that he had bad dreams. Bacon at times stands puzzled, small, frightened for all his indefatigable greatness. Writing his essay, his theme will shoot out into sharp prongs. But beyond the reach of his prongs wander all the old spectres casting uncertain darkness over his systems. As surely as Sir Thomas Browne, Bacon has an Africa and all its prodigies in him. The essay of 'Of Delaies' is no more than a spider's web spun across chaos and old night: 'The Ripeness, or Vnripenesse, of the Occasion (as we said) must euer be well weighed....' Embryon atoms clash and war behind 'Of Vicissitude of Things', and Bacon concludes, 'But it is not good, to looke too long, vpon these turning Wheeles of *Vicissitude*, lest we become Giddy'. And in the essay 'Of Death' the Elizabethan has shrunk to a worm. Miserably small, he contrives a cathedral sonority of phrase. His little mortal tongue tugs at the echoes like bells. But it is mortal nevertheless.

Man might smell of mortality in whiffs, but the Elizabethans were continually busy ignoring it. They had a peculiar kind of mind that could tingle at a mention of the Bermudas and tingle with something like the same heat at the sight of a silk knot tied charmingly. Bacon, or any of them, might lean to dip his quill in the ink, and his velvet sleeve, stretching out, might suddenly bloom in the light. An ordinary action, one of a thousand, and yet an individual item for an anthology of pleasures. Not that Bacon surrendered his mind to the sensation, as Keats would have done. The pleasure was a fringe, and no more than that, to a mind busy with other matters. Bacon did not pause in his serious meditations to watch the sleeve coming and going in the light. But the meditations were the nimbler, the more fiery and delectable for the attendant experience. The Elizabethans all felt that pleasure. The tumult of sensuous metaphor in their English, whether prose or verse, is ample proof. Bacon's imagery alone would testify to the quality of his subsidiary experience.

6

And so, as he writes, his left hand seems to stroke the things which the words represent, his eye to glisten with the colour in his memory. Take this passage:

Ouer the *Arches*, let there bee an *Entire Hedge*, of some Foure Foot High, framed also vpon Carpenters Worke: And vpon the *Vpper Hedge*, ouer euery *Arch*, a little *Turret*, with a *Belly*, enough to receiue a *Cage* of *Birds*: And ouer euery *Space*, betweene the *Arches*, some other little *Figure*, with Broad Plates of *Round Coloured Glasse*, gilt, for the *Sunne*, to Play vpon. But this *Hedge* I entend to be, raised vpon a *Bancke*, not Steepe, but gently Slope, of some Six Foot, set all with *Flowers*. Also I vnderstand, that this *Square* of the *Garden*, should not be the whole breadth of the Ground, but to leaue, on either Side, Ground enough, for diuersity of *Side Alleys*: Vnto which, the Two *Couert Alleys* of the Greene, may deliuer you.

One feels that if Bacon had been confronted with a perfect garden, nothing would have been wasted on him—colours, measurements, ingenuities. He would have found the one planted in the beginning by God intolerably careless. More to his mind would have been that one in Japan contrived 500 years before he wrote. Prince Genji's fastidious horticulture is almost his own (I quote from Mr Waley's translation of 'The Tale of Genji'):

He effected great improvement in the appearance of the grounds by a judicious handling of knoll and lake, for though such features were already there in abundance, he found it necessary here to cut away a slope, there to dam a stream, that each occupant of the various quarters might look out of her windows upon such a prospect as pleased her best.

Words for Princes

To the south-east he raised the level of the ground, and on this bank planted a profusion of early flowering trees. At the foot of this slope the lake curved with especial beauty, and in the foreground, just beneath the windows, he planted borders of cinquefoil, of red-plum, cherry, wistaria, kerria, rock-azelia, and other such plants as are at their best in spring-time; for he knew that Murasaki was in especial a lover of the spring; while here and there, in places where they would not obstruct his main plan, autumn beds were cleverly interwoven with the rest.

Like Prince Genji, Bacon had antennae sensitive enough to know and require perfection, perfection for the mind and body together. A shudder passes through his bones as he warns the makers of houses and gardens to make provision against the intemperance of English weather—otherwise the twin halves of mind and body will not fit together to form the unit:

You are to frame some of them likewise for Shelter, that when the Wind blows Sharpe, you may walke, as in a Gallery.

And

Cast it also, that you may haue Roomes, both for Summer, and Winter: Shadie for Summer, and Warme for Winter. You shall have sometimes Faire *Houses*, so full of Glasse, that one cannot tell, where to become, to be out of the Sunne, or Cold.

And turning back to the longer passage quoted from 'Of Gardens', look at the word *deliuer*. Andrew Marvell's soul glided into the boughs of his garden, and Bacon's, too, crept out a little above his body, far enough to appreciate the cohesion of mind and body. The body indeed could be transformed by the act of union. Bacon did not feel the common walking motion while footing paths of the Perfect Type. He seemed perhaps rather to be standing still. It was the paths themselves that were moving him along, *deliuering* him. But not into *Side Alleys*—such wording would have missed the truth. It was into their *diuersity* that he was being delivered. Bacon would have dismissed the above sentences as 'but Toyes'. Yet in the phrasing of his dismissal would lurk the evidence of his own incurable fancy. More than any other essay that 'Of Maskes and Triumphs' evinces the subtle

38

mechanism of his senses. Again it is the harmony of body and mind together which he is seeking, and seeking with something like anxiety. A Jacobean hall, candlelit, gilded, perfumed, where a masque—perhaps one of Ben Jonson's—was in progress, surely here, one vows, Bacon would confront perfection. But he is sensitive to possibilities rather than to actualities. The wording seems to indicate that he has never happened on all the sleek elements of perfection arrayed together. It is certain, however, that no man has ever brought more of what there was of it away with him, and better provided for its completion:

Let the *Scenes* abound with *Light*, specially *Coloured* and *Varied*: And let the Masquers, or any other, that are to come down from the *Scene*, haue some Motions, vpon the *Scene* it selfe, before their Comming down: For it drawes the Eye strangely, & makes it with great pleasure, to desire to see that, it cannot perfectly discerne.... The *Colours*, that shew best by Candle-light, are; White, Carnation, and a kinde of Sea-Water-Greene.... Some *Sweet Odours*, suddenly comming forth, without any drops falling, are, in such a Company, as there is Steame and Heate, Things of great Pleasure; & Refreshment. *Double Masques*, one of Men, another of Ladies, addeth State, and Variety. But All is Nothing except the *Roome* be kept Cleare, and Neat....

7

The civility that Bacon sought must, like that of Herrick's Julia, be a faintly wild civility. There is no excellent beauty, he said, that hath not some strangeness in the proportion. Light as masques are they must not be too airy. He would have acting not dancing ('a Meane and Vulgar Thing') and 'the *Voices* of the *Dialogue*, would be Strong and Manly, (A Base, and a Tenour; No Treble;) and the *Ditty* High and Tragicall; Not nice or Dainty'. Excellent beauty might be sought in many things, but to be really excellent, its strangeness must incline to the sombre. And it was at some point in this inclination to the sombre that Bacon's attention almost irritably abstracted itself away from the senses into meditation. The sombreness which he sought was little more than

39

a twilight which made meditation easier. Something like the same thing happened to Spenser and Milton. Beauty for them all had to be serious so that they could more easily transcend it. Even the perfection of a masque by candlelight, Bacon had to conclude, was but a toy. He might have struck out the words he had written, but princes would have masques, and so it was clearly his duty to commend the right standards.

1930

V. 'OTHELLO' AND 'THE ALCHEMIST' AT OXFORD IN 1610

I

OUR knowledge of these matters is scanty, and it is probably for that reason that we are surprised to find full honours being accorded to 'Othello' and 'The Alchemist' at Oxford in September 1610, and to have to accept the implication that such professional performances were the ordinary thing. We are indebted for information on this subject to a letter of Henry Jackson's and to William Fulman's transcript, fifty years after, of sentences in it which interested him.

William Fulman (1632–88) made certain excerpts from the Latin correspondence of Henry Jackson. They were both prominent members of Corpus Christi College, Oxford, and both held the college living of Meysey Hampton, Fulman taking it up seven years after Jackson's death in 1662. Presumably the excerpts were made after Jackson's death. They occupy part of Volume 10 of the Fulman Papers. On folios 83ᵛ and 84ʳ come those from a letter headed 'D. G. P.' and dated September 1610. An earlier letter, with the date '1610, Jun. 25', is headed a little more explicitly, 'Amico s. [suo ?] G. P.' I have not yet discovered who 'G. P.' was. He may have been George de St Paul, a benefactor of Corpus Christi College, who died in 1613. The part of Jackson's letter of September which Fulman preserved concerns recent theatrical events in Oxford:

D. G. P.

—Postremis his diebus adfuerunt Regis Actores Scenici. Egerunt cum applausu maximo, pleno theatro. Sed viris piis et doctis impii merito visi sunt, quod non contenti Alcumistas perstringere, ipsas sanctas Scripturas fœdissimè violarint. Anabaptistas scilicet yellicabant; ut sub hac persona lateret improbitas.—

—Theologos nostros, qui (pudet dicere) avidissimè confluebant.—

41

'Othello' and 'The Alchemist' at Oxford in 1610

—nusquam majori plausu theatra nostra sonuisse, quam cum intraret personatus ille nebulo, qui, ut fictam Anabaptistarum sanctitatem spectatoribus deridendam proponeret, scripturas impie, et prodigiosè contaminavit. Habuerunt et Tragœdias, quas decorè, et aptè agebant. In quibus non solùm dicendo, sed etiam faciendo quædam lachrymas movebant.—

—At verò Desdemona illa apud nos a marito occisa, quanquam optimè semper causam egit, interfecta tamen magis movebat; cum in lecto decumbens spectantium misericordiam ipso vultu imploraret.—

Sept. 1610.[1]

There can be no doubt that the first play referred to is Jonson's 'Alchemist'. No other play owned by the King's Men would have combined the themes of alchemists and Anabaptists. And even in the Quarto text of 1612 there is enough 'violation' of the Bible to scandalize men like Jackson. The Anabaptists use scripture 'prodigiosè', and, among other instances, Adam, Moses, Miriam and Solomon are given as authors of alchemistic books. Moreover, it is possible that the text of 1612 represents a play at the far end of a process of expurgation, the Folio of 1616 attempting to complete the process. 'Gad' remains, for instance, in 1612, and a reference to swearing on the '*greeke* Testament'; but in the folio these have become 'IOVE' and '*greeke* XENOPHON'.

One cannot be certain that Henry Jackson attended these performances. 'Sonuisse' certainly might mean that Jackson is reporting from hearsay. But there can be little doubt that Jackson attended at least 'Othello' and possibly the other tragedies. A detail like 'ipso vultu', for example, is not the sort of thing preserved from a friend's comment and repeated in a letter afterwards. If Jackson did not attend 'The Alchemist' himself, the *viri pii et docti* may have done so.

2

This letter constitutes the earliest evidence yet found of the conditions under which professional players acted at Oxford. In his 'Shakespeare and the Universities' (1923) Dr F. S. Boas put the

1 Printed by permission of the librarian of C.C.C.

position clearly, so far as common knowledge and his own findings then went. He showed that the declared policy of the University was to prohibit players, even if necessary by bribing them to keep away. But the players would not always be bribed. They preferred to act, though where and how has remained a puzzle. Dr Boas thinks they acted in inn yards. Direct evidence for this, however, is very late. Anthony Wood in 1657–59 records performances of plays in the yards of Oxford inns, and when, in July 1661, he speaks of the Duke of York's players at the King's Arms in Holywell, he notes that they 'acted on the stage in the yard' (Boas, p. 32). The definite article, 'the stage', suggests that by this time there was a regular structure for playing on. Wood mentions plays being performed in tennis courts. Jackson's remarks would lead one to expect something better than an inn yard.[1]

'Theologi' flock to 'The Alchemist', at least, with the utmost eagerness: *avidissimè confluebant*. These theologians may be students merely or may include D.D.s: we are told nothing specific. But whatever the audience for 'The Alchemist', the tragedies were almost certainly attended by Jackson, and if by Jackson, then by the University at large, excepting extreme Puritans. If men like Henry Jackson, M.A., puritanical cleric, the friend and editor of Rainolds and Hooker—if such men attended non-academic plays performed by professional actors, it would seem that no one paid attention to the University Statute of 1584 which forbade this attendance.

Ben Jonson's dedication of 'Volpone' to the two Universities in 1607 is a dedication completely above board and dignified as a Chancellor's speech. Such a dedication would have been impossible if the authorities had still meant what they said in 1584. Jonson speaks of 'Volpone' as having been 'seene, iudg'd, and to

1 These statements overlook earlier evidence. Dr Boas, in a letter to the 'Times Literary Supplement' of 31 Aug. 1933, pointed out that players were acting in the yard of the King's Arms in July 1634, and that by 1630 this inn had already become the recognized headquarters for professional acting.

my crowne approv'd' by those '*most learned* ARBITRESSES' ('The Alchemist', by the way, appears to have been given even more thunderous applause than 'Volpone': 'nusquam...' etc.). If the University was ready to flock to such plays, it looks as if better accommodation could have been found for them than the casual noises, insecurities and draughts of an inn yard. The tone of Jackson's remarks about the tragedies, and especially about 'Othello', which was more affecting than anything else, though the others moved tears—all this suggests an intense and intimate performance which would surely have been impossible out of doors. Jackson uses the phrases, 'pleno theatro', 'theatra nostra' and 'apud nos'. These seem to imply something better than a yard and certainly state that there was more than one place recognized as available for players. We know from the minutes of the Oxford City Council (February 1579–80) that players were forbidden to play 'within the Guilde Hall or the Lower hall', and though there is only one recorded instance of this decision being waived (1586, Boas, p. 16) it may have been forgotten. 'I have not been able to find', writes Dr Boas, '...any evidence that the enactment was repealed: probably during the Civil War it was simply forgotten' (p. 33). But it may well have been forgotten earlier, and within the quarter of a century separating 1586 from 1610. If Masters of Arts are ready to hear music, they do not rest satisfied with minstrels at street-corners.[1]

1 Dr Boas's letter backed up his theory of an inn-yard performance by noting that the Oxford City audited accounts for the year Michaelmas 1609–Michaelmas 1610 record that ten shillings was paid by the Mayor to the King's Men: 'it is a natural inference', Dr Boas contends, 'that it is to these ["rate-aided"] performances] that Henry Jackson alludes.'

In a private letter to me of 20 July 1933 W. J. Lawrence wrote: 'Of course the fact that most players appearing in Oxford before 1629 acted in inn yards in nowise detracts from the possibility that the King's Men acted within the precincts of Christ Church in 1610. They would seem to have enjoyed special privileges.' He also noted that: 'Dr Boas [in 'Crosfield's Diary and the Caroline Stage', 'Fortnightly Review', April 1925] quotes a passage from Crosfield's diary in which, after enumerating the heads of the five London theatrical companies in 1634 beginning with the King's Men, he goes on to say: "Of all these companies yᵉ first if

'Othello' and 'The Alchemist' at Oxford in 1610

One can be certain from what Jackson says that the Oxford performance of 'Othello' was as finely managed as at the Blackfriars, or even as at Court. Oxford gave Jonson a degree in 1619. This degree, the culmination of an honourable relationship of long standing, carries with it the approval of the colleges. And such approval may have extended to allowing the use of college halls to professional players. With the evidence of Jackson's letter behind it, it may mean that the King's Men in 'Volpone' and 'The Alchemist' were as welcome on a college stage as Scholars and Fellows in a Latin comedy. And if 'Volpone' and 'The Alchemist', then 'Othello' and 'Hamlet'. (We know from the title-page of the first Quarto of 'Hamlet' that the play·'hath beene diuerse times acted by his Highnesse seruants in the Cittie of London: as also in the two Vniversities of Cambridge and Oxford, and elsewhere.') Jonson, according to Wood, was associated with Christ Church before receiving his degree. 'Dr. Rich. Corbet of Ch. Ch.', Wood writes, 'and other Poets of this University, did reverence to his parts, invite him to Oxon, where continuing for some time in Ch. Ch. in writing and composing Plays, he was, as a Member thereof, actually created M. of A. in 1619.' If 'The Alchemist' were acted in a college hall, it would almost certainly have been in the hall of Christ Church, the hall in which most of the academic plays were produced. Christ Church takes Ben Jonson in in 1619. The same college may have taken in his plays ten years earlier.

---

they please may come to Oxōn, but none without the speciall ltrẽs from the Chancellor obteined by meanes of yᵉ Secretary to the Vice Chanc'loʳ".'

Lawrence considered Dr Boas's interpretation of these words erroneous: 'Dr Boas...takes it to mean that even the King's Men could not come without special permission. To my mind, we are bound to read "else" after "none", since there would be no sense in excepting the King's Men if they had to go through the same routine as the others. There can be little doubt that the King's Company enjoyed immunity because of the terms of their patent, which specifically allowed them to act in University towns.'

45

3

Certain conclusions which affect literary history follow from this performance of 'The Alchemist' in September 1610. It has been found a difficult matter to assign a precise date to the action of the play. Ananias's two references to dates by day of the week of the numbered month do not tally with each other, and perhaps were not intended to. But the play clearly is supposed to happen (*a*) in 1610 (Dame Pliant, born some three years after the Armada, is nineteen years old); and (*b*) on a day during the heat of the plague of that year. So much is clear. But Ananias makes difficulties. Subtle, at III, ii, 129–30, gives 'some fifteene dayes' as the period for the perfecting of the 'Magisterium' and Ananias calculates that this would mean 'about the second day, of the third weeke, In the ninth month'. Mr C. M. Hathaway, who edited the play in 1903, begins to reckon the year at March and so arrives at 16 November as the date for the Magisterium, fifteen days before that giving the date of the action—i.e. 1 November. The Oxford editors accept this (II, 88). But there is another of these scriptural reckonings to be taken into account. At V, v, 103–4 Ananias gives 'the second day of the fourth weeke, In the eight month' as the date on which the elders' money was paid; and this, beginning the year at March, would mean 23 October. Unless there was a payment before the action began, Ananias ought to have said 'this morning', since the action happens within one day. It does not seem that much attention can be paid to Ananias's arithmetic. The Oxford editors conclude that 'The two dates may be taken as fixing the supposed day of the action in the last days of October'.

Now that we know 'The Alchemist' to have been performed in September, this conclusion can only be correct if the play as we have it does not exactly represent the text that was performed in Oxford, or if Jonson, while composing the play, bore in mind only his post-plague London audience. Obviously an Oxford audience would not be given future dates for what was supposed to be happening in the near past. If Jonson meant Ananias to talk arithmetical sense, and thought of the year as beginning in March, then the text as we have it is not identical in its dates with the text which was played in Oxford in September 1610.

The discovery of the Oxford performance affects the suggested date of Jonson's composition of the play. The Oxford Jonson reads:

> The title-page of the Folio states the play to have been 'acted in the yeare 1610. By the Kings Maiesties Seruants'; and this was undoubtedly the date of its first performance, and also of its composition. It was entered in the Stationers' Register on October 3 of that year, and internal evidence shows that it had been written during the preceding weeks (II, 87).

We can now say that the play was written some time earlier than September 1610. If the figures implying Dame Pliant's age have always been as they now stand, the play was written some time in 1610 before September. If the references to the plague are actually contemporary, as they may easily be, the composition is dated some time between 12 July, when the plague began (Chambers, 'Eliz. Stage', III, 371), and September. Or perhaps a sounder approach is that of observing what other records there are of the activities of the King's Men. 'The autumn travelling took the company to Dover between July 6 and August 4, 1610, to Oxford in August, and to Shrewsbury and Stafford in 1609–10' (Chambers, op. cit. II, 216). Until Henry Jackson's complete letter turns up we do not know on what day in September he wrote to G. P. If the day was early in that month, 'Postremis his diebus' may well mean that 'The Alchemist' was performed late in August. And unless it was rehearsed on tour, it must have been composed before the tour started, at the latest by the early days of July. A few altered dates and the plague referred to could have been taken as that of 1609. Sir E. K. Chambers (op. cit. III, 371) thinks that 'In view of the S. R. entry, one would take the production to have fallen in the earlier half of the year'. And this after all may be correct. The King's Men were in Oxford in

'Othello' and 'The Alchemist' at Oxford in 1610

1609–10, but they did not perform 'The Alchemist' (Jackson's phrasing, 'nusquam majori plausu theatra nostra sonuisse quam cum...', implies a first Oxford performance). 'Volpone' had been so much applauded a year or two earlier that not to have performed 'The Alchemist', if they had had it, would have been unthinkable. It appears, then, that the play was written between the early months of 1610 and July–September.

4

The date September 1610 has not the same importance for 'Othello' as for 'The Alchemist'. Hans Jacob Wurmsser von Vendenheym saw a performance of 'l'histoire du More de Venise' in the preceding April (E. K. Chambers's 'Shakespeare', II, 336). The interest of Jackson here concerns the actors, and in particular the way they performed tragedies. Evidently it was gorgeous tragedy that was felt to be sweeping by: 'Tragœdias, quas decorè, et aptè agebant.' The very face of the boy who played Desdemona, even after death, implored pity. This is the kind of acting which produced Hamlet's second soliloquy:

> ...all his visage wann'd,
> Teares in his eyes, distraction in's Aspect....

There was all the intensity of that in the acting of 'Othello', but the fire was tempered to a 'decorè et aptè'. 'Othello' has none of the Marlovian parody of the player's speech, and so the playing, being apt, was decorous, stately. Moreover, as with the 'Hamlet' player, the 'whole Function' of the actors suited 'With Formes, to [their] Conceit': 'non solùm dicendo, sed etiam faciendo', they suited 'the Action to the Word, the Word to the Action'.

1933

VI. TWO PRODUCTIONS OF ELIZABETHAN PLAYS

REVIEWING M. St Denis's Old Vic production of the 'Witch of Edmonton', Mr Desmond Macarthy praised it as an ideal instance of the kind of production ideal for Elizabethan plays:

It has caught the spirit of that drama so completely and projected it so vividly (thanks to a most judicious use of modern pictorial devices) that, speaking for myself, the performance has unskinned my eyes...no production of Shakespeare, let alone of his inferiors, is worth a dump that does not reproduce [the proper] atmosphere; [an atmosphere which] is not to be achieved by reproducing *as exactly as possible* the conditions of the Elizabethan and Jacobean stage.[1]

Mr Macarthy, therefore, can have little use for the productions of Mr Robert Atkins who, at the Ring, is now busy providing a scratch team of Sunday-evening actors with a rough and ready, and therefore adequate, approximation to the conditions of the Globe (except for the roof and consequently artificial light). Mr Macarthy ranges himself virtually with the ordinary theatre-goer who would be loth to miss scenery (or so he would assure us, if asked), who would be loth to sacrifice the picture stage for what Mr Atkins gives him instead: the actual ring of the boxing stadium with a balcony and inner stage at one end. M. St Denis is, therefore, 'wise' in not attempting an Elizabethan setting literally: his audiences, who do not know that any other is possible, and who might react too violently against novelty as novelty, are the more numerous.

But it is surely true that in presenting Shakespeare and his fellow-dramatists there are two methods, both of which ideally are indispensable. Ideally there should be both the Elizabethan

1 The quotation comes from the 'New Statesman and Nation', Dec. 1936 (XII, 1026–7).

way and the modern (of which M. St Denis's was a simple example but not therefore less a modern one). It is a pity that plays of such excellence as those of Shakespeare, Jonson and half a dozen others should not be given a performance as closely like their original as the labours of archivists can make them: and it is equally a pity that producers striving towards new principles, methods and effects should not be allowed to try their hand on Elizabethan poetic drama. Professor Wilson Knight's recent book, 'Principles of Shakespeare Production', is an admirable example of what it would be criminal to deny to the modern-producer-with-ideas—the opportunity to use Shakespeare's verbal basis for poetic effects of his own, effects which Shakespeare (not being Bacon) never dreamed of as possible, but which, had he lived in our time and had he also still been a dramatist-producer, he would have encouraged. At the successive hands of this kind of producer, Shakespeare's plays have always been found legitimately turning into new plays. These metamorphoses have pleased their audiences Augustan, Victorian or modern (I am thinking of such productions as Mr Tyrone Guthrie's 'Love's Labour's Lost' four years ago at the Westminster and recently at the Old Vic).

But because this kind of new production has always drawn its producers and audiences, it need not exclude the Elizabethan kind. And this not simply because the Elizabethan kind is the only one that can recreate effects in the plays which otherwise remain puzzling, because only this method can show us why Shakespeare carpentered his plays just as he did. But also because there can be no doubt that both Shakespeare (the poet-dramatist) and his actors get their due from Mr Atkins in a way that they do not from 'modern' producers. The words of the plays mean far more to an audience for whom they and the physical presence of the actors are almost the only channel for the grand total of the play. In the Victorian productions the romantically elaborated realism of the setting sirened attention away from the words, and though modern sirens are more fashionable, they are sirens still. At the Ring there is no scenery, and the audience, which almost surrounds the actors, watches the actors and receives their words with an unencumbered directness of attention which gives its proper meaning to the term 'poetic drama'. It is because of this literary and human focus that, in Mr Atkins's production, scenery is not missed. The audience quickly adopts the new standards forced on it by the full impact of the actors' presence. (The audience does not say 'I feel the lack of painted canvas', nor 'I do not feel the lack of painted canvas': it forgets that painted canvas is usual in theatres.) We know that the Elizabethans did trim up their stage with odds and ends of scenery, but it was little more than make-believe and left the audience free to attend to look, voice, skip and gesture, and to the sumptuous clothing which enhanced them.

One wonders which kind of production the actors themselves would favour. Their choice, I should say, would be determined by the pitch of their skill. The standard demanded by a performance at the Ring is extraordinarily high: the audience almost infringes on the stage, and its demands are like those of a camera filming close-ups that can't be shot twice. Since actors nowadays are regarded as a race 'out of the star' of ordinary people, to have them acting a yard or two away is to feel the awe of children in the presence of royalty. Unless, therefore, the acting is superb, the fall is that of Icarus, and the embarrassment acutely personal.

The acting of the King's Men, no doubt, reached the necessary standard, and the best proof of this is that Shakespeare always crabs players:

> Life's but a walking shadow, a poor player
> That struts and frets his hour upon the stage

is the kind of thing. This crabbing of his own profession has been read as a rooted dissatisfaction with it. The reverse, however, is nearer the truth. Consider the context: on the intimate stage of the Globe or the Blackfriars, the actors themselves voice the charge against themselves. This they would surely have refused to do, had the cap fitted. Indeed, at the Globe, if the charge had been deserved, missiles early on would have made it redundant.

Two Productions of Elizabethan Plays

Shakespeare's dissatisfaction with playing is a luxury emotion permitted by the excellence of the playing: it is as if Schnabel, turning away from the last chord of a late Beethoven sonata, murmured 'Oh, these poor mortal fingers!' Mr Atkins has managed to rake together some decent actors: Margaretta Scott, for instance, was an admirable Beatrice. But if he could have got Maurice Evans to play Hamlet, Charles Laughton Angelo, or Emlyn Williams Richard III, one could wager that M. St Denis and Mr Macarthy would have been among the loudest to applaud.

Mr Macarthy mentions Shakespeare's inferiors, his many fellow-dramatists. That they are a brilliant constellation far below him goes without saying. But we must remember that we have not yet seen them as they wrote to be seen, and that, until we have, literary criticism and evaluation are academic, lucky guesses at the most.

1937

VII. EIGHTEENTH-CENTURY POETIC DICTION (I)

I

IN the greatest poetry of the ages of Dryden and Pope the question of 'poetic diction' scarcely arises.

> When I consider Life, 'tis all a cheat;
> Yet, fool'd with hope, men favour the deceit;
> Trust on, and think to-morrow will repay:
> To-morrow's falser than the former day....
>
> Yes, I am proud; I must be proud to see
> Men not afraid of God, afraid of me....
>
> Slow rises worth by Poverty depress'd:
> But here more slow, where all are slaves to gold,
> Where looks are merchandise and smiles are sold....

In these passages there is no use of prescribed words, nothing in the vocabulary which the subject has not directly and of itself suggested to the poet. These poets wrote their best poetry with man as theme. For them the proper study of mankind was man. Whatever else they spoke of, it was with man as stated reference. They stood at the human centre and saw the horizon and the sky in a way analogous to that in which Ptolemy saw the universe. Man was the centre, however wide the circle described by his stretched compass. Wordsworth thought of the poet as a 'man speaking to men', and clearly this is the implied view of all poets. It depends on what the poet means by 'man' and what by 'men'. If the late seventeenth and early eighteenth centuries had used this phrase, as they might well have done, they would have meant by 'man' the poet in his capacity as member of a civilized society, and by 'men' the other members of that closed society who resembled him in all but poetic gifts.

53

2

For the reception of their discoveries and considerations on the human theme these poets had perfected one metre in particular, a version of the heroic couplet. This version, consciously inaugurated by Waller and steadily improved on by Dryden (at his best) and by Pope, became the most precise metre ever used in English verse. The laws which were evolved for its use have never been fully stated. The ten feet of the couplet were to be kept as closely iambic as possible, the metrical surprises accordingly being of fine gradation. The rimes were to fall on monosyllabic words which therefore received, and could bear to receive, the full terminal accent of the line. Marvell's rime in

> And yonder all before us lye
> Desarts of vast Eternity,

would have been a blemish in one of Pope's poems since *-ty* was a weak syllable. The monosyllabic rime-word, if possible, should have a long vowel, and it was best if one of the two rime-words of the couplet were a verb. Within the couplet the poet worked out as many contrasts and parallels as he could, providing the maximum number of internal geometrical relationships. Denham's lines on the Thames had fascinated later poets with the possibilities of this kind of configuration. They were frequently imitated—too frequently for Swift's pleasure. Their kind of verbal manipulation was improved on, until in Pope a couplet will often suggest a difficult figure in Euclid, its vowels and consonants, its sense-oppositions and sense-attractions, fitted together like arcs and lines.

> A Fop their Passion, but their Prize a Sot;
> Alive, ridiculous, and dead, forgot!

A manner such as this keeps the reader's brain active, fetching and carrying. It is a metre for educated people. No meaning is possible for the 'mind' to review, or for the 'spirit' to kindle at, till the 'brain' has mastered the Euclidean relationships. This

manner and metre were evolved to receive the discoveries and
observations which these poets made concerning man. They saw
man as an oxymoron, a cross-hatching, a contradiction in terms:

> Chaos of Thought and Passion, all confus'd;
> Still by himself abus'd, or disabus'd;
> Created half to rise, and half to fall;
> Great lord of all things, yet a prey to all;
> Sole judge of Truth, in endless Error hurl'd:
> The glory, jest, and riddle of the world!

To say what they saw inevitably required the couplet. And the
fearlessness of their meaning as inevitably required that they
should use words freely.

3

What they saw in external nature was limited and influenced in
statement by the metre they were finding so perfect for their
human materials. This metre of contrasts and concision was un-
fitted for the large freedom of landscape. That large freedom they
saw and valued but did not much use, certainly not much in the
couplet. When they did use it in the couplet its powerfulness
shrank, because of the very 'correctness' of their versification.
But if they had felt the large freedom strongly enough, they
would have found a right metre for it. John Philips and Thomson
found the metre when they wanted it. Dryden and Pope kept to
the couplet in their best poems because their philosophical scheme
entailed nothing to make them reject it. Pope was under no delusions about the beauty of the external world; Dryden and he
were under no delusions about its splendour. Pope stated to
Spence his belief that a tree was a nobler object than a king in his
coronation robes. Yet he has no description of a tree to put beside
that of Belinda's exquisite 'petticoat'. He thought that a fine lady
would like the stars because they reminded her of candles, and
that this would be a pity. Yet in his poems the star he gave most
attention to was a fictitious one, the translated lock of Belinda.
And the court decoration ('Bare the mean heart that lurks

beneath a star') was of more value to his work than Hesperus. Even in the superb line

> The sick'ning stars fade off th' ethereal plain,

it is not the actual night he is thinking of, but the night in the mind of man when the curtain of a universal intellectual darkness is being let fall. The poet does not choose to write of external nature in the way Shelley does, because no man he ever knew, or ever wished to know, so dissolved his 'godlike reason' in ecstasy. Such a man for Dryden and Pope would have been, almost literally, a lunatic, an 'enthusiast'. In so far as man's experience concerned external nature, Dryden, Pope and the rest admit it freely to their verse. And when they admit it they may do one of two things. They may admit it with words newly chosen for itself, or they may provide it with 'diction'. If the poet is a good one, he will bestow or withhold diction as his subject demands. And whether he does one or the other will depend on his meaning. It will depend on whether he is looking at external nature for what new experience it can add to his human sum, or whether he is not so much looking at it as using remembered scraps of it for his own human purpose and pleasure and for those of his readers. Dryden and Pope most often look on it for what it can give, or, since it is never their main theme, show by the quality of their incidental allusions that they have so looked at it. This is Dryden's description of a storm:

> ...the hollow sound
> Sung in the Leaves, the Forest shook around,
> Air blacken'd; rowl'd the Thunder; groan'd the Ground.

This account is obviously individual. (There is something in Dryden's descriptive poetry that recalls Uccello—the heraldic brightness of the colour, the uniform density of the things as represented, the ponderous neatness and jolly gravity.) As an example from Pope one might take:

> As to soft gales top-heavy pines bow low
> Their heads, and lift them as they cease to blow.

Eighteenth-Century Poetic Diction

4

This is how they saw external nature when they wanted to. But at times they were concerned with seeing it not so much as they knew it deserved to be seen but as they wanted to see it. They superimposed on nature what they considered at certain times to be desirable. They made a selection from nature of elements that suited their interests. This is what all poets do. Dryden, Pope and the rest differ only in what they superimpose and in what they select. They superimposed on nature some of their own humanity. Shakespeare, to take an Elizabethan instance, had superimposed human qualities on nature. He saw waves, for example, as striving, as if they were beasts or men (or, more truly, perhaps, as if they were boys). Romeo even sees the severing clouds as envious—that is, as partaking of a primitive emotion common to men and perhaps to beasts. But the humanity which Dryden and Pope project on to nature is more intellectual and sophisticated, more like the humanity they valued in themselves. In 'Windsor Forest' comes:

> O'er sandy wilds were yellow harvests spread,
> The forests wonder'd at th' unusual grain....

Their regard for man made them a little haughty among stars, trees and animals. For them 'man superior walks Amid the glad creation' (the words, surprisingly, are Thomson's). They are interested in nature as it is controlled by man. In this they resembled their hero Virgil, whose 'Georgics' rejected the belief of Lucretius that the productiveness of nature was on the wane for the belief that, in Sellar's words, 'the earth if rightly dealt with would never refuse the "imperium" of man'. Charles II's rigidly controlled garden at St James's, with its Mall, its rectangular sheet of water (the 'canal'), its borders of equispaced limes, showed that man's control of nature could be virtually complete within limits, just as for Virgil it could be as complete as Rome's control over a conquered people. They controlled nature perfectly in their gardens. The landscape proved less tractable, though the Kents and 'Capability' Browns did what they could. But their mental control over landscape could be complete at will. And this is what happens in their pastorals, by a kind of wish-fulfilment.

5

The theme of the pastoral was one of man, but it was man at his faintest. An age which valued satire could only amuse itself in pastoral. Man is the theme still, but it is man as a pretty creature, provided with set and toy emotions which last only to the end of the poem. The melodious tear was shed, the lips were silked with a smile, and all this was done out-of-doors. The traditions of pastoral forbad this out-of-doors to be a garden. It had to be landscape. But the landscape, in verse at least, could be perfectly made to own man's imperium.

The pastoralists therefore controlled its appearance in their verse with the same rigid hand that King Charles's gardeners had used on the configuration of St James's Park. They 'methodized' it by taming it in diction, by caging it in a small group of words which satisfied their garden-bred sense of elegance. This sense of elegance required simplification. The landscape, always limited in pastoral, was further limited by being robbed of all characteristics except those which proved its gentleness, its 'tamedness'. The brook could be there but should be a stream. The qualities of the word *stream* cleared away all the pebbles and angles of the brook, canalized it. The stream should purl rather than babble. If the purl of the stream was for some reason undesirable in a line, its purity would be chemically certified as *crystal*. There should be meadows or meads. There should be woods, but not so near that you could see any 'knotty, knarry barren trees old'. The woods should be beheld distantly and seen as a whole, and seen as *waving*. This is how they composed their 'sylvan scenes', a phrase which they borrow from Milton. The imperium of man was further insisted on by the frequent allusion to nature in terms of what man adapted from it for his own use: lawns were *velvet*, sheep *fleecy*. Nature was shown as imitating art—even the fields of heaven for Isaac Watts 'stand *drest* in living green'. The landscapes of Broome and Fenton, both published in the 'Miscellany' of 1712, show with what uniform completeness external nature could be commanded. Broome writes:

> Thee, Shepherd, thee the pleasurable Woods,
> The painted Meadows, and the Crystal Floods,
> Claim, and invite thee to their sweet Abodes.

And a little later he goes on with 'Here Fountains warble...'. Fenton, some thirty pages farther on, has the line

> Ye warbling Fountains, and ye Chrystal Floods.

The motto of both these passages is *Everything of the Best*. Broome and Fenton are self-elected Tweedledum and Tweedledee. They are two poets playing for safety. But among the better pastoral poets, though the material is virtually the same, the sense of the ready-made is defeated. The pastorals of Pope, of Ambrose Philips, and of Gay (when he outgrows his wish to parody) employ the recognized diction, but their styles are as distinct as the different flavours of cheese. To amplify one instance: Mr C. V. Deane, in his thoughtful study,[1] shows how Pope's manuscript of the 'Pastorals' exhibits the contemporary diction seeking ⟨...⟩ng exactitude of music and statement. 'It cannot be ⟨...⟩ in the *Pastorals* Pope's poetic diction becomes a substit⟨...⟩ etic feeling.' The eighteenth century liked a restrictio⟨...⟩ operated before the poem was begun, which operated ⟨...⟩ ion of the 'inspiration'. Inside that restriction they coul⟨...⟩ iday and the best of them did. And they took advantage ⟨...⟩ which operates in poetry as in everything else, the law ⟨...⟩ proportion. They knew that a reader soon scrambles ⟨...⟩ level of the poem and that, when he has reached it ⟨...⟩ becomes his norm. In 'Endymion' everything is so ⟨...⟩ t, to provide a surprise, Keats almost has to burst a bl⟨...⟩ In Gray's 'Elegy' the even tenor of the style gives ⟨...⟩ ke 'tinklings' the equivalent of an 'angelic

1 'Aspe⟨...⟩eenth-century Nature Poetry', Oxford, 1935.

strength', of a 'happy valiancy'. Fenton, small poet as he is, counts on the benefits of this law. A few lines after the line quoted above he introduces the phrase 'living fountains' and with all the more effectiveness after his poetic sleep. Bolder and better poets used this law to the full, especially after the heartening example of Dryden, whose verbs are more habitually energetic than those of any other English poet.

6

The use of diction by these poets offered a major difficulty to nineteenth-century readers, and still offers difficulty. If that use is understood, the poetry made out of it may be seen at least for what it was. Virgil in his 'Georgics' had been troubled by the unpoetical frankness of his material. His problem, as Dryden translated it, ran:

> Nor can I doubt what Oyl I must bestow,
> To raise my Subject from a ground so low:
> And the mean Matter which my Theme affords,
> To embellish with Magnificence of Words.

The poetic conscience behind that weighed heavily with poets who treated Virgil with awe. Virgil had got over his difficulty partly by ignoring it and writing straight ahead of scabs and foot-rot, and partly by relying on phrases consecrated to the epic and on the spell of his versification. There is in the georgic poetry of the eighteenth century and in the allied local poetry which began with 'Cooper's Hill' a tendency to be stately as befitted Virgil's conception of poetry. The poets of the eighteenth century attain gracefulness, as Virgil did, by their metre. And more than Virgil needed to do, they attain it by restricting their vocabulary and by preferring phrases like 'fleecy care'. The reasons behind their choice of these phrases are complex. In the work of good poets they are not there simply as a means of avoiding the mention of low material, nor even for the acquisition of full-vowelled music ('fleecy care' is beautiful in this way). The good poets discriminate their use. When a poet like Milton takes up a fashion, he does so because he wants to. He spoke of a moonlit 'finny drove' because he wanted the reader to be aware of an exquisite battery of fins. And in 'Windsor Forest' and the 'Seasons', phrases based on his formula are used only when the meaning calls for them. This is not as often as the meaning of *fish* (plural) and *birds* appear, but only when fish or birds are being thought of as distinct in their appearance from other groups of creatures. Both Pope and Thomson use *fish* and *birds* whenever they want to. And they specify in uncompromisingly straightforward terms what particular fish or bird they mean when they mean it—carp, pike, pheasant, lapwing, woodcock. But when they are thinking of fish as fish are distinct from birds or beasts, they employ the formula which embodies their distinction. When Thomson speaks of the sportsmen with 'gun' and 'spaniel' who

> Distress the Feathery, or the Footed *Game*

he is not merely decorating his poem, but differentiating the game that is hit flying from the game that is hit running. When Thomson calls birds 'the glossy kind' it is because he is going on to show how that glossiness counts in the mating season, when the male birds

> ...shiver every feather with desire.

When Thomson speaks of young birds as 'the feathered youth', he means that the birds though young are not too young to have feathers. He is compressing into two words a long meaning, compressing it in a way common at the time for other materials than those of external nature. Pope in 'Windsor Forest' speaks of 'the leaden death' (death by bullet) and 'the iron squadrons' (a group of warships). It is part of the concentration learned from the Roman poets that often shows itself also in a constricted syntax within the couplet.

Eighteenth-Century Poetic Diction

7

These poets knew that the pastoral was a deception. Dryden knew that even the pastorals of Virgil were playthings, and vented the denied interests of his mind by translating

> est mihi namque domi pater, est iniusta noverca

by

> A Stepdame too I have, a cursed she,
> Who rules my Hen-peck'd Sire, and orders me.

The gusto even of human triviality was powerful enough to break into Dryden's pastoral, even into man's chosen holiday from life. And the force of the tempest was more powerful still. For all man's forethought, for all his art, there might fall a 'universal darkness', ruining more than his shielded pastoral: Pope's

> The fox obscene to gaping tombs retires,
> And savage howlings fill the sacred quires,

and Gray's adaptation

> Purg'd by the sword and beautifyed by fire,
> Then had we seen proud London's hated walls,
> Owls might have hooted in St Peter's Quire,
> And foxes stunk and litter'd in St Paul's,

and, later, there are Cunningham's lovely lines

> The lizard and the lazy lurking bat
> Inhabit now perhaps the painted room....

In passages such as these, in Dryden's and Thomson's storms, in Gray's dread and courage among mountains, the 'age of reason' acknowledged the enormous forces of man's environment.

1935

EIGHTEENTH-CENTURY
POETIC DICTION (II)

IT is true of most of those who are likely to read this article that they approach eighteenth-century poetry by way of nineteenth-century poetry. They have been brought up to expect poetry to be written in a certain way, its words to be chosen in accordance with certain principles. They know what Wordsworth said about Pope before they read Pope. And this means that when they read Pope and other eighteenth-century poets, they apply the wrong criteria: criteria which are wrong because irrelevant. These wrong criteria are often applied to the poetic diction of eighteenth-century poetry.

In using the terms 'eighteenth-century' and 'nineteenth-century' I do not intend to imply that they carry any well-defined meanings for the historian or critic of the poetic diction. Blake, who uses almost none of the diction, is an eighteenth-century poet. On the other hand, poets born later are not necessarily immune from the waning infection. The passionate attack on the diction made by Wordsworth and Coleridge, whom we think of as nineteenth-century poets, is all the more passionate because the eighteenth century is in their blood and will not be expelled. Byron, of course, glories in the ancestral germs. Keats and, to a smaller extent, Shelley use the diction more than is generally seen, and even Tennyson does not cut himself off from it, though he seems to discover it again for himself rather than to use it from habit. Browning appears to be the first poet of the nineteenth century who is not indebted to the diction.

The generalizations made below will apply in various degrees to the poets of the two centuries and also to poets of the seventeenth and the sixteenth, since the methods of forming the diction, and even part of the diction itself, are already found in Spenser, in Sylvester's translation of Du Bartas, and in most succeeding poets except, broadly speaking, the metaphysicals.

Eighteenth-Century Poetic Diction

2

It is generally true that the vocabulary of nineteenth-century poetry is restricted only in so far as the vocabulary of any poetry is restricted, i.e. only in so far as the subject-matter is restricted. Poems in the nineteenth century tend to be written on what were then considered 'poetical' subjects. The reservation is a serious one when we consider the poetry of other centuries, including our own since 1920; but, barring it, there is no limitation of vocabulary. There still remains, therefore, a great deal of the dictionary out of which the nineteenth-century poet can choose his words. The nineteenth-century poet may be said to provide each poem (whatever the subject, whatever the form) with new diction. He writes almost as if he were the first and the only poet in the world:

> As if he were Earth's first-born birth,
> And none had lived before him.[1]

The nineteenth-century poet discovers a new poetic territory and maps it out by himself.

Writing poetry was different in the eighteenth century. Then the *kinds* of poetry were still seen as distinct. And these different kinds entailed the use of different kinds of vocabulary, of diction. In the eighteenth century, writing poems was a communal art in the sense that the poet was not free to write as he chose. Much had to be learnt before he could write correctly, without offending the rules and distinctions acknowledged by poets and readers. A poet did not have to create the taste by which he was enjoyed to the same extent as a nineteenth-century poet was conscious of having to do so. The kinds were ready waiting for him and, if the rules for the kinds in which he elected to write were properly complied with, the products were recognizable as poems of those kinds. It goes without saying that for the products to be good poems the 'material' to which the rules were applied had to be good. The kinds included epic, tragedy in verse, pindaric, elegy, heroic and

[1] Wordsworth, 'Expostulation and Reply', ll, 11 f. (adapted).

64

Eighteenth-Century Poetic Diction

familiar epistle, pastoral, georgic, occasional verse, translation and imitation. Pope chooses to tackle all these kinds in turn. He sees them as distinct. He tells Spence, for instance, how he takes a poem and corrects it:

> After writing a poem, one should correct it all over, with one single view at a time. Thus for language; if an elegy; 'these lines are very good, but are they not of too heroical a strain?' and so *vice versa*. It appears very plainly, from comparing parallel passages touched both in the Iliad and Odyssey, that Homer did this; and it is yet plainer that Virgil did so, from the distinct styles he uses in his three sorts of poems. It always answers in him; and so constant an effect could not be the effect of chance.[1]

This observation is modified later:

> Though Virgil, in his pastorals, has sometimes six or eight lines together that are epic: I have been so scrupulous as scarce ever to admit above two together, even in the Messiah.[2]

Sometimes Pope keeps the kinds distinct: when he introduces different kinds into the same poem, he knows what he is doing and marks off the component parts by the use of different kinds of diction (diction includes larger matters such as personification, apostrophe, exclamation). These rules and principles may seem curious pedantry after the practice of nineteenth-century poets. But they were based on first-hand scrutiny of good poetry in the past (witness the above quotations from Spence) and so were as unpedantic, in the hands of a poet, as, say, the study of Spenser was unpedantic in the hands of Keats: or in the hands of Dryden or Pope, for that matter.

For Pope, then, poetic diction would cover all the words used in all the kinds (which meant virtually all the words in the dictionary, except those which nobody knew the meaning of without intense specialization in technical fields). When Pope speaks of words in the 'Essay on Criticism' his criterion of their correct use is appropriateness. He makes no reference to poetic diction.

1 J. Spence, 'Anecdotes, Observations, and Characters, of Books and Men', ed. S. W. Singer, 1820, pp. 23 f. 2 Ibid. p. 312.

He does use the term, however, in the 'Preface' to his translation to the 'Iliad', but not in Wordsworth's sense.[1] He uses it to mark the difference between the vocabulary of poetry and prose, and his instances are figures and compound epithets:

> If we descend from hence [i.e. from remarking Homer's descriptions, images and similes] to the *Expression*, we see the bright Imagination of *Homer* shining out in the most enliven'd Forms of it. We acknowledge him the Father of Poetical Diction, the first who taught that *Language of the Gods* to Men. His Expression is like the colouring of some great Masters, which discovers itself to be laid on boldly, and executed with Rapidity. It is indeed the strongest and most glowing imaginable, and touch'd with the greatest Spirit. *Aristotle* had reason to say, He was the only Poet who had found out *Living Words*; there are in him more daring Figures and Metaphors than in any good Author whatever. An Arrow is *impatient* to be on the Wing, a Weapon *thirsts* to drink the Blood of an Enemy, and the like. Yet his Expression is never too big for the Sense, but justly great in proportion to it: 'Tis the Sentiment that swells and fills out the Diction, which rises with it, and forms itself about it. For in the same degree that a *Thought* is warmer, an *Expression* will be brighter; and as That is more strong, This will become more perspicuous: Like Glass in the Furnace which grows to a greater Magnitude, and refines to a greater Clearness, only as the *Breath* within is more powerful, and the *Heat* more intense.[2]

What follows in the next paragraph must be read in the light of this:

> To throw his Language more out of Prose, *Homer* seems to have affected the *Compound-Epithets.* This was a sort of Composition peculiarly proper to Poetry, not only as it heighten'd the *Diction*, but as it assisted and fill'd the *Numbers* with greater Sound and Pomp, and likewise conduced in some measure to thicken the *Images*.[3]

This statement concerning the diction of poetry has a general validity. It would be subscribed to by almost all poets and

1 Dennis apparently invents the term (see 'Poetry and Language', by F. W. Bateson, 1934, p. 71 *n*.): Dryden had used the phrase '*dictio Virgiliana*' (see below, p. 75) and ten years before, in 1685, had halı anglicized it: 'diction, or (to speak English)...expressions' ('Essays ed. Ker, 1900, I, 266).
2 Pope, 'The Iliad of Homer', I (1715: folio ed.), D 2ᵛ.   3 Ibid. E 1ʳ.

critics, except Malherbe. 'In the same degree that a *Thought* is warmer, an *Expression* will be brighter....' Even Wordsworth, despite statements implying the contrary, is found allowing Pope's general position. He seems indeed to be repeating Pope's words—it was to be expected that he should pay attention to Pope's 'Preface' before attacking the diction which he considered to have sprung from the translation which that 'Preface' introduced. Wordsworth writes:

> The earliest poets of all nations generally wrote from passion excited by real events...feeling powerfully as they did, their language was daring and figurative.[1]

Pope's use of the term poetical diction has nothing to do with the narrower sense in which it was used by Wordsworth and others in relation to the poetry of the eighteenth century.

3

Poetic diction, in Wordsworth's sense, only applies to certain kinds of eighteenth-century poetry. As Wordsworth and Coleridge saw, there is little or no poetic diction in the satires, familiar epistles, and occasional verse. (In the elegy and the heroic epistle the poetic diction is of a kind which has passed almost unnoticed by the critics: this diction includes such words as *sad, beauteous, trembling, pensive.*) In the satires and familiar epistles the vocabulary is as free in principle as that used in any nineteenth-century poem—the 'Ring and the Book', for example. The vocabulary of all nineteenth-century poetry cowers into a corner when the 'Dunciad' walks abroad, seeking whom it may devour. And this applies even to those parts of the 'Dunciad' where the subject is a favourite one of nineteenth-century poetry, where the material is external nature. In the same way that the primary human emotions tended to mean for Matthew Arnold only the noble primary human emotions, external nature tended to mean for the

1 'Appendix' (on poetic diction) added in 1802 to the 'Preface' (1800) to the 'Lyrical Ballads' (Oxford Poets ed. 1916, p. 942).

5-2

nineteenth-century poets only what was 'beautiful' and noble in
it. But Pope knew no such distinction. In the 'Dunciad' there
are the isles of fragrance, the lily-silver'd vales, but there are also
other things:

> So watchful Bruin forms, with plastic care,
> Each growing lump, and brings it to a Bear.[1]

Or

> Next, o'er his Books his eyes began to roll,
> In pleasing memory of all he stole,
> How here he sipp'd, how there he plunder'd snug,
> And suck'd all o'er, like an industrious Bug.[2]

The nineteenth-century poets were squeamish about external
nature. So that even on their chosen ground the eighteenth
century can beat them in variety of appreciation. There is
obviously no poetic diction in the 'Dunciad': except of course
where Pope is deliberately mimicking the epic manner. When
writing satire the eighteenth-century poet chose his words as
freely as any poet. And the same is true when he is writing several
of the other kinds.

But when writing epic, pastoral, and georgic the eighteenth-
century poet was not so free.[3] No eighteenth-century poet of
much distinction writes an epic (Pope started to write one). But
Milton wrote one, and Dryden translated one and part of another:
here the term eighteenth-century extends itself backward
spiritually as for certain nineteenth-century poets it extends itself
forward. Pope follows Dryden's example. There is, however, no
need to examine the epic diction here because the nineteenth-
century attackers, though they single out Pope's 'Homer' as the
source of the diction, select for examination that passage which
could have stood equally in a pastoral or georgic. Coleridge, it

---

1 I, 101 f. Cf. Dryden's inventive translation (ll. 559 ff.) of Ovid's
  'Metamorphoses', xv, 379 ff.
2 I, 127 ff.
3 I denote by the terms *pastoral* and *georgic* not only poems like Pope's
  'Pastorals', Thomson's 'Seasons', Grainger's 'Sugar-cane' but local
  poems like 'Windsor Forest', and Goldsmith's 'Traveller'.

seems, was the first to examine the 'popular lines' from Book VIII of the 'Iliad'—

As when the moon, refulgent lamp of night....[1]

Southey followed in the 'Quarterly Review' (October 1814), and Wordsworth, a year later, in his 'Essay, Supplementary to the Preface' of the 'Lyrical Ballads'.

It was in the pastoral and georgic, then, and in pastoral and georgic material intruding into other kinds, that the diction of the eighteenth-century poets came to be most despised. This fate was inevitable since it was by jealously extending the descriptive element in these two kinds that the nineteenth-century poets found the form for much of their own best writing. The champion of eighteenth-century diction must take his stand on pastoral and georgic, insisting, of course, that the eighteenth-century poets, unlike those of the nineteenth century, did not do their best work in those kinds. The best poetry of the eighteenth century is generally that of man (any man of a liberal education, of a certain reach of mind) and his fellow-men. The best poetry of the nineteenth century is generally that of man (an individual man of unusual distinction) and external nature: that is, the poet himself in a world of dawns and sunsets, streams and trees, mountains and sea. This difference of favourite subject-matter is at the root of all the differences between the poetry of the two centuries. In discussing poetic diction, therefore, we are comparing the best poetry of the nineteenth century with the less-than-best poetry of the eighteenth.

4

The nineteenth-century poets have a strong sense of the individual quality of each moment of experience. Late in their day, the 'Epilogue' to Pater's 'Renaissance' enunciated this part of their creed with exquisite finality. The nineteenth-century poets are humble—one is forced to the conclusion—because they see the

1 'Biographia Literaria', ed. J. Shawcross, 1907, I, 26 f.

external world as more startlingly beautiful than anything they have of their own, than anything they themselves can make. When they experience any natural phenomenon, they offer as white a mind as possible to receive it. They tremblingly hold up the mirror to nature. Their business as poets is to prove to their readers that they have been worthy of a unique experience. And so they write of skies, for instance, in the following ways:

> ...the western sky,
> And its peculiar tint of yellow green.[1]
>
> Deep in the orange light of widening morn.[2]
>
> ...a bed of daffodil sky.[3]
>
> The orange and pale violet evening-sky.[4]

Coleridge, in the first of these quotations, feels it necessary to excuse his perception of a green sky by allowing that it was 'peculiar'. Later poets (green skies are frequent in the eighteen-nineties and in the earlier twentieth century) make no apology.

The eighteenth-century poets were not so humble. They saw external nature, not as culminating in its own most exquisite moments, but as culminating in man. Thomson, for instance, who looked at external nature as long and as lovingly as any nineteenth-century poet except Wordsworth, considered that

> ...Man superior walks
> Amid the glad creation.[5]

Thomson forgets this superiority at times and so do many eighteenth-century poets, but this is their attitude in the main. The glad creation provides them with many instances of individual beauty, but they differ from the nineteenth-century poets in being impressed only up to a point. They seldom present a white mind to experience. They present a mind already coloured

---

1 Coleridge, 'Dejection: An Ode', ll. 28 f.
2 Shelley, 'Prometheus Unbound', II, i, 18.
3 Tennyson, 'Maud', I, XXII, ii, 4.
4 Arnold, 'Thyrsis', XVI, 9.
5 'Spring', ll. 170 f.

with all their past experience of all kinds: experience of other past instances of the beauty of external nature (they tend to generalize a description), experience of man, and experience of books (man's record of his experiences). Whereas the nineteenth-century poet is interested in the freshness of his response to experience, the eighteenth-century poet is interested in that response at a later stage: when the new has been welcomed by the old, when it has been accommodated to the existing harmony. It is this presence of a stage intermediary between the fresh response and the written poem that accounts for much of the difference between an eighteenth-century nature-poem and a nineteenth-century one. In every eighteenth-century pastoral and georgic there is something expected, predictable. And it is this element which requires and receives its poetic diction. The poetic diction represents the existing mind, the new words represent the freshness of the response. The poet's value is measured by the quality of the new, and also by the quality of the new art with which he manipulates the old. Bergson held that fresh experience is itself poetry. The mere fact that there is seen to be an orange and pale violet evening sky is poetry. The art in that phrase is negligible, the fact is everything. But an eighteenth-century nature-poem depends for half its existence on its paper and ink, on its words as words. When you read Arnold's line it is the thing, not the words, that you are given. Arnold—for all his mind—does not exist except as a finger pointing to a unique sky. We praise him for his discovery.

It is another matter when we read the following lines from Pope's juvenile pastoral, 'Spring':

> Soon as the flocks shook off the nightly dews,
> Two Swains, whom Love kept wakeful, and the Muse,
> Pour'd o'er the whitening vale their fleecy care.... [1]

Here in the first and third lines (we must neglect the second because the slight human element in 'Thyrsis' is unrepresented in

1 ll. 17 ff.

the line selected) we find a combination of new and old. Actually there is such a combination in Arnold's line: Shelley, as my quotations show, had already seen an orange sky. But the combination in Arnold's line is accidental. His line is not, so to speak, built on Shelley's,[1] and he does not expect us to remember Shelley's 'orange'. He expects us to think both 'orange' and 'pale violet' original and striking. Pope knows of course that the reader will recognize 'fleecy care' as a common phrase in pastorals. And whereas 'fleecy care' is old, a quotation from the poetic diction, there is new and old simultaneously in the preceding phrase: 'Pour'd o'er the whitening vale.' Here *vale* (for *valley*) is old, a quotation from Spenser. *Whitening* is old, but also new. It goes back to Virgil where it is used of the light of dawn (*ut primum albescere lucem Vidit*).[2] Pope, indeed, appears to count on our knowing this, otherwise we might take his phrase to mean that the valley was whitening with daisies, or by being spread with lime, or whitening by the fleeces of the sheep themselves: a flock of sheep can appreciably alter the general colour of a field. But *whitening* is not merely a quotation from Virgil, since it is applied to *vale* and not to *light*. Pope counts on the reader's remembering Virgil's phrase and so not applying the word literally. A valley cannot whiten in the light of dawn except in the sense that the light of dawn itself can whiten. Then again, take *pour'd*. It is startlingly new. Pope seems to have been the first and only poet to observe the effect of sheep bursting out of a fold: they seem to be poured out, like porridge from a pan. Then in the first line there is the unpredictable verb, *shook off*.

1 Keats, and to some extent Shelley, seem to build on the poetic diction of the eighteenth century. Following an age which, for example, delighted in *soft, blooming, sylvan, trembling, purple, blush*, Keats writes with a recognizable variation: 'While barred clouds bloom the soft-dying day' ('To Autumn'), 'Sylvan historian' ('Grecian Urn'), 'trembled blossoms' ('Psyche'), 'a thought...in his pained heart Made purple riot' ('Eve of St Agnes'), 'scutcheon blush'd with blood' (ibid.). There are many more instances. In the same way Coleridge's lines in the 'Ancient Mariner': 'As idle as a painted ship Upon a painted ocean' dealt a contemporary shock by using *painted* literally.
2 'Aeneid', IV, 586 f.

Eighteenth-Century Poetic Diction

In summary, then, we can say that Pope has observed something new, as Arnold has. His discoveries are as valuable, though not as spectacular, as those of Arnold. But the record of the discovery is all that there is in Arnold, whereas in Pope the discovery represents only a part of the whole. Pope is using his whole mind.

5

One of the major elements included in the whole mind which is evident in eighteenth-century pastorals and georgics—what is 'old' in it—may be compendiously stated as Virgil's 'Georgics'. It is the 'Georgics' more than anything else that prepare the mind of the eighteenth-century poet for writing his nature-poem, which are responsible for the element of the old. Virgil helped the eighteenth-century nature-poet in something like the same way that the Bible helped Bunyan. And the value of eighteenth-century nature-poetry suffered in the nineteenth century, when the reverence for Virgil faded, in the same way that the value of 'The Pilgrim's Progress' suffers whenever there is a decline in Bible reading. Not that the nineteenth century did not honour Virgil. Keats as a boy translated the 'Aeneid' into prose. Tennyson saluted Virgil's centenary with a remarkable ode. In Max Beerbohm's cartoon, the nineteenth-century 'Statesman...[makes] without wish for emolument a...version of the Georgics, in English hexameters'. But that version is confessedly 'flat but faithful'. And we find Hazlitt recording in his 'First Acquaintance with Poets' that on one occasion 'Coleridge spoke of Virgil's "Georgics", but not well. I do not think he had much feeling for the classical or elegant.' Keats as a boy may translate the 'Aeneid' into prose. But Dryden as an old man translates not only the 'Aeneid' but the 'Pastorals' and 'Georgics', and not into prose but into splendid verse. The eighteenth century feels Virgil as a divine presence. Hazlitt's 'classical or elegant', even when allowance is made for contemporary usage, were words too cold to describe their reverence for 'the best of the Ancients'.[1] He is

1 J. Oldmixon, 'Amores Britannici' (1703), A 7r.

73

Pope's favourite poet, and one of the four busts in his garden is Virgil's. Gray habitually reads him under the beeches at Burnham.[1] Shenstone has his Virgil's Grove at the Leasowes. They arrange part of their very lives about him. Thomson in the first edition of 'Winter' cries:

> Maro, the best of poets, and of men!

In the second:

> Maro! the glory of the poet's art!

Later editions read:

> Behold who yonder comes! in sober state,
> Fair, mild, and strong as is a vernal sun:
> 'Tis Phœbus' self, or else the Mantuan swain![2]

The same thing is even true of prose writers: Gilbert White's mind is haunted by the classics. He sounds a Latin phrase now and then as if to tune his English. The echo that was so famous a feature of Selborne seems of its own accord to boom out 'Tityre, tu patulae recubans...'. It was with Virgil in his mind that Gilbert White described the women making rush candles at Selborne.[3]

And it is the 'Georgics' that for Dryden, and so for most eighteenth-century poets, are 'the divinest part' of Virgil.[4]

Virgil helps the eighteenth-century nature-poets in a dozen ways. He helps them technically. They try to get his 'strength', 'sweetness',[5] and smoothness of tone, to write lines the music of which is as solid, as exquisite, as his. In his translation of Virgil Dryden seems at times to be trying to suggest something of the Latin versification by letting the stress of the lines fall on syllables with long vowels.[6] Virgil also helps them to concentrate their

1 Letter to Walpole, Aug. 1736.
2 Oxford Poets, ed. 1906, p. 205.
3 Virginia Woolf, 'White's Selborne' ('New Statesman and Nation', 30 Sept. 1939, p. 460).
4 Op. cit. I, 16: cf. I, 259.
5 Two qualities Dryden insists on as essential in poetry.
6 Dryden also sometimes appears to be imitating lines like those of Chaucer's 'Knight's Tale', ll. 1747 ff., where the stresses fall on boldly alliterative syllables.

meaning into fewer words, to combine words in new ways. He shows them how subtly meaning may be embodied in appropriate sound (a lesson they usually find too difficult). He furnishes them with many actual words: *liquid, involve, purple,*[1] *irriguous, refulgent, conscious, gelid, crown* (verb), *invade, painted* (used adjectivally). *Care* comes straight from the 'Georgics': *cura* is Virgil's constant word for the job of the shepherd and farmer. *Fleecy care* itself, in an age of poets who liked adjectives ending in *-y* and invented them by the hundred,[2] springs readily from the juxtaposition: 'superat pars altera *curae, Lanigeros* agitare greges'.[3] The phrase *sylvan scene* comes from another juxtaposition, this time in the 'Aeneid': 'silvis scaena coruscis'.[4] Dryden spoke for many of these poets when he praised 'the *dictio Virgiliana*', adding 'in that I have always endeavoured to copy him'.[5]

And while Virgil improved the eighteenth-century sense of metre, the diction which he contributed to forming was found useful in a more readily practical way. Many of the nouns in the diction are monosyllables: *race, tribe, train, gale, vale, swain, tide,* and so on. They also have long vowels. And so for poets who held that rhyme should have just those qualifications,[6] here was a body of words suitable for the rhyme position in which they usually placed them. It has also been pointed out that the trochaic adjectives belonging to the diction, when linked to nouns of one or

---

1 'used in the Latin sense, of the brightest, most vivid colouring in general, not of that peculiar tint so called' (Warburton's note on Pope's 'purple year', 'Spring', l. 28, in his edition, 1751).
2 The practice of inventing them begins at least as early as Chapman's 'Homer' (see the list in Professor de Sélincourt's 'Keats', 1907 ed. p. 577). A list from William Browne occurs ibid. p. 579, and from Dryden at p. 65 of Mr Van Doren's 'Poetry of John Dryden', ed. 1931.
3 'Georgics', III, 286 f.
4 I, 164.
5 Op. cit. II, 148. Dryden is writing late in life, in 1695.
6 It was by these qualifications that rhyme escaped Milton's disdainful charge: 'the jingling sound of like endings'. Dryden considered that Milton turned to blank verse because his own skill in rhyme was clumsy: 'he had neither the ease of doing it, nor the graces of it' (op. cit. II, 30). Cf. G. Sewell, 'The Whole Works of Mr John Philips' (1720), p. xxiii.

two syllables, formed convenient units for getting that balance in a line which was considered musically valuable.[1]

By virtue of the words and phrases borrowed or adapted from Virgil, the nature-poems of the eighteenth century have a quality which is usually denied them, the quality of 'atmosphere'. The diction is coloured with Virgilian connotation. Critics have been too apt to dismiss the words merely as derived from Latin, as if their previous life lay only in the double-columned pages of the dictionary. But it is because these words leapt to the eye whenever the poet opened his Virgil that they appear whenever he writes nature-poems for himself. Too much attention has been paid to that perceptive dictum of Crabbe on Pope: 'actuality of relation, ...nudity of description, and poetry without an atmosphere'.[2] The dictum only applies to eighteenth-century nature-poems when the reader fails to supply the Virgilian connotation. As the reverence for Virgil faded, the capacity to supply the connotation faded with it. In the eighteenth century the meanings of the favourite Virgilian words are not defined in the dictionaries. They are beyond definition in the same way that Keats's words are, though often for other reasons. They are indefinable because the dictionary cannot assess the Italian light they derive from the 'Georgics'. Take, for example, *gelid*. Johnson defines it as 'extremely cold', and this is sometimes its meaning: Professor Sherard Vines, for instance, comments as follows on the use of the word in Thomson's 'Winter':

> The horizontal sun
> Broad o'er the south, hangs at his utmost noon
> And ineffectual strikes the gelid cliff,

tells us in words what Claude would have told us on canvas; he would have seen, not as Ruskin, the tertiary cliff with inclined strata, or glacial curvatures, particular after particular, but in all its essential and generalised dignity, the gelid cliff.[3]

1 T. Quayle, 'Poetic Diction: A Study of Eighteenth Century Verse' (1924), p. 30.
2 Preface to 'Tales' ('Works', 1834, IV, 144).
3 'The Course of English Classicism' (1930), p. 98.

Gelid sometimes has this zero temperature in the 'Georgics': it is applied, for instance, to *antrum*. But it is a warmer word on other occasions, when, for instance, it describes valleys that Virgil longs to idle in.[1] And it has this warmer connotation when Goldsmith writes in 'The Traveller':

> While sea-born gales their gelid wings expand
> To winnow fragrance round the smiling land.

(*Smiling*, a common word in eighteenth-century pastoral, may be considered the equivalent of *laetus*, which Virgil constantly applied to crops.) When Joseph Warton translated *gelidi fontes* (among *mollia prata*)[2] he was right to render it as 'cooling fountains'.

6

Virgil suits these poets for another reason. The 'Georgics' are an exaltation of human control over the stubbornness and fertility of the earth and of the beast. The men of the eighteenth century, like those of any other century, admired this control, but sought more intelligently to refine and enlarge the amount of it which had already been secured: witness their landscape gardening, the improvements in agriculture and in the breeding of stock. But the control which is most worthy of celebration by poets is that of a stubbornness and fertility which almost have their own way, which need a ceaseless vigilance. Virgil, therefore, had also celebrated the severe act of labour which is the means to the control. He had experienced the realities of the land on his own farm. And, further, he had laboured like any peasant on the furrows of his poem: the 'Georgics', we are told, cost him seven years to perfect. But it must be confessed that in the georgics of the eighteenth century there is not always much evidence of a struggle. The control which they assume is dry-browed and sometimes almost automatic. A stubbornness which is shown so thoroughly tamed risks the suspicion that it was never stubborn

1 II, 488.   2 'Ecl.' X, 42.

enough. The poets of the eighteenth-century georgics are too much like the absentee gentleman farmer who comes down from town and does his controlling with a straight back and a walking-stick. What Virgil won with pain, they take with a bow. More-over, it is often the same bow: because, whereas you know that minor nineteenth-century poetry will be bad, you know that minor eighteenth-century poetry will be bad in a certain way. And it is partly because of their more facile harvest that the eighteenth-century poets take certain lines in the 'Georgics' too seriously. Writing for Augustus and Maecenas, and being himself a poet naturally prone to grandeur rather than to simplicity, Virgil did not always feel that he could write straight ahead as if he were writing merely for farmers. At least he feels the need for an apology before doing so:

> Nec sum animi dubius, verbis ea vincere magnum
> Quam sit, et angustis hunc addere rebus honorem.[1]

But after this apology his words say frankly what he means. It is not because of any abstention that Virgil's poem remains poetical: he uses the words he obviously needs. It is what may com-pendiously be called the versification that sheds the glory on the poem. By virtue of the richness of the sound, Virgil, in Addison's words, 'breaks the Clods and tosses the Dung about with an Air of Gracefulness'.[2] Some of this glory is present in Dryden's translation, and perhaps it is not without significance that we find Beattie censuring him for 'being less figurative than the original [and] in one place exceedingly filthy, and in another shockingly obscene'.[3] The georgic writers of the eighteenth century may not have been writing for the great of Rome, but no more than Virgil

1 III, 289 f.
2 'Essay on the Georgics' ('Works of Virgil...Translated...by... Dryden', ed. 1763, I, 207).
3 'Essays: on Poetry and Music, as they Affect the Mind' (1778), p. 257. Dryden (not *mirabile dictu*) certainly heightens the original, but his fiery additions are not made without generous encouragement from Virgil. Virgil may be more 'figurative', but Beattie forgets that the figures are often pictures.

were they writing simply for farmers. They had in mind readers of poetry who had also, actually or potentially, the interests of gentlemen farmers, farmers in a comfortable mood of contemplation. They also, therefore, had their problems of vocabulary, and, of course, they often take the easy path of solving them by glossing. But it must be remembered that their problems were real ones, and that they had at least two strong reasons for being squeamish about using 'low' words in 'serious' poems. Even if they realized that Virgil was often using realistic words, they were conscious that these words were more 'sounding' (to use Dryden's epithet) than their English equivalents. Beside Virgil's Latin, the Saxon and 'low' element in English seemed like human life itself, 'nasty, brutish, and short'. In his life of John Philips, George Sewell put his finger on

the great Difficulty of making our *English* Names of Plants, Soils, Animals and Instruments, shine in Verse: There are hardly any of those, which, in the *Latin* Tongue, are not in themselves beautiful and expressive; and very few in our own which do not rather debase than exalt the Style.[1]

And it was not only the words 'in themselves' which were the trouble. During the latter half of the seventeenth century and the

1 Op. cit. p. xxv. In the preface to the translation of Virgil by himself and Christopher Pitt, Joseph Warton writes: 'But, alas!...what must become of a translator of the Georgics, writing in a language not half so lofty, so sounding, or so elegant as the Latin, incapable of admitting many of its best and boldest figures, and heavily fettered with the Gothick shackles of rhyme! Is not this endeavouring to imitate a palace of porphyry with flints and bricks? A poem whose excellence peculiarly consists in the graces of diction is far more difficult to be translated, than a work where sentiment, or passion, or imagination, is chiefly displayed. ...Besides, the meanness of the terms of husbandry is concealed and lost in a dead language, and they convey no low or despicable image to the mind; but the coarse and common words I was necessitated to use in the following translation, viz. *plough and sow, wheat, dung, ashes, horse and cow*, &c. will, I fear, unconquerably disgust many a delicate reader....' ('The Works of Virgil' (1753), I, vi f.) This passage introduces another subject. Words in a dead language, even when they are realistic, fasten themselves more lightly than words should to the equivalent objects of the here and now, and may end by making the objects themselves less real. The small poets of the eighteenth century did not guard against this

earlier eighteenth century, burlesque was busy blackening the Saxon elements in the English language. These words were being rotted by gross ridicule. None of the 'serious' kinds of poetry were exempted from brutal parody, and to use any of the enemy's words would be to instigate the laugh you dreaded. It is not too much to say that in the eighteenth century part of the English language was rendered temporarily unusable in 'serious' poetry. Dr Johnson discussing the passage from 'Macbeth' (a passage he greatly admires) which includes the words *dun, knife,* and *blanket,* finds that he 'can scarce check [his] risibility', and one of the reasons for this lies in his sensitiveness to the occasions when these words or their like have occurred in amusing or offensive contexts which he personally cannot forget:

if, in the most solemn discourse, a phrase happens to occur which has been successfully employed in some ludicrous narrative, the gravest auditor finds it difficult to refrain from laughter....[1]

So that for the 'serious' eighteenth-century poet, a periphrasis was often a means for skirting the company of such parodists as

---

enough. Wordsworth (who is probably speaking of Latin and Greek proses) realized the danger strongly after he had escaped it:

'......In general terms,
I was a better judge of thoughts than words,
Misled as to these latter, not alone
By common inexperience of youth
But by the trade in classic niceties,
Delusion to young Scholars incident
And old ones also, by that overpriz'd
And dangerous craft of picking phrases out
From languages that want the living voice
To make of them a nature to the heart,
To tell us what is passion, what is truth,
What reason, what simplicity and sense.'

('The Prelude', ed. E. de Sélincourt, 1926, p. 176
[the version of 1805–6].)

1 'Rambler', 168. Cf. Beattie, op. cit. pp. 256 ff. for a justification of Pope's translating Homer's 'swine-herd' as 'swain'. Cf. also Wilde, 'The Importance of Being Earnest', Act II:

'*Cecily*:...When I see a spade I call it a spade.

Gwendolen (satirically): I am glad to say I have never seen a spade. It is obvious that our social spheres have been widely different.'

Eighteenth-Century Poetic Diction

(to name only the greatest) Cotton, Butler, Gay, and Swift.[1] It is inevitable that when there is no other reason for a periphrasis than this strictly temporary one, the periphrasis itself will seem ludicrous to a later, cleaner age. But this does not alter the fact that the periphrasis did once seem preferable. Pope, anticipating ourselves, laughed at the periphrasts.[2] The remedy, he saw, was sometimes worse than the disease. But the disease was a real one. Some of the poets use the diction as stilts to escape the mud. But not the good poets. It is true to say that the good poets of the eighteenth century use language, including the poetic diction, with a scrupulousness far in advance, say, of Shelley's use of language. Examine, for instance, this excerpt from a snow scene in Thomson's 'Winter':

> ...The foodless wilds
> Pour forth their brown inhabitants. The hare,
> Though timorous of heart, and hard beset
> By death in various forms, dark snares, and dogs,
> And more unpitying men, the garden seeks,
> Urg'd on by fearless want. The bleating kind
> Eye the bleak heaven, and next the glistening earth,
> With looks of dumb despair; then, sad-dispersed,
> Dig for the withered herb through heaps of snow.[3]

Here the diction is parcel of the meaning. 'Brown inhabitants' is a neat way of grouping creatures which inhabit the scene described and whose brownness is the most evident thing about them in the snow. 'Bleating kind' is anything but an unthinking substitute for 'sheep'. Thomson is saying: we think of sheep as creatures who bleat, but they are silent enough in the snow; it is the dumb eye and not the voice that tells us of their despair.

---

1 We can appreciate this linguistic repugnance by examining our own over such a word as *blooming*. It is Saxon, and 'beautiful' (i.e. pleasant to say, having pleasant original associations); it was overused by eighteenth-century poets and, therefore, vulgarized; it was 'successfully employed in some ludicrous' parody; it even became slang and a euphemistic swear-word; it therefore seems ludicrous whenever it is now met in eighteenth-century poems.
2 'Peri Bathous', xii.   3 ll. 256 ff.

7

There is at least one more reason why the diction is called for. It helps to express some part of the contemporary interest in the theological and scientific significance of natural phenomena. If external nature was not much regarded for its own sake, it was often regarded for the sake of a straightforward theology and an everyday science. The creatures were a continual proof of the wisdom and variety in the mind of the Creator, and a continual invitation for man to marvel and understand. The eighteenth-century theologian and scientist (they were frequently the same man) often see themselves in the position of the writer of Psalms viii and civ, which appear as follows in the version of George Sandys:

> ...O what is Man, or his frail Race,
> That thou shouldst such a Shadow grace!
> Next to thy Angels most renown'd;
> With Majesty and Glory crown'd:
> The King of all thy Creatures made;
> That all beneath his feet hath laid:
> All that on Dales or Mountains feed,
> That shady Woods or Deserts breed;
> What in the Airy Region glide,
> Or through the rowling Ocean slide....

And

> ...Great God! how manifold, how infinite
> Are all thy Works! with what a clear fore-sight
> Didst thou create and multiply their birth!
> Thy riches fill the far extended Earth.
> The ample Sea; in whose unfathom'd Deep
> Innumerable sorts of Creatures creep:
> Bright scaled Fishes in her Entrails glide,
> And high-built Ships upon her bosome ride....[1]

1 'A Paraphrase upon the Psalms', ed. 1676, pp. 14 and 178.

82

Like the Psalmist, they are conscious of the separate wonders of the different elements:

> Whate'er of life all-quick'ning æther keeps,
> Or breathes thro' air, or shoots beneath the deeps,
> Or pours profuse on earth...
> Not man alone, but all that roam the wood,
> Or wing the sky, or roll along the flood....[1]

And above all they are interested in the adaptation of life to environment. To draw only on one instance. The Rev. William Derham in 1713 published his Boyle lectures with the title 'Physico-Theology: or, a Demonstration of the Being and Attributes of God, from his Works of Creation'. The book went into many editions. One chapter concerns the *Clothing of Animals* 'in which we have plain Tokens of the Creator's Art, manifested in these two Particulars; the *Suitableness of Animals Cloathing to their Place and Occasions*, and the *Garniture and Beauty thereof*'.[2] The poetic diction is obviously a means of differentiating the creatures in this way: *the scaly breed, the feather'd race*, and so on. It is not surprising to find it cropping up in brief descriptions of the genesis of the world: see, for instance, Sylvester's 'Du Bartas';[3] John Hanson's 'Time is a Turnecoate':

> The winged-people of the various Skie,
> The scalie Troupe which in the Surges lie;[4]

1 Pope, 'Essay on Man', III, 115 ff.

2 9th ed. 1737, p. 215. Cf. Montaigne, 'Of the use of apparel': 'My opinion is, that even as all plants, trees, living creatures, and whatsoever hath life, is naturally seen furnished with sufficient furniture to defend itself from the injury of all weathers:

> *Proptereaque fere res omnes, aut corio sunt,*
> *Aut seta, aut conchis, aut callo, aut cortice tectae.* (Luc. I, iv, 932)

> Therefore all things almost we cover'd mark,
> With hide, or hair, or shells, or brawn, or bark.

Even so were we.'

3 I, v, 33.   4 1604, p. 33.

Davenant's 'Gondibert':[1] Dryden's 'State of Innocence', where the newly created Eve, seeking to distinguish what she is, sees

> from each Tree
> The feather'd Kind peep down, to look on me;[2]

and Blackmore's 'Creation'.[3] The notion of the great Scale of Being, which Professor Lovejoy has so thoroughly interpreted for us,[4] provided for an infinite scale of creatures, ranging from angels, whom Dryden calls 'Th'Etherial people'[5] to

> ...the green myriads in the peopled grass.[6]

All these 'people' were variously adapted to their place in the sublime chain. Life manifested itself on every link, and the grouped bearers of that life (*people, inhabitants, race, train, troop, drove, breed*) are clothed in appropriate bodies. Derham, for example, uses terms such as *vegetable race, winged tribes, watery inhabitants*.[7] The diction, then, is not simply 'poetic' diction: it is also 'physico-theological' nomenclature. All this tells against Owen Barfield's suggestion in his brilliant book on 'Poetic Diction':

> No one would have dreamed of employing the stale Miltonics [Barfield followed Sir Walter Raleigh in deriving the poetic diction from Milton], which lay at the bottom of so much eighteenth-century 'poetic diction', in *prose*, however imaginative.[8]

The evidence, however, runs the other way, and we must allow for this in estimating the degree to which the poetic diction was poetic to contemporary eyes. Among Derham's terms for dividing the creation into groups of creatures is the term 'heavenly bodies'. This term alone has survived into the scientific usage of our own century. We should not suspect any poet who dared to

1 II, vi, 57.   2 1677, p. 13.
3 II, 150.
4 Arthur J. Lovejoy, 'The Great Chain of Being' (1936).
5 'State of Innocence' (1677), p. 37.
6 Pope, 'Essay on Man', I, 210.
7 Op. cit. p. 9.
8 'Poetic Diction: A Study in Meaning' (1928), p. 177.

use this term of attempting decoration. And with this as evidence we may believe that those terms of the poetic diction which were also the terms of the moralists and scientists had an intellectual toughness about them as well as a neatness and fashionable grace.

Enough has been said of the poetic diction of the eighteenth century to indicate that when it comes to be examined as thoroughly as it never yet has been, much of eighteenth-century poetry will be seen more clearly. The reasons why eighteenth-century poets use the diction share in the central reasons why they write poetry at all.

1939

VIII. ALEXANDER POPE (I)

THE career of Pope is important in several ways. It is the career of the greatest poet of his time, and consequently the career of English poetry over the first half of the eighteenth century. And since Pope was frequently a poet exercising his genius on the literary affairs of his time, his life inevitably entails important aspects of the lives of all men of letters of his time. Reading the life of Pope, one will be reading the life of everybody who mattered during the length of fifty years, and during a fifty years unparalleled for literary machination and assault.

The life of Pope is that of one who suffered intensely and who yet was master. The alternation of pain received and pain given, of the physical-mental imprisonment of deformity ('this long disease, my life') and the triumph of writing poetry, of friendships and hatreds—all these are unusually strong colours for a biography. But, strong colours as they are, they exist mysteriously. Pope's own hand throws tormenting shadows over them. His biographer must guess what becomes of this and that, but before he guesses he must have observed the whole chiaroscuro with laborious sensitiveness. The mere amount of research necessary for anyone concerned with Pope's biography is almost overpowering. Professor Sherburn acknowledges that his book[1] has occupied him over 'a shocking number of years'. But, with the pleasant exception of Miss Sitwell's, his biography is the first since Johnson's to be built on the understanding that research must begin, continue and end in a religious spirit of fairness. Even Professor Sherburn is not wholly clear of prejudice: the indecent verses of Pope need not have troubled *his* conscience. But the beauty of his book is the modesty of its claims, the 'multiplicity and complexity of the facts', the refreshing fairness of its interpretation of those facts, and the argumentative charity where

1 'The Early Career of Alexander Pope', by George Sherburn, Oxford, 1934.

facts are not completely retrievable or retrieved. Pope emerges from these three hundred pages as the recognizable successor of the Pope whom Spence knew and whom Johnson found worthy of one of his finest biographical tributes. Professor Sherburn's book 'is in no sense an attempt at a definitive treatment of Pope's early life'. Adequate materials are still wanting: a critical text of the poems and a critical text of the letters. It is doubtful, however, if discoveries and revaluations will take any other form than that of pendants to this biography, at least for a long time. Paragraphs may in time need to be changed here and there, but one can scarcely predict anything more serious than that. And someone will need to take the life down from 1728, where this book leaves it, to Pope's death in 1744. That someone, let us hope, will be Professor Sherburn.

Professor Sherburn is good at recreating people, a gift rare in the research scholar. His portrait of Addison, for example, is admirably penetrating. His attitude in approaching the obscured and fascinating subject of Pope's character is summed up in his remark: 'Critical suspicion should exist in the mind of anyone studying Pope, but such a state of mind should not dominate one's whole attitude.' Miss Sitwell, with little scholarship but a great deal of sympathy, got nearer the true Pope than any biographer since Johnson. She seems to have looked at his portraits and discovered that they could not be the portraits of a blackguard:

> If to his share some human errors fall,
> Look on his face, and you'll forget 'em all

What she discovered by intuition Professor Sherburn has been able to add to and improve on by a brilliantly intelligent use of the more reasonable method of scholarship. His work on Pope's character and on that of his many associates is more interesting than a detective story, since it coordinates material which is partly, and puzzlingly, known already.

Professor Sherburn shows how literary criticism of Pope has been warped by misconceptions of his character and by preoccupations with it, a warping that reached the point of crack-brained laughter in the edition of which Elwin was part editor. Professor Sherburn hopes his biography 'will serve as a preliminary to better criticism of Pope'. It certainly could not have come at a better time. Two new editions are announced. Mr Ault has discovered new unsuspected early poems. Pope is becoming, and is to become, better known. There is a chance that he will become known for the poet he is.

Professor Sherburn's biography helps one to see the elements of continuity in Pope's writing. One of the most neglected of these elements is Pope's sense of beauty and his use of it as material for poetry. Pope may be considered to exemplify, especially as a young poet, certain qualities of two other London-born poets, the Milton of the Horton period and the young Keats. Pope's early conception of the poet is as much as Keats's one of enthusiasm. The ideal poet as he frets through the surface of the 'Essay on Criticism' is a bold and fiery spirit with some of the qualities which Pope in the preface to his 'Iliad' saw in Homer. A poem for Pope is one

> Where Nature moves and rapture warms the mind;

and in 'Windsor Forest' there is the apostrophe:

> Ye sacred Nine! that all my soul possess,
> Whose raptures fire me, and whose visions bless....

And Pope and Keats both did their poetic reading in the same spirit: Pope

> Glows while he reads, but trembles while he writes,

he confesses. The sonnet on Chapman's Homer sprang from a similar glow and, to take one of Pope's two senses, was written with similar trembling. Pope differs from the young Keats by having a much more continuous regard for orderliness. A poem must be bold but regular. The poet must know when to let fly and when to hold the poem tight. This sense of structure is a rare and valuable thing in English poetry. 'Endymion' lacked it, fatally by any high standard. And Pope very nearly produced his own 'Endymions'. He told Spence that he 'had some thoughts of writing a Persian fable', in which he would 'have given a full loose to description and imagination. It would have been a very wild thing....' And these thoughts were amplified in a letter to Judith Cowper:

> I have long had an inclination to tell a fairy tale, the more wild and exotic the better; therefore a *vision*, which is confined to no rules of probability, will take in all the variety and luxuriancy of description you will....

There is a strong element of wildness in the 'Temple of Fame', but it is restrained, and wisely restrained.

Like Keats and the young Milton, Pope was a country poet before he was a town poet. We have heard too exclusively of Pope's urban preoccupation with morals and satire. His world of experience was as extensive as that of any other poet. Pope is held to be deficient in a sense of beauty, in the amount of beauty he experienced and in the quality of that experience. Actually he was as sensitive to aesthetic experience as the young Milton, and probably as sensitive to it as the young Keats. Spence preserved some important fragments of his aesthetics. He shows Pope on the Thames receiving 'That Idea of the Picturesque, from the swan just gilded with the sun amidst the shade of a tree over the water'. And another remark, almost Wordsworthian in imputing to education the spoiling of the natural instincts:

> A tree is a nobler object than a prince in his coronation robes.... Education leads us from the admiration of beauty in natural objects, to the admiration of artificial (or customary) excellence....I don't doubt but that a thorough-bred lady might admire the stars, *because* they twinkle like so many candles at a birth-night.

Pope is seen in Professor Sherburn's second chapter (1705–1715) to be as completely environed with lane, wood and field as Milton was in the vacations and after leaving Cambridge, and as Keats

liked to be. Gay in 1713 inscribed his 'Rural Sports' to
Pope: to

> You, who the sweets of rural life have known,
> [And] despise th' ungrateful hurry of the town....

In the 'Pastorals' and 'Windsor Forest', Pope is as warmly in love
with natural sights and sounds as any of those pastoralists and
country-drawn poets who are always breaking into seventeenth-
century poetry with their sunny landscapes. Pope asks for:

> ...sequester'd scenes,
> The bow'ry mazes, and surrounding greens:
> ...Thames's banks, which fragrant breezes fill,
> Or where ye Muses sport on Cooper's Hill....
> I seem thro' consecrated walks to rove,
> I hear soft music die along the grove.
> Led by the sound, I roam from shade to shade,
> By god-like Poets venerable made....

Pope made the most of the usual training for a poet, things of
acknowledged beauty to see, things of acknowledged beauty to
read.

The thoroughbred lady might like stars because of candles.
Pope preferred stars, but had his aesthetic use for candlelight. He
carried his sense of beauty further than any previous poet by
taking it indoors with him and employing it on anything made
by the inspired hand of man. This was one of the easy means of
transition to 'town' poetry. In the work of utilitarian silversmith
or carver Pope took a delight which is new and valuable for
English poetry. George Herbert, Herrick and Waller had touched
part of this new area for poetry, but Pope is the first poet who
shows himself worthy of looking at the work of the anonymous
Inigo Joneses and Grinling Gibbonses of the silver workshops.
Pope provides a logical extension of one aspect of renaissance
humanism. The Elizabethans were fond of describing their
dolphin chambers. Pope sees the things on a sophisticated table

to be lovely, man's hand being god-like even in the common-place:

> For lo! the board with cups and spoons is crown'd,
> The berries crackle, and the mill turns round.
> On shining altars of Japan they raise
> The silver lamp; the fiery spirits blaze.
> From silver spouts the grateful liquors glide,
> While China's earth receives the smoking tide....

It is part of the way that everything for Pope is centralized in man, in men, in human character and the visible instruments upon which human character orchestrates its fine or broken music. Pope is often laughing at man-made beauty since it is so often misused by man, since it so often exemplifies the proud canker in his soul. But in itself he finds it beautiful.

This experience of indoor beauty—or of beauty contrived by man out of doors, in gardens, for instance—was included no doubt under 'plains' in Wordsworth's famous remark about Pope's neglecting the heights—Wordsworth allowed that the heights were within Pope's reach. But it is what one sees in the plains that matters, as it is equally what one sees in the heights. One might as well quarrel with Manet for wasting time with the bar of the Folies Bergère when there were mountains sawing the skies, as quarrel with Pope for the Hampton Court interior.

Besides this extension of beauty on one of its boundaries, Pope may claim to be a 'nature poet' in a way disconcerting to the romantic nature-poets. In the same way that Swift saw more in animals than any previous writer except the author of 'King Lear', so Pope saw more in insects than any other poet except perhaps Gray. Insects are everywhere in Pope's poetry. Swift sees men often as beasts, as rats or wolves or yahoos. Pope sees men often as insects, and there is no doubt about the natural liveliness of his vision:

> Satire or sense alas! can *Sporus* feel?
> Who breaks a butterfly upon a wheel?

and the answer that neglects the implied denial:

> Yet let me flap this bug with gilded wings,
> This painted child of dirt that stinks and stings...
> [Who] at the ear of Eve, familiar Toad,
> Half froth, half venom, spits himself abroad....

Man is 'a puny insect shivering at a breeze', 'an industrious bug',

> And lo the wretch! whose vile, whose insect lust
> Laid this gay daughter of the Spring in dust.

The first motto chosen for the 'Dunciad' was the famous stanza of the 'Faerie Queene', in which the shepherd 'mars' the play of gnats, a stanza Pope recollected in the 'Epilogue to the Satires':

> Ye tinsel Insects! whom a Court maintains,
> That counts your Beauties only by your Stains,
> Spin all your Cobwebs o'er the Eye of Day!
> The Muse's wing shall brush you all away....

One might take these instances to show to what use Pope put his perception, whether of beautiful or unpleasant things. Pope is seldom exclusively interested in beauty, and in his greatest poetry he is seldom interested in beauty for its own sake. (This is true even of his strong interest in the beauty of versification.) To speak more precisely, Pope's interest in beauty is only allowed to be total on momentary occasions. If his poem has brought him to a point where he can write with his eye full on beauty and forget all else, he takes the chance to be as purely a poet of beauty as ever Keats was. Pope's favourite couplet of all his thousands was the one Keats would have chosen:

> Lo! where Mæotis sleeps, and hardly flows
> The freezing Tanais thro' a waste of snows.

Pope's excursion into pure beauty may be limited by its place in the poem. It is tied, so to speak, at both ends. But inside that prescribed space, or rather time—perhaps the five seconds of a couplet—the chance for the perfect realization of beauty is infinite. The astonishing thing is that in these flashes Pope can cover such

large areas. In the early poems he gives himself, as he saw later,
too many chances. He came to see later, as Keats came to see, that
'pure description' should not hold 'the place of sense'. But the
descriptions which he did write are fine and varied. The partridge
in 'Windsor Forest' is as brilliantly done as Chaucer's chanticleer.
Then there is the throne of Fame, and this northern simile raised
on a basis of Pope's reading in books of travel:

> So Zembla's rocks (the beauteous work of frost)
> Rise white in air, and glitter o'er the coast;
> Pale suns, unfelt, at distance roll away,
> And on th' impassive ice the light'nings play:
> Eternal snows the growing mass supply,
> Till the bright mountains prop th' incumbent sky:
> As Atlas fix'd, each hoary pile appears,
> The gather'd winter of a thousand years.

It is noteworthy in the later works that when Nova Zembla is
mentioned it is by name only. In the later works the element of
beauty is restricted. The point here is that that element is as intensely perceived as in the works of any great poet. Because it is
all controlled, critics have been apt to think there was nothing to
control.

Pope controls the element of beauty not only in its amount but
in its manner of expression. He formularizes the expression of it
to fit the geometrical subtleties of his couplets. And, moreover,
he often itemizes it by a process analogous to deduction. He
begins with a general idea and applies it to the external world,
selecting by a process of itemization. This is really Ovid's way in
the 'Metamorphoses'. Daphne, Mirrha or Dryope become trees
and the process is followed item by item. This is part of Dryden's
translation of the tenth book:

> For while she spoke, the Ground began to rise,
> And gather'd round her Feet, her Leggs, and Thighs;
> Her Toes in Roots descend, and spreading wide,
> A firm Foundation for the Trunk provide:

Her solid Bones convert to solid Wood,
To pith her Marrow, and to Sap her Blood:
Her Arms to Boughs, her Fingers change their Kind,
Her tender Skin is harden'd into Rind.

This becomes the method of much of Pope's description—Sandys's Ovid was a favourite book of his childhood, Dryden had translated several of Ovid's stories, and Pope himself did early translations from Ovid. Here are some of his itemized descriptions:

Oft in her glass [i.e. a stream's] the musing shepherd spies
The headlong mountains and the downward skies,
The wat'ry landscape of the pendant woods,
And absent trees that tremble in the floods;
In the clear azure gleam the flocks are seen,
And floating forests paint the waves with green,
Thro' the fair scene roll slow the lingering streams,
Then foaming pour along, and rush into the Thames.

Later it is the manner of the 'Eloisa' setting:

But o'er the twilight groves, and dusky caves,
Long-sounding aisles, and intermingled graves,
Black Melancholy sits, and round her throws
A death-like silence, and a dread repose:
Her gloomy presence saddens all the scene,
Shades ev'ry flow'r, and darkens ev'ry green,
Deepens the murmur of the falling floods,
And breathes a browner horror on the woods.

Later still it is the manner of the 'Moral Essays':

Grove nods at grove, each Alley has a brother,
And half the platform just reflects the other.
The suff'ring eye inverted Nature sees,
Trees cut to Statues, Statues thick as trees;
With here a Fountain, never to be play'd;
And there a Summer-house, that knows no shade;
Here Amphitrite sails thro' myrtle bow'rs;
There Gladiators fight, or die in flow'rs;
Un-water'd see the drooping sea-horse mourn,
And swallows roost in Nilus' dusty Urn.

94

Alexander Pope

Pope's sense of beauty is almost always incorporated into his sense of interest. He sees meaning among things. This is one of the several seventeenth-century elements in his poetry, and its presence forbids him to discard entirely the metaphysical process. Not that Pope's meaning is of the same kind as that of Donne or Herbert. His process, however, is often theirs. The sensuous world is as important to him as it is to them because it coordinates itself with the strength of his meaning. This is often the explanation of his similes. They are seldom decorations for their own sake, even when they are parodies of epic similes. They are usually sudden and surprising intricacies of the external world which an intricate meaning has magnetized to itself. They are the same in kind as the fine 'homely' similes in the 'Biographia Literaria'. The material of these similes may be beautiful or unpleasant, but whether it is one or the other is irrelevant, accidental. The meaning has been sufficiently intense and defined to amalgamate itself with that detail of the external world which is, so to speak, the sole example of its law:

> For wit and judgment often are at strife,
> Tho' meant each other's aid, like man and wife.

Or the law may have two manifestations:

> Or, if to Wit a coxcomb make pretence,
> Guard the sure barrier between that and Sense;
> Or quite unravel all the reas'ning thread,
> And hang some curious cobweb in its stead!
> As, forc'd from wind-guns, lead itself can fly,
> And pond'rous slugs cut swiftly thro' the sky;
> As clocks to weight their nimble motion owe,
> The wheels above urg'd by the load below....

Pope uses his acquaintance with beauty or 'interest' where it is needed. And so with every other element in his poetry. One of the most subtle things in poetry is the way in which a poem by Pope is multiple in its layers of significance. Pope is usually doing several things at once. He is writing what he wants to say on his theme. This, of course, is what any author is doing; but for Pope the saying of what he had to say entailed the saying of it in an intensive manner which has seldom been completely that of any other poet. Shenstone said that, more than any other writer, Pope had the art of condensing sense, though Dr Johnson, sitting wet through in a hut in Scotland, did not agree with him. Then Pope was concerning himself with the fine mechanics of his verse. Again, every poet must, of course, be attentive on this point. But Pope was unusually attentive. He distinguished, he told Spence, between sweetness and softness in versification, which will serve to indicate the gradations of his sensitiveness to sound. Then, usually he was writing in imitation of some poet or poetic form. The 'Rape of the Lock' and the 'Dunciad' are miniature epic poems, and the detailed tallying is effected by a technical mastery which recalls Mozart. The speech of Clarissa, added in the 1717 version of the 'Rape', is a close parody of Pope's own earlier translation of the speech of Sarpedon to Glaucus in the 'Iliad'. The 'Imitations of Horace' show the poet bound hand and foot and yet dancing as if free. These do not exhaust the sum of his activities. Pope is always eager to adapt the phrases of earlier poets. It was almost a principle with him. As an example of this one might take the line:

[Till] Alma Mater lie dissolv'd in Port.

This expression derives in the first place from Ovid. Line 612 of Book XII of the 'Metamorphoses' reads:

Quo cubat ipse Deus, membris languore solutis.

Sandys translates by:

Here lay the lazie God, dissolu'd in rest.

When Dryden came to the same line in his translation he avoided the literal perfection of Sandys, and wrote:

...where lay the God
And slept supine, his limbs display'd abroad.

But he remembered the phrase when translating the story of Cymon and Iphigenia from Boccaccio, and at line 550 spoke of

...Men dissolv'd in ease.

So far, in Sandys and Dryden, the phrase has remained virtually static. Pope provides it with its culmination. His line requires the cooperation of the reader's memory for all its juices to be at their most piquant. This kind of imitation was as important for Pope's verse as any other element. And finally, added to all these, there was his continuous attempt to control his poem into shapeliness.

Since all these activities are usually found working together in a poem of Pope's, this is the best answer for anyone who considers a simple cause like ill-nature to have accounted for his satiric poetry. Pope had his hatreds as his contemporaries had theirs for him. But his sense of the strenuous requirements of his verse promoted the personal grudge into a larger emotional context, the disinfecting context of hard work, and finally of great poetry. When one reads the character of Sporus, one's eyes are not on Hervey. It is as much as they can do to receive the fire of the words. Hervey's-character is for Pope an entrance into a brilliantly sensuous world every atom of which is vital, a world as exciting to the aesthetic sense as those of the 'Nun's Priest's Tale' or of 'Lamia'.

Moreover, hatred as an inspiration for Pope's satire has been overstated in importance. The emotion of pity is often as powerfully at work:

> Who would not weep, if Atticus were he?

Or this from 'Of the Characters of Women':

> Asham'd to own they gave delight before,
> Reduc'd to feign it, when they give no more:
> As Hags hold Sabbaths, less for joy than spite,
> So these their merry, miserable Night;
> Still round and round the Ghosts of Beauty glide,
> And haunt the places where their Honour died.

Satiric poetry such as this affects the primary human emotions, even in Matthew Arnold's sense which limited the meaning to the nobler of those emotions. The terms 'moral' and 'satiric' poetry have put off readers for too long. One's face, if it responded to this poetry (and the face is apt to respond privately to Pope) would wear a complicated smile, or a look of complicated solemn intensity. Hazlitt, the profoundest of all critics on the 'Rape', did not know whether to laugh or to weep over the poem. Pope added a 'moral' to it in the 1717 edition:

> Oh! if to dance all night, and dress all day,
> Charm'd the small-pox, or chas'd old-age away;
> Who would not scorn what huswife's cares produce,
> Or who would learn one earthly thing of use?
> To patch, nay ogle, might become a Saint,
> Nor could it sure be such a sin to paint.
> But since, alas! frail beauty must decay,
> Curl'd or uncurl'd, since locks will turn to grey;
> Since painted, or not painted, all shall fade,
> And she who scorns a man, must die a maid;
> What then remains, but well our pow'r to use,
> And keep good humour still what'er we lose?...

This is indeed (to use a phrase that comes twice in his poetry) 'the language of his heart'. And that language is habitual with him. No other poet has found his sense of beauty so closely and continuously allied to his sense of human values. No other poet has put or answered the question how to live with tenderer concern and more pointed wisdom. In his trembling eye a virtue was as dear as a flower.

1934

ALEXANDER POPE (II)

ONE has only to think of Blake, who stands in the other half of Pope's century, to see that Pope was in no sense revolutionary. No poet has ever been more dependent than he on the tradition established by his immediate predecessors. He carries on the work of those seventeenth-century poets of whom Denham and Waller were early examples and Dryden the latest and greatest. Recalling an early glimpse of Dryden, Pope used the words, *Virgilium tantum vidi*, and his salute indicates how, for him, the seventeenth century in England and the poets of Rome were two sides of the same medal. Almost all Pope's work is done in forms which the poets of Rome and of the seventeenth century in England (and France) had invented or practised. Pope begins as a boy by translations mainly from Latin. His earliest 'original' poems were pastorals. His 'Essay on Criticism' looks back to Horace's 'Ars Poetica', to Boileau's 'Art Poétique' and to English verse essays on the aims and technique of writing. His 'local poem' 'Windsor Forest' imitates Denham's 'Cooper's Hill'. His 'Temple of Fame' has many French and English predecessors besides Chaucer's 'Hous of Fame' which is its immediate source. The 'Rape of the Lock' and, later, the 'Dunciad' belong to that mock-epic tradition which begins, as far as extant work is concerned, with Homer's 'Battle of the Frogs and Mice'. 'Eloisa to Abelard' follows Ovid's 'Heroides'. The 'Essay on Man' and the 'Moral Essays' are virtually Horatian epistles, and the 'Imitations of Horace' describe themselves accurately. Like Dryden, Pope hankers after writing an epic, and whereas Dryden translates the 'Æneid', Pope translates the 'Iliad' and the 'Odyssey'.

In all this Pope was doing what any of his contemporary poets could have chosen to do. He may be said to have allowed his age to dictate what poems he should write. And in the same way, there is nothing revolutionary in his metre. During the whole of the seventeenth century—to go no farther back—there had been conscious and continuous attempts to make the most of the heroic couplet, to discover or develop the 'rules' by which poets could be guided to write it 'correctly'. Pope seldom uses any other measure. His 'ten thousand verses', marvellously varied within their couplets, crown the experiments of a century.

Furthermore, there is nothing revolutionary in the 'content' of his poems. Pope deliberately drew his material from what was then called 'Nature', i.e. from that considerable part of every intelligent man's mind which is virtually identical with a considerable part of the mind of his fellows, past, present, and future.

To invent an instance. If Pope, like Keats, had listened to a nightingale and had found himself believing that 'Now more than ever seems it rich to die', he would not have put the idea into a poem. He would have considered that, deeply as the idea might stir him, he was in this too much unlike his fellows to speak of it to them. He would also have seen that the idea had more force for him—Keats was consumptive—than for his fellows, and that tuberculosis, whatever it meant to him, was a barrier between him and them. When Pope heard nightingales, he heard them, of course, more sensitively than his fellows, but he only used that element in his perception which was, in kind at least, that of every man. And because such subjects did not often come in the way of ordinary men, he did not often write of them. The interests of ordinary men may be summarized as other men, personal relationships, manners, morals, politics, books, houses, food, etc. And so it is these themes with their loads of pointed, brilliant detail which occupy him most. It is for this reason that he looks back on the 'Pastorals', 'Windsor Forest', the 'Rape of the Lock' as so much wandering 'in Fancy's maze', and on his essays and satires as 'truth', as concerned with fact, with 'WHATEVER IS'. Pope's later work, therefore, is rooted in Man.

Within this human bound his poems explore a great variety of topics. To begin with, there are Pope's friends and men like the Man of Ross, who are praised; and there are his 'enemies' who are analysed as if with the sharpest instruments of the vivisectionist. The friends may seem to be posed in too golden a light, the enemies in too poisonous a limelight: Pope's scorn can be so intense that he seems to overstep the elected bounds of 'Nature' and write personally as a 'Romantic' poet. But his merciless, at times feminine, emphasis and his deadly quiet have the effect of sharpening the moral, the general truth. The immediate object is burnt up in a wider illumination. The praised or condemned figures do not remain individuals. They expand into summaries, into types. Often Pope arrives at types by another route, less personal than friends and enemies. 'Of the Knowledge and Characters of Men'

Alexander Pope

begins by considering the data offered by all individuals. Their characters are bundles of incoherent details: and yet continued scrutiny may discover some central spring which controls the whole ramshackle apparatus. And when more of these springs are found, resemblances among them will pattern out the type. Pope touches the apex of the human pyramid when he leaves types for Man. Man is summarized with unexceptionable authority in the opening lines of the second Epistle of the 'Essay on Man'.

Pope for the most part abides by what *oft* was thought, and his task is to express it *ne'er so well*.[1] He deliberates over the material existing in every man's mind till he finds that his own sense of its quality is prompting the perfect expression. It is in this best expression that Pope's originality most obviously shows itself. He is not out to surprise by his thoughts, his metre, his 'form'. And yet his poetry is full of surprises. These are often the surprises of finding a hot fire made out of a few sticks, and made out of the sticks which in the hands of other poets had remained uninflammable. The elements of his poetry are commonplace but suddenly rare. Pope, to use Joubert's words, was one of those 'spirits... who when they have an idea to put forth, brood long over it first, and wait patiently till it *shines*, as Buffon enjoined, when he defined genius to be the aptitude for patience'. Pope was tireless in his brooding over the inches of his poems. He found it 'as pleasant... to correct as to write'.[2] But one feels that the series of his revisions have all the 'inspiration' that is associated with freer work. They often take the form of a partly transparent element added on top of an old, and it is this superimposition of strata that makes Pope's work difficult to see to the bottom of. Some of his most famous lines—for example, 'To err is human, to forgive, divine'—are no doubt crystal clear. But usually Pope intends his meaning only to complete itself when the things attracted to

---

1 True Wit is Nature to advantage dress'd,
  What oft was thought, but ne'er so well express'd.
                                        ('Essay on Criticism', ll. 297–8.)
2 Contrast William Morris, p. 141 below.

it from outside are allowed their full say. He is sometimes spoken of as a poet without 'atmosphere', without 'suggestion'. But in truth he is a poet whose suggestion is unusually elaborate. The suggestion, however, is usually not so much pictorial as literary. Before one can appreciate Pope properly one has to know what contemporary readers knew. One needs a head full of earlier poetry and prose. Pope's very meaning; his tone, depend often on a comparison between what he writes and what his writing is echoing. In the 'Dunciad', for example, occur these lines:

> Silence, ye Wolves! while Ralph to Cynthia howls,
> And makes night hideous—Answer him, ye owls!

Without any special knowledge, the reader is instantly aware of the excellence of the comedy. But the comedy is deepened when he finds that Ralph wrote a poem called 'Night'; that the first line parodies Waller's 'Paraphrase on the Lord's Prayer':

> Silence, you winds! listen, ethereal lights!
> While our Urania sings what Heaven indites....

and that the second line quotes Hamlet's hysterical address to the ghost (and consequently implies 'ghosts are not the only things to appal human beings at midnight, for there is now Ralph'). The comic effect is still further deepened when one becomes aware that the couplet strikes on the great bells of the 'Psalms' and of the prayer in Book v of 'Paradise Lost'. The sixteen words of that couplet pile Pelion on Ossa: the howls of Ralph jar a whole universe. One can never be sure that one has discovered everything that Pope put into his verses, and this is perhaps the reason that Lamb could read him 'over and over for ever'.[1]

But Pope was not always out for these layers of effect. Sometimes he elicits a simpler response, a response much more nearly

[1] There are, of course, other and less complicated reasons why the mind welcomes the frequent recurrence of Pope's couplets: cf. e.g. W. Macartney's 'Walls have Mouths' (1936), p. 213: 'One wild Leeds youth, Henderson [a convict] had a passion for Pope and would recite heroic couplets for hours and hours...while digging spuds.' There could be ño finer tribute than this to the vigour and memorability of the heroic couplet when written as Pope wrote it.

confined to the emotions. In 'Eloisa to Abelard', for instance,
and 'The Elegy to the Memory of an Unfortunate Lady' the
litc ary echoes (they never cease in Pope) are intended to be heard
much less clearly, to have the vaguer emotional values they would
have in nineteenth-century poetry. In these 'pathetic' pieces—
the word was equivalent to our 'emotive'—Pope found an outlet
for the extraordinary tenderness of feeling that is so amply
attested by his friends. But even in these poems, moved as he
himself is, he is still thinking of 'Nature', of how not only he, but
all people, feel. He is still providing a human, rather than a
personal, document. He seldom says directly that his own feeling
is running high, except when he is standing publicly proud or
indignant. He insinuates his own mood into a 'dramatic' piece,
into the plight of Eloisa, or into an 'Elegy' on a lady who never
in fact existed. And it is because of this use of the 'objective
co-relative' that his feeling never gets out of control. Nor does
it exist apart from a sound 'sense'. When Eloisa cries,

> Ah hopeless, lasting flames! like those that burn
> To light the dead, and warm th' unfruitful urn,

the lines do not merely set us feeling their subtle blending of
upheaval and resignation. They set us thinking. Feeling, indeed,
deepens as thinking grows clearer. Eloisa's love *is* hopeless and
lasting (Abelard is incapable of union with her, and she is incapable of forgetting him) and the images (not new in themselves
but newly applied) which develop, and so reanimate, the commonplace image of 'flames' are not used merely because of their
music, their 'atmosphere', their pictorial and literary suggestiveness. Nor are they used merely because they are, literally, flames
which are hopeless and lasting. They are used also because they
light the dead and warm the unfruitful. Pope's poetry exhibits
always an equilibrium of many separate forces.

There is, then, a solid prose content in Pope's poetry. But
that prose content, unlike the prose content in prose, is thickly
elaborate. If we think of it for a moment as metal, we think of

it not as an ingot but as a metal tree. And a radiance is playing on the strong interlacing lines of silver, and they are coloured and delicate as Shelley's. Or put it this way: Shelley's words give us their swamping colour before they give us their pittance of sense. Pope's words pay us their sense down, generously and with a variety of coin; but when we look up into the face of the giver we see it as a face 'ensky'd and sainted', the face of a poet.

1938

IX. WILLIAM SHENSTONE

I T would be impossible to imagine Shenstone living at any other time than the mid-eighteenth century. He was, more than many men, the product of a particular age, and a means of guiding that age into the age which succeeded it. The gentle hour was favourable to his particular combination of gifts, or rather to the manifestation of his single gift in a maximum number of ways. He was a poet, an essayist, a writer of *pensées*, a letter-writer ('I look upon my letters as some of my *chef-d'œuvres*'), a landscape gardener, a small artist in calligraphy and decoration, an executant on the harpsichord, a discriminating collector of *objets d'art*. It did not very much matter which medium he happened to choose to divert him at which hour of the day.

The giants of the Renaissance often had various media at their command, but their media were those which have supplied the world with its great works of art: stone, paint or words arranged metrically. Pope had an even wider range of media, though of these only poetry and painting could be considered noble. And, in spite of Pope's calling his garden the greatest of his works, there was never any doubt about the relative unimportance of everything except poetry, about the distinction between work and hobby. With Shenstone there is a further decline from the Renaissance phenomenon. Among his many media only the medium of words could claim to rank among the arts. But whereas with Pope there was no confusion of emphasis, with Shenstone the media seem all about equally insistent. For example, he writes to Jago that he has 'an alcove, six elegies, a seat, two epitaphs, three ballads, four songs, and a serpentine river, to shew you when you come'. The list was, of course, arranged with the tongue in the cheek, but its arrangement has serious significance. It was not vitally important for Shenstone which came first. With equal satisfaction he might add another stanza to an elegy or to a

'Levity', might design yet another memorial urn or superintend the making of another 'root-house'. Pope may have spoken of his garden as the greatest of his works, but however much its maturing delights contrasted with the outside world, the outside world still meant a great deal to Pope. He was by nature a moralist and satirist (though he drew his poetical material from all the usual poetic sources) and therefore, garden or no garden, a man of the world.

With Shenstone one feels that the garden shuts out too much of the world, or shuts it out for too long stretches at a time, or falsifies some part of what it admits. It provided Shenstone with a life too calm for the development of his best qualities. His *ferme ornée* had been given its Gothic hermitage at too early a date— Shenstone had had it scooped out of the gravel pit at the corner of a field among some hazels, and had set a little cross of wood over its door. He accepted the facile refuge too readily. In his 'Egotisms. From My Own Sensations', he acknowledged that something was wrong:

I begin, too soon in life, to slight the world more than is consistent with making a figure in it. The 'non est tanti' of Ovid grows upon me so fast that in a few years I shall have no passion.

And 'Elegy XIX', written when he was twenty-eight, contains these lines:

Another spring renews the soldier's toil,
And finds me vacant in the rural cave.

The retreat from the world was neither physically nor mentally complete, since complete seclusion, if indeed it had been possible, would not have suited Shenstone's temperament. His pleasure came not so much from vanishing out of the real world, as from translating real life into artifice. He arranged that the world was never too much with him. It did encroach on to his happiness rudely at times, but many of these intrusions could be tamed by the exercise of philosophy or philanthropy. The thief who burst into his precious garden and stole his purse actually contributed

William Shenstone

to his calm: Shenstone had him followed to his home, where, through the keyhole of the door, the rascal provided a fairylike compensation: Shenstone's servant was benefited by a scene which might have come from the pages of Goldsmith:

As soon as the man entered [his house] he threw the purse on the ground, and addressing himself to his wife, 'Take', said he, 'the dear-bought price of my honesty', th⬛⬛⬛g two of his children, one on each knee, he said to them⬛⬛⬛⬛⬛ l my soul to keep you from starving', and immediat⬛⬛⬛⬛⬛⬛⬛ of tears. Shenstone inquired after the man's charact⬛⬛⬛⬛⬛ was a labourer, who was reputed honest and indus⬛⬛⬛⬛ v want and a numerous family. He went to his ho⬛⬛⬛⬛ eled down at his feet, and implored mercy. Shens⬛⬛⬛⬛ him, but gave him employment as long as he live⬛

Or there was the consump⬛⬛⬛⬛⬛an. Dr Alexander Carlyle's autobiography report⬛⬛⬛⬛d to the Leasowes:

At the end of a high walk, from w⬛⬛ce we saw far into Gloster and Shrop shires, I met with what struck me most,—that was an emaciated pale young woman, evidently in the last stage of a consumption. She had a most interesting appearance, with a little girl of nine or ten years old, who had led her there. Shenstone went up and stood for some time conversing with her, till we went to the end of the walk and returned: on some of us taking an interest in her appearance, he said she was a very sickly neighbour, to whom he had lent a key to his walks, as she delighted in them, though now not able to use it much....

One has the suspicion that the pale young woman was partly given the freedom of his walks since she contributed to the 'interest' of the place, helped to purvey the mood which Shenstone and his distinguished visitors cultivated. Mason's 'English Garden' counselled the use of rustic children as landscape material:

> call the loiterers into use,
> And form of these thy fence, the living fence
> That graces what it guards....

And in his 'Prefatory Essay on Elegy' Shenstone wrote:

There is a truly virtuous pleasure connected with many pensive contemplations, which it is the province and excellency of elegy to enforce.

107

This, by presenting suitable ideas, has discovered sweets in *melancholy* which we could not find in *mirth*; and has led us with success to the dusty *urn*, when we could draw no pleasure from the sparkling *bowl*.

Shenstone seems to have been able to change the nature of real experience so as to give sanction to his retirement. The enthusiasms of philanthropy, the pathetic charm of being kind to a consumptive and of shedding the 'sadly pleasing tear'[1] on a memorial urn of one's own design—these were as much retreats as the frank recesses of the gravel-pit. If Curll's scurrilous biographies had 'added a new terror to death', these urns, by their sensitiveness to the wrong things, added a new callousness.

But the intrusion of the world sometimes caused havoc which his fragrant herbs could neither properly heal nor disguise. There are the terrible implications of the poem asserting that he had found his warmest welcome at an inn, a poem which moved Johnson 'with great emotion'. There is the evidence, too, of Shenstone's few hundred aphorisms, his best work and as near as anything in English to the *pensées* of La Rochefoucauld. This too-brief collection shows that Shenstone did not escape having to rub up against a good many fools, that he felt impelled to note many human weaknesses for what they were. And then there were the deaths of close friends, and of his brother. For some months after his brother's death it seemed that neither the Leasowes nor his poetry could ever amuse him again, and though pleasure did in time return, its quality was found to have changed. Writing to his friend Graves, who had just married, he is discovered confessing 'I have lost my road to happiness'. One of his most telltale remarks, pathetic in being so assured, is that 'inanimates, toys, utensils, seem to merit a kind of affection from us, when they have been our companions through various vicissitudes. I have often viewed my watch, standish, snuff-box, with this kind of regard, allotting them a degree of friendship which there are some men

[1] The first use of 'sadly pleasing' which I have noted is Dryden's, 'Hind and the Panther', III, 35.

who do not deserve.' This leads directly to the snuff-box incident in the 'Sentimental Journey':

> ...he [the monk] begged we might exchange boxes.... In saying this, he presented his to me with one hand, as he took mine from me in the other; and having kissed it,...with a stream of good-nature in his eyes, he put it into his bosom,...and took his leave.
> I guard this box as I would the instrumental parts of my religion....

Shenstone is, therefore, a pioneer in sentimentalism. There had been sentimentalists before him (though most were to come after), but there had been no sentimentalist of this kind before. He gave to small personal objects more than their due place in his mind. He either valued them too highly for their own sakes, or made them bear too melancholy a weight of private connotation.

And yet Shenstone's sentimentalism is partly justified. It has an occasional quality of perfection. Shenstone may have moved along trivialities, but, as his essay on Taste shows, he had a strictness and subtlety in his choice. If he liked inferior things, he always discriminated the degree of their imperfection:

> Where the discernment is predominant, a person is pleased with fewer objects, and requires perfection in what he sees. Where the appetite prevails, he is so much attached to beauty, that he feels a gratification in every degree, in which it is manifested.

Shenstone frankly admits that he belongs to the latter class, but the very drawing of the distinction between discernment and appetite proves his kinship with the former. Dr Johnson, who preferred even Hebridean hardships to the making of an ornamental garden, accorded to Shenstone the praise of doing 'best what such multitudes are contending to do well'. And Percy, in a letter of obituary summary, writes phrases which demand their full emphasis: 'the delicate sensibility of his writings, the consummate elegance of his taste'. Nothing is easy, if you have Shenstone's standards, though a less perfect creative artist who makes rapid sallies into his art may satisfy more people more completely. Shenstone had no use for the empyrean climate of the 'Night Thoughts'; 'Dr Young...has relapsed into "Night the Fifth"'. I take his case to be wind in great measure, and would advise him to take rhubarb in powder, with a little nutmeg grated amongst it, as I do.' Shenstone's one or two ambitious poems are failures. Reading his letters, humorous and carefully pretty, his 'School-Mistress', a paragraph or *pensée* from his essays, or the description of his grounds by a delighted visitor, one sees that, though he touched nothing of permanent importance, many things that he did touch he left perfect.

And his sentimentalism is saved, too, by his fanciful fun or humour. (It is one of the many qualities that link him with Gray.) Shenstone can write of his exquisitely laboured garden as 'my hole', or inform Lady Luxborough of the latest Gothic news as follows:

Old Pedley [Shenstone's urn-maker] is now at Work for me. The Devil take all Gothicism! I was told (and by an experienced Judge) that I might have two pinnacles hewn in my Gothic Building, for a trifle. They are now done, and have taken more stone than wou'd have built me an Urn.... This last week they have hewn me also an Urn, almost big enough for yᵉ Bacco-stopper of an Inhabitant of Brobdignag.

Shenstone's best poems are among his 'Levities or Pieces of Humour', excepting the 'School-Mistress', which could go into that group as easily as into the 'Moral Pieces', among which Dr Johnson found it incongruous. One can allow Shenstone the 'substantial happiness' he found among his 'genteel urns', his seals, snuff-boxes and busts, when that happiness is seen to be founded partly on laughter.

1935

X. 'RASSELAS' AND THE 'PERSIAN TALES'

I

IN Chapter IX of 'Rasselas' Imlac, continuing his life story, tells of his travels into Persia. 'The Persians', he says, 'are a nation eminently social, and their assemblies afforded me daily opportunities of remarking characters and manners, and of tracing human nature through all its variations.' Johnson's knowledge of the East was that of the unspecialized man of letters of his time. He frankly confessed its shallowness in one of his letters to Warren Hastings.[1] But his imagination, like that of many eighteenth-century authors, felt itself free to shuffle on a Persian coat and to dilate itself at ease in fable or fantasy. The seventeenth and eighteenth centuries had become more and more aware of what the East could offer their travellers and merchants, their authors and scholars, the authors finding in the ideas of it they had derived from books a chance for escape, sometimes for head-long escape.

As early as 1635 Davenant furnished his best masque, 'The Temple of Love', with its 'company of noble Persian youths', its 'Brachmani' and its magi. The controversy of ancients and moderns entailed repeated surveys of the greatness of Eastern empires and Eastern learning. Pope's 'Temple of Fame' displays Ninus, Cyrus, Zoroaster and Chaldaeans, Magi and Brahmans. Beginning with Addison's visions of Mirzah comes a host of writings taking advantage, for moral purposes, of the freedom of Oriental stories. Pope, who concludes no. 61 of the 'Guardian' with one of Pilpay's fables, told Spence that he had once intended to write a Persian fable and that it would have been a very wild

1 'Boswell's Life', ed. G. B. Hill, IV, 68–9.

thing; and in his letter to Judith Cowper of 26 September 1723 he confesses

> I have long had an inclination to tell a fairy tale, the more wild and exotic the better; therefore a *vision*, which is confined to no rules of probability, will take in all the variety and luxuriancy of description you will; provided there be an apparent moral to it. I think, one or two of the Persian tales would give one hints for such an invention. . . .

European knowledge of these tales derived mainly from the French translation of some of them by Pétis de la Croix, whose 'Mille et Un Jours' appeared in five volumes during 1710–12. Ambrose Philips translated these into English at the rate of half-a-crown a section: a payment which, according to Johnson, was very liberal, but which earned him several contemporary hits.[1] The first date I have been able to discover for Philips's translation is 1714: the Bodleian Catalogue (1843) includes an edition of this date. Lowndes and the 'D.N.B.' give the impossible date 1709. Another translation, the preface of which mentions Philips's translation as just published, came out in 1714, and was the work of 'the late Learned Dr. *King*, and several other Hands'.[2] Philips's translation, according to title-page evidence, was reprinted for the second time in 1722, for the sixth in 1750, again in 1783 and lastly in 1848. In 1892 J. H. McCarthy, who had come upon Pétis de la Croix accidentally, retranslated the tales. He considered them almost unknown in England, having only met with a 1714 edition of King's translation and a 1738 one of Philips's which he took to be the first.

1 Cf. Pope, 'Ep. to Dr Arbuthnot', 179 f.:
> 'The Bard whom pilfer'd Pastorals renown,
> Who turns a Persian tale for half a crown';

As Johnson noted ('Life of Philips'), the sum 'had a mean sound': it was commonly understood as the price of a woman of the town.
2 For precise dates see R. H. Griffith's note in 'Times Literary Supplement' 16 Nov. 1935, and Mr Duncan B. Macdonald's note, 14 Dec. 1935.

The 'Persian Tales', all of which provide examples of true love, are supposed to be told to the Princess of Cashmir by her nurse, Sutlumeme, in an endeavour to overcome the princess's aversion for men. The second and third of Philips's three volumes are mainly taken up with a section of stories completely framed in itself. They relate the search for a happy man made by Bedreddin Lolo, King of Damascus, and his vizier, Atalmulc, surnamed the Sorrowful Visier. These stories, in effect, show 'Rasselas' as a fulfilment of the intention which Pope disclosed to Judith Cowper. The following summary of them disregards the frequent philosophizings which, even more than the actual incidents, find their counterpart in Johnson.

Bedreddin's inquiry for the reason of Atalmulc's unhappiness meets with the general explanation that all men are unhappy. Bedreddin cannot credit this, though the story of Atalmulc's misadventures in love certainly seems an adequate explanation of their particular effect. The king instances his favourite as a proof that the happy man is easy to find, but the favourite's answer and story match Atalmulc's. A search among local tradespeople ends in a merry weaver's undergoing examination, but when one more instance of inward misery is disclosed, Bedreddin refuses to let his faith weaken. The refusal is maintained in face of the similar disclosures of his generals, courtiers and household officers. A royal proclamation of the question receives no affirmative answer. So Bedreddin, Atalmulc and the favourite pursue the subject by travelling. A preacher in the streets of Bagdad seems evidence for the king's contention, but private conference at his home undoes the illusion. Two men in a *fiquaa* shop, accidentally overheard discussing the cares of human life, name Hormoz, King of Astrakan, as a 'king without sorrow'. Even Bedreddin is shaken by the unlikelihood of this, and a visit to Astrakan reaches the old conclusion: the continual festivity of Hormoz is only a cloak. So the travellers decide to return home. A last flicker excites

Bedreddin when a great traveller, encountered on the way, seems as happy as he has been successful. But his wife, though perfectly dutiful, loves another. On reaching Damascus, Bedreddin makes an announcement:

> I am convinced there is not a Man in the World but has something or other to trouble him. Those are the happy Persons whose Troubles are most supportable. Let us for the future remain here in Quiet. If we three are not entirely contented, let us consider that there are others more unhappy.

3

It is uncertain how early Johnson knew Philips's translation. He does not seem to have mentioned the 'Persian Tales' in writing or conversation, except in the 'Life of Philips', when he wrote bibliographically of the book in a way suggesting that he had handled it. But that was in 1781 and 'Rasselas' was written in 1759. During those 'evenings of one week', under the immediate sorrow of his mother's death, Johnson had neither time nor inclination for consulting 'sources'. The 'power' of his memory, however, in Boswell's phrase, was 'almost incredible', and we know from Nichols that the criticism of Rowe in the 'Lives of the Poets' was written without consulting plays he had not read for thirty years. His memory of the 'Persian Tales' may have had to extend farther back than this. But though Johnson owes no verbal debt to them, some of their phrases were worth remembering for their touches of Johnsonian solidity and liveliness, or for their human reference. The King of Astrakan, for example, tells his son Hormoz to distribute largesse freely when on his travels, adding as reason, 'The People, dazled with his Bounties, will often praise him for Virtues which Heaven never gave him'.

There can be little doubt of Johnson's debt to the 'Persian Tales' for the subject and outline of 'Rasselas'. The role of Rasselas resembles that of Bedreddin. Both are attempting, incognito, to find happiness, though for different ends, since Rasselas is a young man trying to make the best 'choice of life'.

'Rasselas' and the 'Persian Tales'

The role of Imlac is that of Atalmulc, the wiser man who foresees the end of the search and whose scepticism provides a chorus for each further step in it. The method of narration is similar, since both contain stories within the story. And there is a conclusion to both in which nothing is concluded—Bedreddin and his associates remain frustrate lovers, a rare fate in these tales. Some of the details suggest that Johnson's debt may have extended further than this outline. Atalmulc, in two of his bouts with Bedreddin, tells him to judge of others' condition by his own, but Bedreddin does not agree that different cases are comparable. Nor does Pekuah in 'Rasselas' when, after imputing misfortunes to the old astronomer, she remarks that 'nothing... is more common than to call our own condition the condition of life'. Imlac is of the same opinion and develops it into the aphorism 'Envy is commonly reciprocal'. Bedreddin allows immediately that a king cannot be happy. This is the attitude which Rasselas comes to adopt in his 'Disquisition upon Greatness' (Chapter xxvii). This chapter falls alongside the passage in the 'Tales' in which Bedreddin elicits the secret complaints of his officers. Rasselas, like Hormoz and the weaver, lives amid 'the song of joy, or the laugh of carelessness', and, like them again, is 'only loud and merry to conceal [his] sadness'. The speech overheard in the *fiquaa* shop resembles at one point the opinion of the old man in 'Rasselas' who hopes 'to possess in a better state [after death] that happiness which here I could not find'. Like the Persian experimenters, Rasselas comes upon a preacher who assures his throng that happiness is in the power of those who live according to his advice. Rasselas gives him gold, goes home with him and finds his theory upset by the sudden death of his only daughter. Atalmulc's story shows his happiness shattered on one occasion by a similar, though less fatal, *contretemps*.

But the reading of these two books side by side shows how much Johnson added through the exercise of a mind habitually engaged in enriching philosophy by a play of material instances. He improved the darkness in the scepticism and made it cover everything, the framework and all the stories inside it—even Pekuah's adventures with the Arab add to the philosophical sum of the book, since for Johnson they are a commentary on the theory which a brigand's life implies. Atalmulc had this kind of interest in his story. He saw it throughout as jerking between sumptuous happiness and savage misery, and did not forget the condition in which the final jerk had left him. The other unhappy men had no such controlling attitude towards their autobiographies. All these stories dealt too freely in magic to yield any respectable human law for Johnson. His own magus, the astronomer who has learned how to control the weather, is miserable because of the social responsibility involved. His condition moves Imlac to say, with all Johnson's own fear in his words, 'Of the uncertainties of our present state, the most dreadful and alarming is the uncertain continuance of reason'. The story which the weaver tells has in it a mechanical chest. This chest works: it carries its owner through the air. In 'Rasselas' the end of a similar invention is immediate, flat and final:

> In a year the wings were finished, and, on a morning appointed, the maker appeared furnished for flight on a little promontory: he waved his pinions a while to gather air, then leaped from his stand, and in an instant dropped into the lake. His wings, which were of no use in the air, sustained him in the water, and the prince drew him to land, half dead with terrour and vexation.

The only things which frighten the timid, rather 'unidea'd' Pekuah are pyramids, Arab marauders and catacombs. Johnson's depreciation of marvels in fiction, stated in number 4 of the 'Rambler', held good even for an Eastern tale.

1935

XI. ON GRAY'S LETTERS

I

GRAY scarcely pretended to write poems: he actually stated that he '[did] not pretend to write prose'. Yet nowhere in English is there such perfect informal prose as in these letters. Gray never wrote poetry easily, except humorous poetry. He would not have thought it worth adding that he wrote prose easily, though this would have been true. But easily as word hopped to word in his prose, it was never with the sketchiness of inaccuracy:

> True ease in writing comes from art, not chance,
> As those move easiest who have learn'd to dance.

His movement in prose has the beauty one thinks of as naturally easy, though here and there it may flourish a wing, sure of its technique. Gray never wrote any sentence without a lightning calculation as to its effect as words. The grace of words for him could be either formal or informal. His poems, or some of them, are the product of his fine sense of the formal, his letters almost always the product of his fine sense of the informal. There is no stiffness in the prose even when it is at its most formal. (The eighteenth-century writers hated stiffness, though not all of them were able to keep stiffness out of dignity.)

He was indeed master of the informal grace of prose long before he was master of the formal grace in verse. Indeed, the astonishing thing about these letters, which range from 1734 to 1771, is that their easy grace is almost perfect from the start. Gray has not mastered his mood, his character, in the early letters. He speaks out to his social superior, Walpole, in such a way as rather to taint himself with toadying. But even the toadying is dexterously, and often boisterously, manipulated on to the paper. The informal grace of Gray can be seen by comparing his young letters with those of Pope. Pope is master of grace in prose as in poetry,

117

but never so much as Gray of informal grace. There is too small a gap, one feels, between Pope's early verse and his early letters. Later, of course, Pope's prose and poetry achieved a miracle of formal and informal grace combined, a single grace formal as Milton and informal as 'Hudibras'. But it is as seldom that Gray's letters are formal as it is that Pope's are informal. Gray can open a letter to Mason with:

A life spent out of the World has its hours of despondence, its inconveniences, its sufferings, as numerous, & as real (tho' not quite of the same sort) as a life spent in the midst of it....

But less than a month before he had opened a letter to Mason with 'Why you make no more of writing an Ode, & throwing it in the fire, than of buckling and unbuckling your shoe'. He can discourse on 'the grand beauties of lyric poetry' or on the difference between French and English versification, in paragraphs of essay-like finality, but such anthology pieces are rare. What is usual is a closely knitted monologue of personal comment on persons and things, the evidences that life is continuing for Gray and that Gray is continuing to meet it with day-to-day wakefulness. The poetical traces of his journey were things he had to brace himself up to leave. The letters are the traces he could no more help leaving than he could help making the journey.

2

Gray's journey could not well have been a quieter one. Even the removal from Peterhouse to Pembroke marked 'a sort of Æra in a life so barren of events as [his]'. But there was little that passed without a precise annotation. Most of the light may be shed from solitary candles, but its clearness is that of daylight as it falls on the edges of the chairs, on the harpsichord and the nine volumes of manuscript music copied in Italy. It gives to anything and everything that water-clearness which distinguished the Cumbrian hills in Gray's prospective glass. He may be trusted to record with an accuracy 'exact as diamond' whatever comes his way—the undergraduate who 'looks like toasted Cheshire cheese, stewed with brown sugar', the 'green Velvet Sac' of Queen Caroline, the 'peaked' doorway at Strawberry Hill, the flagellants at St Peter's with 'backs and arms so raw we should have taken it for a red satin doublet torn, and shewing the skin through'. For Gray's friends so sharp a pen fills a gap in experience which was decreed by place: for us it fills a gap which is decreed by place and by time.

It is among such things that Gray, like Jane Austen and Lamb, was most at ease. If he did not speak out very much, it was because there was not very much to speak out about. He sought a journey in the 'ample room and verge enough' of the middle way, a way existing for him in its own right, not the negation of what lay farther on either side. He counselled Wharton to 'be rather slow to hope, as well as to despair'. His taste in life was his taste in towns. In the Alps he is brilliant with excitement, but Rome is for him, as for Addison, 'the place in the world which best deserves [to be seen]'. Calais for him is an 'exceedingly old, but very pretty town'. He speaks of 'the quiet ugliness of Cambridge'. At Rheims the old houses have 'a melancholy aspect'. Not till he reaches Turin does he find real content: 'streets all laid out in line, regular uniform buildings, fine walks that surround the whole, and in general a good lively clean appearance'. It was to this aesthetic that his life was plotted. And yet there were flashes which seemed to blaze up the whole geometry of his path. His middle way would suddenly leap out into the wildest of détours. 'The Progress of Poesy' and 'The Bard', the translations from outlandish tongues, are evidences of it among the poems. In his daily life it was his early passionate affection for Walpole, his almost delirious affection in middle-age for the brilliant young Bonstetten. And it was his travels.

Gray's passage over the Alps epitomizes a whole century of outdoor enthusiasm. Walpole, his companion, also had his ecstasies, but hoped he would never again have to see 'such uncouth rocks and...uncomely inhabitants'. Walpole's relief at finding himself again on the plains is that of Addison thirty years earlier. Gray's ecstasy is more than descriptive. Like Wordsworth and Coleridge he is moved to philosophy as well as picture.

Not a precipice, not a torrent, not a cliff, but is pregnant with religion and poetry. There are certain scenes that would awe an atheist into belief, without the help of other argument.

But the remarks which follow do not need to travel outside their own century to find an echo: 'You have Death perpetually before your eyes....' This recoil from danger among 'beauty and horror' is one of the distinctly 'romantic' experiences of the later eighteenth century.[1] Clearly it is a very possible experience, and one permanently possible. But it did not happen to be popular with the poets of the nineteenth century. Gray was never shaken out of his fear, and indeed he would not readily have permitted himself to be shaken out of it. The uncertain capacities of his small and ailing body, his spinster-like dread of damps—these alone would have made fear hard to shake off in any century. In the eighteenth, however, they had their compensations. They were exquisite stimulants to gooseflesh. The value of this sense of fear to the mind of the latter part of the century may be gauged from

1 In her 'Italian Landscape in Eighteenth-Century England' (p. 5) Miss E. W. Manwaring has drawn attention to the following passage in John Dennis's 'Miscellanies in Verse and Prose', 1693: '...The impending Rock that hung over us, the dreadful Depth of the Precipice, and the Torrent that roar'd at the bottom, gave us such a view as was altogether new and amazing. On the other side of that Torrent, was a Mountain that equall'd ours....Its craggy Clifts, which we half-discern'd, thro the misty gloom of the Clouds that surrounded them, sometimes gave us a horrid Prospect. And sometimes its face appear'd Smooth and Beautiful as the most even and fruitful Vallies. So different from themselves were the different parts of it: In the very same place Nature was seen Severe and Wanton. In the meantime we walk'd upon the very brink, in a litteral sense, of Destruction; one Stumble, and both Life and Carcass had been at once destroy'd. The sense of all this produc'd different motions in me, *viz.* a delightful Horrour, a terrible Joy, and at the same time, that I was infinitely pleas'd I trembled' (pp. 133 f.). There is most of the 'eighteenth-century' experience already discriminated here; and, in a similar way, Gray's comments leap forward to the 'nineteenth-century' experience. Dennis has discovered delightful horror, Gray religion and poetry.

On Gray's Letters

Mrs Radcliffe's novels, in which, as Miss J. M. S. Tompkins has pointed out, nothing dreadful happens but something dreadful is always about to happen. Gray's cry peals in his letter. But on the actual precipice it was best to keep silent. Years afterwards, among merely English crags, he remembered to repress the physical cry:

the place reminds one of those passes in the Alps, where the Guides tell you to move on with speed, & say nothing, lest the agitation of the air should loosen the snows above, & bring down a mass, that would overwhelm a caravan. I took their counsel here and hasten'd on in silence.

Non ragioniam di lor; ma guarda, e passa!

Coleridge, in the vale of Chamounix, intrudes more boldly. He is so completely unafraid of the 'bald awful head' of Mont Blanc that he acts the part of an agitator, hectoring the sublime into joining his pantheistic matins:

...Awake, my heart, awake!
Green vales and icy cliffs, all join my Hymn.

The young Wordsworth at nightfall joined in imitating a hunt on the ice:

So through the darkness and the cold we flew,
And not a voice was idle; with the din
Smitten, the precipices rang aloud....

Gray feels it is wiser to cower, or hasten on, in silence, glorying and shuddering. There is no development in this attitude of his. He is the same at Gordale Scar thirty years later: 'it is safer to shelter...I stay'd there (not without shuddering) a quarter of an hour....' Cowering on his crag, Gray seems to have lost his middle way by miles. And yet its narrow pavement is represented even here, in the glued lips and smothered breathing.

There is usually the same recoil in his enthusiasms. He does not trust himself to his instincts. He liked reading stories to the point of fascination. 'Eternal new romances of Marivaux and Crebillon' would, he felt, be necessary in heaven. And yet he fears the comment of the strict intellectual to the point of having to argue it aside:

> However the exaltedness of some minds...may make them insensible to these light things...yet surely they are as weighty and much more useful than your grave discourses upon the mind, the passions, and what not.

When he cannot think, he admits to dreaming. But, again, 'Some people, who hold me cheap for this, are doing perhaps what is not half so well worth while'. When his poems appear he is nervously intent on getting to know how people are receiving them. He hankers after encouragement. He is standing alone but standing timidly. He speaks out but with a quaver. It must have seemed inevitable to him that his enthusiasm for Bonstetten should have been built on the certainty that death was soon to end it.

3

Gray discovered mountains but he did not completely discover the finest way to look at them. Nor did he discover very much of the way the nineteenth century looked at them. His connexions with the romantic poets are not, therefore, of the most profound kind. But where he does connect with them is in the new quality of his observation of particulars, whether on mountain or plain. Fundamentally he sought for the 'general', but he sought for it by the only sure way, through accumulations of the 'particular'. This quality of his observation gets into the poems, but its most ample home is in the letters. The superb letter to William Palgrave (6 September 1758) is its manifesto. When not disturbed by an 'impending' danger, he could see new things with the concentrated accuracy which enlightens and excites and which one associates with the Wordsworths (particularly Dorothy) and with Coleridge: the 'furrow'd sides [of Saddleback] were gilt by the noon-day Sun, while its brow appear'd of a sad purple...the grass was cover'd with a hoar-frost, which soon melted, and exhaled in a thin blewish smoke'; on the side of Crow Park after sunset, he noted the long shadows of the mountains across the lake almost touching the hithermost shore.

But Gray's path soon leaves that of Wordsworth and Coleridge. He does not seek through particular beauty a divine abstraction of all beauty and all goodness. He travels instead 'the journey homeward to habitual self'.

Do you not think [he asks Palgrave] a man may be the wiser (I had almost said the better) for going a hundred or two of miles; and that the mind has more room in it than most people seem to think, if you will but furnish the apartments?

Furnish the apartments. After his glance skyward at the uncertain glory, Gray is back in his rooms at Cambridge.

1935

XII. GRAY THE SCHOLAR-POET

THE extent of Gray's learning caused the Rev. W. J. Temple in 1772 to describe him as 'Perhaps...the most learned man in Europe' and caused Dr Johnson to repeat that estimate. Gray's erudition has always been borne in mind by his biographers and critics, but to see the evidence for it set out as Mr Jones[1] has now set it out is to have quite a new experience of its impressiveness. Among the evidence here printed for the first time is Gray's own catalogue of his library and his notes on learned periodicals. Mr Jones does not believe that he can endorse Temple's superlative. But in the course of his array and discussion of Gray's knowledge of ancient culture, of travel and geography, of the history of English poetry, of English history, heraldry and architecture, and finally of natural history, it becomes clear that Gray's place in scholarship and the history of scholarship is as assured as his place among the English poets. His learning was not merely the discovery for himself of what was already known to the most learned among his fellows. He discovered tracts and crannies of learning for the first time, becoming, in Mr Jones's words, 'an intellectual frontiersman'. His scholarship was ultimately as bold as his Pindaric odes or his travels. The quality of his work was a stand made against intellectual apathy. He writes his own ironic 'Hymn to Ignorance' after reading the close of the 'Dunciad'. He follows Swift, who saw that

we of this age have discovered a shorter and more prudent method to become scholars and wits, without the fatigue of reading or of thinking. The most accomplished way of using books at present is two-fold: either, first, to serve them as some men do lords, learn their titles exactly, and then brag of their acquaintance. Or, secondly, which is indeed the choicer, the profounder, and politer method, to get a thorough insight into the index, by which the whole book is governed and turned, like

1 'Thomas Gray, Scholar', by W. P. Jones, Harvard University Press, 1937.

Gray the Scholar-Poet

fishes by the tail. For to enter the palace of learning at the great gate requires an expense of time and forms; therefore men of great haste and little ceremony are content to get in by the back door.[1]

Mr Jones shows Gray inscribing the following quotation in his commonplace book, and it 'sums up what he himself might have said':

> Our Dictionaries, Bibliotheques, Journals, & a thousand other Books of the same kind, wch are daily swarming among us, & that, while they facilitate to us the Means of appearing learned, keep us from making ourselves really so, seem to be the Forerunners of Barbarism & Ignorance.

The books and manuscripts which Gray read had no indexes. He entered learning by the great gate, crawling in toilsomely as an insect.

He received little monetary reward for his toil. Much money was not included in what he asked of life. He asked to have friends, to receive and answer their letters, to be reconciled to the death first of West and then of his mother, to find what ease was possible from the pain of bodily sluggishness and disease, to see mountains occasionally. For so undemanding a suppliant, the kindest other gifts were great libraries, his papers, his microscope.

His scholarship helped him to live. It also helped him to write his poetry. Matthew Arnold complained that the Romantic poets of the early nineteenth century had 'proceeded without having ...sufficient materials to work with'; they had 'plenty of energy, plenty of creative force [but] did not know enough'. Gray as a poet seems the reverse of this. Arnold's complaint against Gray is that he has not enough creative energy. That complaint, in so far as it is not the sentimental one which everybody feels at the combination of sparseness with quality, was perhaps prompted by Arnold's esteem for the Zeitgeist (he saw the eighteenth century as an age of prose) rather than by Gray's poetry itself. That poetry is of a kind which cannot exist in plenty. Gray said his say. And

---

1 Cf. Pope, 'Dunciad', I, 279 f.:
   'How Index-learning turns no student pale,
   Yet holds the eel of science by the tail.'

that say took much of its inspiration—Mr Jones is able to show how much—from his scholarship. Gray is a learned poet, a poet showing the sublimity and the solemnity of learning. 'The Bard' is a tremendous poem. Its material is founded on difficult knowledge and its metres are those of a poet who has studied Pindar and Welsh poetry. But, more than that, its words come from a mind which has solemnly experienced the sifted layers on layers of human lives which find in chronicles their bleak summary. It is this experience which gives the words a tone of sullen bells. Gray, like the bard, is aware of the innumerable dead and the innumerable to-be-born: ('Ye unborn Ages, crowd not on my soul!') He, too, can cry:

> With me in dreadful harmony they join.

Gray's voice is that of centuries, the voice of Shakespeare's history plays concentrated and deepened. The same voice speaks quietly in the 'Elegy'. Mr Jones traces the interconnexions of Gray's learning and poetry, but he does not end by seeing that ultimately they are the same thing. Wordsworth's 'Preface' was written to rid himself of the verbal influence of Gray and others, but its words concerning true poetry are the best one could find for hinting a description of Gray's:

> The Man of science seeks truth as a remote and unknown benefactor; he cherishes and loves it in his solitude: the Poet, singing a song in which all human beings join with him, rejoices in the presence of truth as our visible friend and hourly companion. Poetry is the breath and finer spirit of all knowledge; it is the impassioned expression which is in the countenance of all Science.

1937

XIII. NOTES ON WILLIAM COLLINS

I

In a useful chapter on personification, Professor Ainsworth [1] fails to make the valid distinction between what is personification and what is not or is not necessarily so. In an age which used capitals freely, not every capitalized abstract noun was seen by the poet as a person. For example, in the line

> The tender Thought on thee shall dwell

'Thought' cannot be personified. One should not, therefore, complain that 'In some instances the personification amounts to no more than the presence of a capital letter' and give as example the lines:

> Where is thy native simple Heart,
> Devote to Virtue, Fancy, Art?

2

Professor Ainsworth has done good work in citing 'sources' for much of Collins's diction. Such sources can never be finally and certainly collected, but there is a serious omission when the verse translations of Homer and the Latin poets are neglected. A fair number of Collins's words have had a previous history in Sandys's Ovid, Dryden's Virgil, Pope's Homer, etc. The use of *substantive* + y as an adjective had been common in English poetry since Shakespeare. Professor Ainsworth has noted this form in Milton, but Milton himself learns it, along with many other things, from the Elizabethans. So that Collins's 'beamy', 'gleamy', 'wavy' (words which play an important part in his characteristic effect of evanescence) are really quotations. 'Beamy' has an interesting history.

1 'Poor Collins. His Life, His Art, and His Influence', by Edward Gay Ainsworth, Jr., Ithaca, 1937.

Dryden uses it in his Virgil mainly (perhaps entirely) in the sense of wooden ('beamy spear') or of a stag's antlers ('Three beamy stags'). Trapp applies 'beamy' to the sun (1709 'Miscellany', p. 379), and again in the same volume (p. 427) the sun for Tickell is 'the Beamy God'. The word had been applied occasionally, though insignificantly, in this way earlier (see 'O.E.D.'). Pope uses the word often in his Homer for javelins (cf. Dryden), blades, falchions, the day, light, and lustre. (Rowe's 'Royal Convert'— 1707—had used it with 'gold'.)

Collins's use, therefore, comes very late in the day. Collins's 'gleamy' has an earlier history in Pope's 'Iliad' and Rowe's 'Pharsalia'. His 'sheeny' has an earlier history in Milton (noted by Professor Ainsworth) and Fenton (see 'O.E.D.').

In discussing Collins's lines:

> Whilst *Vengeance*, in the lurid Air,
> Lifts her red Arm, expos'd and bare,

Professor Ainsworth has noted Horace, 'Odes', I, ii, 2–4, and Milton's 'Arm again His red right hand to plague us', but not the more important passage from Dryden's 'Æneis' (VI, 800–1):

> But he, the king of heav'n, obscure on high,
> Bar'd his red arm....

(Virgil has nothing corresponding to these last four words.) Moreover, Pope's 'Odyssey' (XII, 456) borrows the phrase from Dryden for Jove:

> Lo! my red arm I bare...

and cf. '*Jove*'s red arm' at XXIV, 623.

The word *brede* ('Ode to Evening') has more certain sources than Milton's *braid* ('Comus') which Professor Ainsworth suggests. Milton had used the word in prose, and Dryden in his 'Essay on the Georgics' writes 'in a curious Brede of Needlework'. In poetry the first use seems that of Waller: 'On a Brede of Divers Colours' opens:

> Twice twenty slender virgin-fingers twine
> This curious web....

128

Notes on William Collins

Later, Philips in 'Cyder' (1708) uses 'watry brede' for the rainbow. Pope employs the word for Penelope's web ('Odyssey', XIX, 179) and Akenside in 1744 follows Philips in applying it to the rainbow. The sense of the word seems sufficiently indicated from these three instances; it appears to have been Keats who confused the denotation (see 'Grecian Urn'). Some of the above instances are noted in 'O.E.D.', which seems to indicate that Professor Ainsworth might have consulted it more often.

Pope's 'Homer' is certainly one of the 'sources' for Collins's mood and words of tenderness (*pity, melting, tender, pale*); though even here one must remember that Pope himself is improving on earlier translations of Latin epics which exaggerated their pathos.

The above notes are merely indications of Collins's debt to an area of English poetry which has been neglected by modern scholars. A thorough study would discover much more of the same kind. Until we know what Collins read and remembered, we cannot begin to assess his originality. Even his red-armed vengeance seems a more serious figure when we find whose arms were red before hers.

1937

XIV. THE 'NEW LADY'S MAGAZINE' OF 1786

I

A MAGAZINE of twenty years ago is quite unreadable now. The grains of decay lodged in the cover and paper smell too recent. The binding has not yet commended its dyes and label to the crayoning of time. The print is ugly, not yet curious or significant historically. The inky illustrations just miss being naïve. The prose style of the contributors claps before one's eye the familiar vision of a horse-hair sofa like a trireme and on it an aunt reading bolt upright. The same magazine, as one pushes back into earlier numbers, begins to change gently under one's eyes. The less recent its date, the fresher its air. The outworn gradually awakens into the antique. One knows precisely what would stare back at one from the magazine of 1900. But further back, in 1850, one is not quite so sure. The very horsehair looks glossier, new-varnished like pomfret cakes. And further back still—1820, 1790—one's sense of whereabouts is numb.

When one handles the 'New Lady's Magazine' for 1786 on a second-hand book stall, one's mind spreads almost flat to receive its quality. The title means nothing. 'What would be counted New', one asks, 'in 1786? What did a Lady consist of then? What, indeed, was happening historically, socially, domestically, in 1786?' But as the woolly pages fawn under the hand, as the nostril scents the thin charnel atmosphere, as one's eye roams the foggy print, the yellowed wirelines, focusing on a significant phrase here and there, one feels oneself caught in a fascination. One must hold, smell, scrutinize on and on. And one turns, at last, to one of the monthly title-pages where stray impressions amalgamate and solidify centripetally. I say 'at last', because my copy opens in the middle of the first number, the one for

The 'New Lady's Magazine' of 1786

February, and the margins of the March title-page have so grown into those of adjacent leaves that they defy all but the most patient fingers.

The title-page of any number is a map perfectly projected, packed tight as any English shire with names, drawing on many founts of type, ruled across, ruled downwards, balanced about a middle line as if the folio were indeed a leaf. In the following transcript line endings are not indicated:

THE NEW LADY'S MAGAZINE; OR POLITE AND ENTER-TAINING COMPANION FOR THE FAIR SEX: *Entirely Devoted to their Use and Amusement*. CONTAINING more in Quantity, and a much greater Variety of New, Original, and Select Pieces (in Prose and Verse) on every curious, useful, and entertaining Subject, than are to be found in any other Publication of the Kind whatever. For MARCH, 1786 Embellished with, 1. A most ELEGANT PLATE, containing a VARIETY of LADIES fashionable HEAD DRESSES for the present Year. 2. A fine Portrait of Mrs. JORDAN in the Character of the Country Girl. 3. A beautiful Representation of Miss BRUNTON, as Euphrasia, in the Grecian Daughter; these two admirable Portraits finely engraved by THORNTON. 4. A new and most elegant PATTERN for CLOTH WORK; together with Two fashionable PATTERNS for EMBROIDERY BORDERS, for Waistcoats, Muffs, &c....

and so on towards a fuller list of contents in double columns. After which comes this in guarantee, assurance and invitation:

The Whole Published under the immediate Inspection of THE REV. MR. CHARLES STANHOPE, Of Queen's-Square, Great Ormond-Street...by whom the Communications of ingenious Persons—Post Paid—will be received...and sold by all Booksellers, Stationers, and News-Carriers in Town and Country. [To be continued MONTHLY.— Price *only* Six-pence.]

As the page turns over the title overflows with it, the Royal Licence and Authority are set forth, the Ladies are entreated not to make mistakes when ordering their copies, but to be particular to give the proper title, and their timorous incredulity is once more assured that the price is '*only* 6d.'

That is the title-page of the second number. It seems a pity that the magazine should have been launched in a February. Why

The 'New Lady's Magazine' of 1786

couldn't the Rev. Mr Charles Stanhope have issued his first number simultaneously with the New Year? A magazine is twice a magazine in January, tiding over the bald days after Christmas, loading up the frozen news-carriers with weights that would soon warm them. By February the Lady is again venturing abroad. But late as it was, the Ladies of Great Britain made a New Year Resolution. They resolved to buy the 'New Lady's Magazine'. On the verso of the March title-page (where beat the thrilled editorial heart) romantic figures were announced:

The rapid Sale of the First Number having already carried two large Impressions and the Demand for this NEW LADY'S MAGAZINE still increasing in all Parts of Europe, Notice is hereby given, that This Day is Published, a Third Edition (Revised and Corrected) of Number 1. Price only 6d.

Furthermore a paragraph in the same minute type reads historic:

We were sensible, the extensive Sale of the NEW LADY'S MAGAZINE would materially affect those who are interested in any old Publication of the Kind, and raise an alarm which their own Negligence and Mismanagement have been the just Occasion of. We have accordingly met with a very strong Opposition from a certain Quarter; but the Ladies are no longer to be trifled with. Such unfair Conduct as Mr. R.'s we were obliged to expose, and his Demerits being tried before a Female Tribunal, the Ladies declared against his Tyrannical Behaviour, and left off the old and imperfect Publication, in Favour of our NEW, COMPLETE, ELEGANT, and IMPROVED LADY'S MAGAZINE.

The Ladies were no longer to be trifled with. Mrs Woolf with exquisite humour and imagery has recently shown us the same spirit. The modern woman was embryonically vital as early as 1786. St Paul had spoken memorably of the new man. And owing to the sly non-inflexional syntax of the English language there are indications that 'the new, complete, elegant, and improved Lady's Magazine' could be interpreted by 'ingenious persons' as 'the Magazine of the New, Complete, Elegant, and Improved Lady'. If the Rev. Mr Charles Stanhope, having missed the January of 1786, had only waited two more years, the advent of the New Lady would have coincided with the centenary of

132

that other glorious, bloodless revolution. The date of her début might never then have gone out of mind. As it is, stuffed on the verso of an obscure title-page for February 1786, the historic words lack fanfare. For all its bursting italics the voice does not rise above a whisper. The New Lady slips *in medias res* almost unobserved.

2

Among the first of the New Ladies must be reckoned the Queen herself. The image of her successor, Victoria, wilts like wax in the burning praise of Queen Charlotte. In the opening number a column is devoted to '*A short Sketch of the Character of her* PRESENT MAJESTY'. Superlative goodnesses and greatnesses pile within the draping rhythms. And, finally, her influence sheds downwards—the sketch ending:

> As comparisons are odious, it would be an invidious task to draw parallels between her Majesty and some of the court ladies. Suffice it to say, that such of them as act contrary to the rules of virtue and decorum have ever met with her disapprobation, while the greatest praise which can be given to the best of them, is to say, that they tread in the steps of their royal mistress, and are proud to copy so excellent an example.

After this, of course, it was imperative that H.M. George III should receive a notice. But the pious joy, the hieratic glow fade from the words. The New Lady evidently had not found very much to praise in him. She concludes a tiny sketch with *ifs* and *buts*: 'He is a patron of learning, a perfect admirer of the *belles lettres*, and would certainly rise the Augustus of the age, if he had but a Virgil to celebrate him.'

No, the New Lady had already begun to compare herself favourably with the male. In a dissertation '*On the present Mode of* FEMALE EDUCATION' she readily admitted that it was not incumbent on the fair-sex (the New Lady invariably insulated the expression with a hyphen) to acquire 'the knowledge of a *Bacon*, the oratory of a *Demosthenes*, or the grammatical pronunciation of a *Johnson*'. Merely mental greatness she could well dispense with, although 'A Man of Feeling' assured her in his 'ADDRESS to the LADIES of GREAT-BRITAIN' that she was equal to man in every species of mental or bodily exertion 'not incompatible with the delicate texture of her frame'. Indeed, 'The Female Rambler' noted that 'there is a pleasure that results even from the prattle of a pretty woman, though without meaning'. The New Lady felt sure of her ground. She well knew that, try hard as he would, man could only manage half the world's work. The other half stood waiting for the New Lady. It was enormously incumbent on her, for instance, to excel in housewifery. How she despised the all-too-common young thing who could do nothing beyond waving about in a minuet! The desirability of matrimony, almost her *sine qua non*, decided that she should be equal to making a

good dumplin [*sic*], or *apple-pudding*, and pickle, upon occasion, some *cabbages* or *cucumbers*, the bare mention of which necessary things in a wife would, perhaps, cause the present boarding school Miss *to faint away!*

Matrimony decided all that for her. And the New Lady never stopped to question the good, round, apple-dumplin ideal of wedlock, though she improved on it. She provided herself with the long monthly columns of her first courses, second courses, under the encyclopædic title of '*The* LADY'S ASSISTANT *in the* Whole ART *of* COOKERY'. She embellished the columns with cuts exclusively designed for them, but, with the economy she had admired in her Queen, she made the same cut do for every month. The baking of apple-dumplins soon appeared quite a childish test of her culinary importance. She taught herself how to cook and serve the most Cleopatran dishes: hog's face, boiled tansy pudding, bride pie, fricasee of lamb stones, jesuit pig and ducks disguised. And in the August of that *annus mirabilis*, she discovered the true way of making bread and butter, a lucky hit which laid futurity so deeply in her debt. (The historic recipe ran: 'Spread the best butter on bread, cut it about a quarter of an inch thick, serve it in a plate.')

The 'New Lady's Magazine' of 1786

It was not her fault, then, if matrimony turned to ashes in the mouth. Not with Eve this time lay the blame. 'Man,' cried a correspondent, 'Man... woman's most inveterate foe, when void of that humanity which softens the ferocity of nature, and inspires him with every tender, every grateful emotion!' That hinted man at his worst and, judging by the report 'On the STATE of MATRIMONY in South-Britain', he was frequently at his worst. The report opens with:

If you see a man and woman, with little or no occasion, often finding fault, and correcting one another in company, you may be sure they are man and wife. If you see a gentleman and lady in the same coach, in profound silence, the one looking out at one side, the other at the other side, never imagine they mean any harm to one another; they are already honestly married.

Further examples show that the male is to blame. And then the New Lady's irony towers into statistics:

Wives eloped from their husbands	1362
Husbands run away from their wives	2361
Married pairs in a state of separation from each other	4120
Married pairs living in a state of open war, under the same roof	191023
Married pairs living in a state of inward hatred for each other, tho' concealed from the world	162320
Married pairs living in a state of coldness and indifference for each other	510132
Married pairs reputed happy in the esteem of the world	1102
Married pairs comparatively happy	135
Married pairs absolutely and entirely happy	9
Married pairs in South-Britain, in all	872,514

But the New Lady did not lose heart. After all, the unassembled Northern statistics might reassure her. Moreover her magazine had only been going six months. And, furthermore, statistics were not always indisputable. In the very next number, for instance, she corrected W. Stone's 'computation of the National Debt, which far exceeds the amount he has supposed in his Rebus'.

The 'New Lady's Magazine' of 1786

3

The New Lady was meeting these facts with admirable resources. She was working at her cookery pages. And she was working at her personal charms. No corner of the known earth, for example, was exempt from her researches into toilet properties. Nothing, not even frog-spawn water, seemed too repellent where her complexion was concerned. She invented in June a concoction '*to cure the* VAPOURS' which must have been tedious to prepare and nauseating to apply. In August she powdered together pumice and alum since 'by often rubbing the teeth with it, they, if sound, will become as white as ivory'. In April she realized at last the 'Inconveniences and Disorders arising from Straight-Lacing in Stays'. In October she records with delicate blush that 'the *sandal shoe* is still graced by the foot of beauty' and that 'loose-flowing ringlets begin to fail in their attractions; their fair admirers having now added a *white* ribbon, which ties them together immediately above the shoulders, so as to fall gracefully down the centre of the back'.

But over and over again she realized with full pelt of italics that in external beauty, whether natural or aided, did not lie any final happiness. For that she looked to her mind, to her Intellect. It is probably here that the twentieth century ladies' magazine most miserably diverges from its predecessor. The serials in 1786, for instance, were by no means Miss Dell romances. One—'*A New* SENTIMENTAL JOURNEY *through* ENGLAND'—was probably indited by a bespectacled widow of advanced years. Another unrolled simultaneously the twin scrolls of History and Geography with '*An* ACCURATE *and* COMPLETE HISTORY *of* CAPT. COOK'S *First Voyage round the World*'. Yet another, 'the English Prize Oration at Oxford in 1779', expatiated '*on the Affinity between* PAINTING *and* WRITING, *in Point of Composition*'. Apart from her improving serials, the New Lady read and wrote scores of poems per month. She fountained into lyrics at the slightest touch. She reviewed current literature with malicious brilliance. She studied the effect of music on animals. She looked into the strange report of a rat's being suckled by a cat. She recorded with impersonal phrase the first use of mahogany in England. She catalogued with the industry of a modern research student the varieties of mourning in the world. In addition to her monthly regalement of Foreign and Home Affairs, she discoursed on the curious Golden-Bough habits of primitive tribes, on Pyrenean Hermits, on the Rights of Hospitality among the Arabians, in the state of her backward fellows in the Grand Signor's Seraglio. Moreover, as the following Botanical Conversation exhibits, she had already become proficient in the latter-day art of learning without tears:

INGEANA.

How charming these snow-drops still look; notwithstanding the late frost, and the depth of the snow, with whose whiteness they seem to vie.

FLORA.

The snow, my dear, has preserved both their beauty and life; otherwise they must have fallen a sacrifice to the severity of the weather.

INGEANA.

What elegant simplicity and innocence in this flower! It belongs, I believe, to the sixth class of the Linnean system, called Hexandria, and by our botanical society Six Males, and to the first order of that class: but it seems to me to be two flowers, a less within a greater.

FLORA.

The whole is but one flower; this part, which you suppose to be a lesser flower, is called by our ingenious translaters of the immortal Linneus, the nectary; and indeed emphatically; for if the bee were now stirring, you would see him drink his honey out of it.

INGEANA.

I have often admired the green streaks on each of these shorter petals of the nectary; eight in number; which through a microscope swell on the eye like a piece of beautiful fluted work: but we are called.——

The New Lady attended to her French, contrived and probably solved innumerable enigmas and rebuses. 'An Enigmatical list of

The 'New Lady's Magazine' of 1786

Old Maids in D—t—d' and 'An Enigmatical List of Bachelors of Barnstaple, Devon' and 'An Enigmatical List of Ladies' Names at Eastland Boarding School, Greenwich' must have been hard nuts for ladies not actually located in those vicinities.

The New Lady admired Art. Each month she was given one or more examples of contemporary steel engravings—the chastest, most intellectual of all manifestations of Design. The artists' supreme scorn for perspective suggest that she required more from Art than Sir Joshua had laid down. She was given also a monthly song composed by Mr Hook. These songs, like those of Mr Gustav Holst for voice and violin, are of two parts, the lower part sulking for bars on the same note, the upper (in unison with the voice) frilling out into the airiest of melismas. One might note in passing that the New Lady was always a soprano, and, moreover, one of almost operatic nimbleness. But I doubt if she ever performed these songs. Being printed vertically up the page, and often committing the artistes to an ugly *Volti Subito*, they were as ill adapted to any music stand as to the human grasp.

4

The surprising science underlying cookery and the more innocent toilet preparations, the study of European affairs, of the minutest Beauties of Nature and art—enthralling as these were, the New Lady still had an ear for the not very still but certainly sad music of humanity. It was not an innocent age. But she did not shrink. The crystal charm of her magazine might receive an almost monthly smear—some modern instances of vice might shock her for a moment—but she had supporting knowledge that all men were not like that. There were advisers she could trust implicitly. Men of Feeling, Faithful Monitors, Protectors of the Fair-Sex figuring under various initials never grew tired of issuing warnings against the Male Danger. The rake, the treacherous fop, the decamping seducer were fulminated in the beefy, upright prose of more generous males. Painful anecdotes recreated for the New Lady the reality of evil and the ensuing motto hung up a framed text in her heart. The nine truly faithful husbands of South-Britain seem to have laboured hard for her welfare.

And the New Lady was prepared from another quarter. She believed in the fundamental Goodness of the Deity. The universe, as she saw it, was governed from top to bottom wisely. To illustrate her point she took the common house fly, perhaps the last example that would have occurred to persons less sure of themselves. She believed that the Creator from his foundation of the world had ordained a dramatic visible justice: did not one Weston, a cruel chimney sweep, fall over a bag of soot dropped by his over-driven boy assistant, and expire there in the road?

5

One thing remains. The advent of the New Lady coincides so pat with the revival and spread of Paper Filigree-Work that she and it seem to mingle together in enriched significance. The first time one hears of this art is in 'An Old Bachelor's' letter to the editor in the April number. When he objected to the frequency of his ward's requests for pin money, '"La! Sir," said the sweet girl, "They an't to pin my clothes but for filigree".' On seeing samples, he no longer objected to her expenses in so fine an art. In the July number, there is a 'Candid Review' of ' *The Guiding Assistant to Paper Filigree Work—In Six Weekly Numbers; each of which contains two Sets of various original Patterns, executed in real Paper Filigree. By* Charles Styart, 5s. 3d. *each.*' The review, if candid, is also favourable. In the November number there is a three-column 'Historical Account of the Origin and Progress of Paper Filigree-Work, with an accurate description of the present patterns'. The following definition of an art now, it seems, wholly discarded will acquaint the modern mind with its lost charms: 'Paper Filigree, as now revived by modern artists, consists of narrow slips of paper, either crimped or plain, of various colours with gilt edges, which are artfully rolled or joined together in such a manner, as to form an embellishment suited to any particular work of fancy which the female artist may think proper to ornament.' 'As now revived', says the author, and farther down the column he asserts that, 'It has been supposed by some, and not without some degree of plausibility, that among the cunning works mentioned by Moses in Exodus, paper filigree-work might be one'. However that may be, paper filigree seems to symbolize in frail, tinted impermanence those many lives so nattily busy, so willing, so domestic, so like ever-dripping burettes of rose-water, and yet so knowing, so independent.

1927, 1929

XV. WILLIAM MORRIS
WORD-SPINNER

WILLIAM MORRIS was one of those men who love most not to have things done but to have things still a-doing, and, when the doing is inevitably over, to have things done for good. 'No work,' he said, 'which cannot be done with pleasure in the doing is worth doing.' These instinctive preferences affected the way he used and husbanded his poetic talent. He is the only poet who believed that 'Poetry goes with the hand arts', a dictum which meant that, for Morris, poetry was pleasant to do, as pleasant to do as the hand-loom weaving to which in another dictum he related it: 'If a chap can't compose an epic poem while he's weaving tapestry, he had better shut up.' Most poets find composition lowering and painful, but words for Morris slipped off the pen (or was it the quill?) like thread through fingers. 'I am an inveterate word-spinner', he said. He did sometimes make a few corrections here and there in his verse. But, taking a craftsman's pleasure in a run of work, his usual way of revising, if revision could not be escaped, was to write the thing again from the start. All which means that Morris was restricted to that part of poetic composi-tion which may be called craft. He resented any work which was not pleasurable, which was more difficult than a craft is. To ply a craft is to exercise a possessed and almost automatic skill confident of its power to succeed. Craft is not art. In plying an art, the hand and the mind are often at variance, the one frettingly eager to help, the other troubled in seeking what to ask to have done. Art includes craft, but craft that is curbed and tormented by the indecision and staggering circles of the mind. Morris knew little of this frustration, and so he knew little of what lies on the farther side of it, the achievement of poetry which gives the reader re-peated and fine pleasure. He dissociated himself from modern

William Morris word-spinner

poets, who compose with difficulty, and identified himself with poets of primitive ages, whom he supposed to have been craftsmen composing, like himself, with ease. But there is no reason to suppose that primitive poetry was easier to make than modern, that any good poet was ever able, as a practical proposition, to share Morris's innocent equation of poetic composition with fun. Poetry was never a craft, but always an art; and, notoriously, *ars longa*.

Morris had little use for his place in history. He refused to realize that poetry in the nineteenth century was a sophisticated pleasure experienced in solitude through the eye. (If Morris was consistent, his pleasure in poetry at this stage must have come mainly from the type, illustrations, paper, and binding.) And therefore, since he has made no proper preparations for them, he begins to suffer when his contemporaries and posterity set in. He wrote without an actual audience in view.[1] No one could be said to be trying to reach a literary audience who could permit himself the unpardonable excess of writing seven hundred lines in a single day—Milton, whom Morris always abused, wrote fifty lines in the morning and by evening had reduced that loose fifty to ten. If Morris aimed at an audience at all, it was one composed of figures in his books. Perhaps he imagined himself reciting to them as in 'A Dream of John Ball': 'as I told it, the words seemed to quicken and grow...and they ran almost into rime and measure as I told it'. Or he imagined others reciting the tales as, in his utopia, tales were told of an evening at the Hammersmith guest house, or as rhymes accompanied the streamside laundering in 'The Ring given to Venus'. If Morris imagined an audience at all, it was an audience composed of such coloured spectres. All that was wrong with this audience was, of course, that it did not exist actually. No one would have complained—or, more

---

1 I am speaking of the bulk of his work; obviously the 'Defence of Guenevere' volume considered its readers, and when Morris once again, in his fine socialist songs, considered recipients who were real people, he again wrote excellently.

William Morris word-spinner

exactly, no one would *now* complain—if Morris had found a living equivalent for spectres and taken his verbal wares into public houses or on to village greens. No one would have complained because the result would have meant a much smaller quantity of bad word-spinning poetry and an increased quantity of good poetry. Morris would have found that his half-educated audience had ears ready for stories and brains only too critical of them. For the unlearned stand bad art worse than the learned, and what popular poetry has survived has survived by virtue of its art. A comedian who is much more propitiously equipped than few modern tramp-poets can ever hope to be, does not rely even on his best jokes; he practises hard before his mirror. Morris on the village green would have started with much to commend him: he was the only English poet who could have been mistaken in Kensington High Street for a sea captain ('Beg pardon, Sir, but were you ever captain of the Sea Swallow?'), and he was the only English poet, probably, who felt at home among the cheekiest urchins. But a great deal of practice would have been necessary before his narrative became as acceptable as his person and personality. That practice would have made him into an artist, a sophisticated poet like all other poets who have something complicated to get over. He would have needed an art as did Milton, and, more than Milton needed to, he would have had to face the supreme difficulty of learning to hide it. He might well have continued to compose at his loom. That adjunct of his rhythmical composition must not be taken more seriously than the narcotic adjuncts of other poets—Burns's tipped-back chair, Wordsworth's smooth ground, or Coleridge's rough. But though he might have continued to compose at the loom, he would not have continued to compose at it to the tune of seven hundred verses a day. He would have ceased to say, 'Well, if this is poetry, it is very easy to write', for his eyes and ears, now well rinsed at the village pump, would have known that it was poetry by its being, in Morris's inevitable phrase, 'bloody difficult'.

1934, 1940

XVI. WILLIAM MORRIS AND MACHINES

I

WILLIAM MORRIS turned to the Dark Ages for his enlightenment. It was the same in everything he did. In his poetry he turned to the primitive epic, to the ballad, writing as if he intended his verses to be recited as they recited verses in the Middle Ages. In his prose he wrote mediaeval romances, his one attempt at a contemporary novel proving, as he put it, 'just a specimen of how not to do it'. In his designs he went for inspiration to the Middle Ages. He revived or continued the practice of mediaeval arts, painting tiles, weaving tapestry and carpets, printing by hand, cutting book decorations on wood, making stained glass. He exhausted the manual possibilities of all arts except that of music.

William Morris considered that the maximum pleasure when things were being made was experienced by hands using simple tools. For him the skilled handling of tools provided the best pleasure work can offer. Looking back at the Middle Ages, and for him the Middle Ages must have lasted well into the eighteenth century, he saw man as daily in a state of happiness, since up to the industrial revolution things were created independently of machines. According to Ruskin and Morris, machines brought misery and boredom into workshops which, up to then, were jolly as any scene out of 'News from Nowhere'.

The nineteenth century, now we can see it telescoped, was as much a period of transition as any other. Nineteenth-century reformers were so near to the machine that they saw only its ugliness, the ugliness of its contemporary products, and the ugliness which the new conditions of industry were forcing people into. Seeing

William Morris and Machines

that ugliness, they did not realize that the machine had come to stay, whatever the reformers could bring up against it. Those reformers ought to have seen that machinery, even by 1850, had done enough good work to justify itself, in principle at least. Ruskin and Morris, for instance, did not need to travel either in coach or on horseback. Distance was very conveniently diminished for them by the aid of steam transport. Morris uses a train to go to Glasgow. Moreover, when he finds the efficiency of trains failing him, as he did once in the company of Bruce Glasier, what he does is to blow up the guard, behaving, as Glasier puts it, like a pillar of Olympian wrath. When his railway company fails him, Morris does not say, 'I told you so; we ought to have come by coach'. Instead, he demands more efficient service in machines. Ruskin and Morris ought to have seen that if those who distrusted machinery had, through pure convenience, to accept of its benefits, then the people with no grudge against it would see to it that machinery had come to stay.

Obviously what the nineteenth century wanted was not fewer machines, but more and better ones. We cannot stop the progress of the machine. Even D. H. Lawrence, a primitive in so many things, saw, or made two of his characters see, that machines constitute an improvement. In 'Lady Chatterley's Lover', Sir Clifford says:

'I ride upon the achievements of the mind of man, and that beats a horse.'
'I suppose it does' [replies his wife]. 'And the souls in Plato riding up to heaven in a two-horse chariot would go in a Ford car now....'
'Or a Rolls-Royce: Plato was an aristocrat!'

The workshops of to-day employ the achievements of the mind of man. Morris found he could not do without machinery if life was to be lived with economy. But he considered that by using machinery he was aiding and abetting the devil. Unless you made the things you wanted by hand, then your relationship with industry was immoral. The users of machines were removing beyond the reach of man one of his few permanent and satisfactory sources of pleasure. It is perfectly true that a craftsman takes pleasure in his work. The evidences of that pleasure in the things left over to us from the Middle Ages and from all centuries before the nineteenth are overwhelming in proof of this. There must have been pleasure present at the carving of the minstrels' pillar at Beverley, for instance, or at the making of chairs in the workshops of Chippendale or Sheraton. But this pleasure is not the only one where work is concerned. The advent of the machine has proved this. It has proved that man is a mechanical animal. The percentage must be very high of men who derive satisfaction from observing, examining and participating in the working of complicated pieces of machinery. Looking back, one can see the vaunted Middle Ages as so much the poorer for their unconscious lack.

If the Middle Ages had had the wit to make machines, they would have made them and used them. Chaucer's pilgrims would have delighted in a charabanc. One can see the Wife of Bath perfectly on the back seat. And the Squire on his motor-bike. That this is not fancy can be seen by turning to the tale the Squire tells. There we see the Middle Ages faced with a machine, a horse of brass. Chaucer shows the crowd gaping around it, each man with his own opinion confidentially whispered to his neighbour:

> But evermore hir moste wonder was,
> How that it coude goon, and was of bras.

In the end we find that it goes if you 'trille a pin'. This indicates that before the advent of machines the potential interest in them was strong. One thinks of how the mechanical imagination has always been moving, if fantastically. The conception of Pegasus, for example, a horse with wings, is really a mechanical conception. It is an attempt to improve on nature by combining materials furnished by nature. In the mediaeval romance of Alexander the aeroplane and submarine are both suggested. Impossibilities in their day, but obviously ready to be accepted when machinery made them possible.

William Morris and Machines

Clearly the human race loves the results which machines provide. And as clearly it loves the machines themselves. Machines do not strip labour of its pleasure. They provide pleasure different from that provided by handicrafts, but not necessarily inferior pleasure. Moreover their cult liberates the strong instinct of certain men for invention. Before an invention becomes a commercial proposition, a great deal of hand labour has to go to its materialization. There is no fear that the handicrafts will die because of machines. Nor does the pleasure end when the finished machine leaves the showroom for the factory. Or rather, the pleasure *should* not end when the machine reaches the hands of those who are to use it. It is often only too plain that the pleasure does end there. The uncensored version of the speech which the B.B.C. recently invited from a workman showed that there was little pleasure in his workshop. Workshops vary in this matter. If a master printer takes you over his workshop, he is not bored, nor does he expect you to be bored. He knows that he can make an educational film look childish by confronting you with the superb machines which cope with modern printing. The men you see in the workshop are not bored. To enter a workshop as an apprentice often does mean, and always should mean, that the pleasure a boy has experienced over his Meccano set suddenly becomes significant, practical. A monotype machine is much more pleasant to work than a composing stick. But many workshops undoubtedly are degrading both to body and mind: they are degrading because their machinery involves automatic human activity. I have blamed the nineteenth century for blaming machines before the human race had learned to use them wisely. And the twentieth must blame them no more than the nineteenth. The nineteenth century needed more and better machines, and so do we. If any machine entails human labour which is so regular as to be monotonous, that is the indication that another machine should be doing the labour. It is a law in the application of machines to labour that if any action has become 'mechanical', as we put it, giving the show away, then it should be taken over by machines. This taking over will depend, of course, on other things, on politics—whether the State will equalize the unemployment machines have caused, making the working day shorter and employing everybody for that shorter day. The machines are waiting to be used wisely.

2

The Ruskins and Morrises denied that man takes pleasure in tending a machine, in participating in a scheme of superhuman practicality, in controlling powerfully the virtual labour of an army of brilliantly efficient hands. One might have argued them out of this belief. But one would have found it more difficult to argue them out of their belief that only things made by hand have real aesthetic value. Clearly, chairs made under a system of mass production will not usually be as beautiful to look at as chairs lovingly tooled by a fine craftsman. They will frequently be more beautiful than those made by a second-rate craftsman. But to expect mechanically made chairs to be beautiful in the same way that Chippendale's are beautiful is unreasonable. One must not expect an impersonal machine to produce a personal object 'by itself'. But we can expect a machine to produce an object appropriate to the capacities of a machine. And these capacities are high and valuable. A steel tube is as good machine-made as when made by human hands. ('Human hands' is, of course, inaccurate: human hands can make few things without tools of some sort. By 'human hands' I mean hands guiding simple tools.) And though it is impersonal, it is only impersonal so long as it is not used by an artist as part of his material. The works of art made by machines will not be less works of art because they have not been 'lovingly' fingered by a workman all through their history. They will become works of art when they have been co-ordinated under the supervision of an artist. So that the modern artist is a designer creating his thing by setting a machine to do it for him, instead of being a designer who carries out his creation with his own hands.

William Morris and Machines

The conception of an artist with machinery at his call fulfils the dream men have always dilated their imagination upon. It realizes Hamlet's renaissance cry about man—'how infinite in faculty!'—better than Hamlet's experience could realize it. It puts Hamlet in the position of Prospero, the man-magician. In using machines, man rides on the achievements of the mind of man. Morris, in these views of his, was not a prophet crying in the wilderness. He was an echo sounding in a wilderness created by his fancy.

3

In 'A Dream of John Ball' come these words:

> But while I pondered all these things and how men fight and lose the battle and the thing they fought for comes about in spite of their defeat and, when it comes, turns out not to be what they meant and other men have to fight for what they meant under another name....

This is certainly Morris's best epitaph. The thing that Morris fought for is coming about, is already visibly on the way. Only it is not coming about in his way, nor is it quite what he dreamed.

We cannot go back to the Middle Ages for our conditions of labour. It is impossible for the world not to go on revolving in the same direction. And it would be quite foolish, as well as impossible, to go back. Machinery is the natural outcome of man's genius. It is a natural development from tools to machines, since tools are machines in their simplest form. The genius in man that devised a knife or an arrowhead has devised in later ages the electric paper slicer, for instance, and the aeroplane. The happiness Morris dreamed of for the worker will be got not by scrapping machinery, but by developing it fearlessly, while at the same time developing politics fearlessly, for the sake of the worker.

When all 'mechanical' jobs are being done by machinery, man will have leisure forced upon him, and leisure properly used will mean pleasure. In the proper use of that leisure Morris's example will be useful. The handicrafts he advocated will be the sort of thing people will take pleasure in, say of a wet afternoon. It does not appear ever to have rained in Morris's utopia, but since, out of it, rain is certain, the leisured population of the future may prepare for a rainy day by learning some of Morris's crafts after him. They may bind a few books, or paint tiles, or copy out verses on vellum—not because vellum is 'quaint' but because it is a perfect medium for penmanship like Edward Johnston's or Alfred Fairbank's. But except for people like Morris himself who would use their fingers in crafts anyhow, handicrafts may never grow more important than the work of the small group of cultured ladies who, with the pretty patience of Penelope, nowadays weave scarves on hand looms. Most of the inmates of Utopia will probably prefer a leisure of sports and hiking and picnics, like the heroes in the Greek or Roman heaven.

Much more important is the influence Morris has already had on the things of everyday life. We do not make many ordinary things by hand: books, chairs, bedspreads. We make them by machines, but we are learning more and more to make them beautiful. Morris is largely responsible for that beauty. He made a stand for design in an age so fascinated by the capabilities of the machine that it neglected design for ornament. Since the machine did anything you set it to, the nineteenth century set it to do work as elaborate as possible. In the nineteenth century a kitchen range made entirely by machinery was hideous with the festoons of fruit that would have been beautiful if Grinling Gibbons had carved them on the oak of a reredos, but which were ugly when badly copied by machines and applied indiscriminately to iron and to oven doors. Morris's understanding of the principles of design and of its appropriateness underlies the modern value placed on those principles. Broadcasting House is full of machine-made things, but it is no less beautiful for that, since those things have been made with full knowledge of what machines can and can not do. Eric Gill was called in to do the carvings. The nineteenth century would have let a machine do those carvings and would have covered the building with their reiterations. We differentiate between the work machines ought to do and the work artists ought to do with their hands. The result, since an artist supervised the machine labour, is something as fine for its object as a Gothic cathedral, and one less guilty of human sweat. The magnificence is one more completely of brain than of brawn, so far has man and his machines 'progressed' since the days of the pyramids. Morris was out for integrity of design. The design in dull blues and yellows which is reproduced on the posters of the Victoria and Albert Exhibition is one of the finest designs made outside Persia. Morris might have rested after having made that design, and after seeing it in the hands of capable machinists who would apply it to weaving. That he was a craftsman who wanted to see the thing through with his own hands was, in the history of industry, accidental.

But the quality of the design was there, and remained there whether or not that design materialized by means of the human hand or by means of the human control of humanly devised machinery. The quality which Morris demanded in his designs, a quality from which Gothic elements were often absent and if present irrelevant to the principle underlying the design—this quality has had its influence on industry. The world is getting more thoroughly accustomed to beauty in ordinary things. The elaborate and preposterous furniture still crowding the second-rate windows along Tottenham Court Road represents the last gasp of the Victorian ideal which made machines a short cut to pomp. The synthetic marble beds, raised on a dais of synthetic marble, which can be secured by paying three shillings and six-pence per week for a prescribed number of years—these things show machines working without the benefit of Morris's sense of fitness in design. But the better shops are selling furniture sensibly designed with an eye to beauty. Both kinds are machine made, but the latter kind are made by machines fulfilling a sense of beauty and fitness which Morris in his finest moments understood profoundly. We have to thank Morris more than any other man for the growing pleasantness of our rooms, our printed books, our handwriting, our scarves and teacups. Not so much because of what he achieved as for what he stood for. Many of his actual productions (his type designs, for instance) ceased to be pleasing at least twenty years ago. What has lasted has been his example, the example of a man who applied himself to making agreeable the overlooked portions of daily life.

1934

XVII. ERNEST DOWSON

IN 'New Bearings in English Poetry', Mr Leavis finds no place for
even a mention of Dowson. The thesis of the book is that only
certain of the good poets of the last century counted in the development of English poetry. It is equally true to say that every good
poet, as well as every great poet, develops the work of his predecessors and contributes towards forming the poetry that is written
after him. Certainly Dowson might have been given his place in
Mr Leavis's survey. For he is a poet who is characteristic of his
time and who, because of that modernity, is as closely allied with
other good poets coming after him as he is with the good poets
who preceded him and with the good poets who were his contemporaries.

Like all good poets he epitomizes significant developments in
the poetical history of perhaps a hundred years. He clearly derives
part of his quality from Swinburne and so also allies himself with
Pater, Wilde, and the early Yeats in the belief that the value
of a work of art is in proportion to the nearness with which it
approaches 'the condition of music'. Arthur Symons recorded
that Dowson's favourite line in English poetry was Poe's

The viol, the violet and the vine.

But it would be a mistake to over-emphasize the importance of
verbal music in Dowson's scheme. When he copies the effect of
that line in such a line as

Vine leaves, kisses and bay

he is not only trying to assemble beautiful words but is saying
something exact. The line contains a symbol each for wine,
women and song. Dowson derives from Swinburne, but he does
not snatch at the first things that come to a poet's eyes for the sake

153

of saying them divinely, does not transform a modicum of complex but limited impressions into a thousand lines of lyric. He may be dreadfully intent on writing poetry that shall be flawless as verbal music, and that music may be of an exacting and subtle kind, but all this is only half his activity. Dowson does give minute attention to working over and over his lines, to punctuation, to placing capital letters as a refinement for indicating accent; and yet, beside all this, he is putting in an equal amount of work on improving his meaning. He succeeds in the use of forms like the villanelle because he can write lines which are substantial enough to bear repetition, or to make minute variation worth while. It is the same with certain contemporary materials. Even his lilies and roses seem of a more expensive kind than those in the pages of his fellow-poets. A letter of Oscar Wilde's might refer to 'your slim gilt soul'—a poetical letter of Wilde's has more literary value than a poem of Wilde's. Dowson writes and repeats a profounder phrase, 'her golden face'. He was too fond of his Latin lyric poets to be too much enchanted with a flash or a cadenza.

This reading in Catullus helps to connect Dowson with another 1890 poet who might appear almost too timeless a figure for the historian of poetry. Professor Housman also read Catullus. There are passages in Dowson which are almost 'Shropshire Lad'; and the first explanation is that both go back to Catullus. Other similarities are too difficult to explain without more facts. The 'Shropshire Lad', published in 1896, made use of the following stanza form:

> Lie down, lie down, young yeoman;
> What use to rise and rise?
> Rise man a thousand mornings
> Yet down at last he lies,
> And then the man is wise.

Dowson's first volume of poems, 'Verses', published in 1896, uses virtually the same stanza, though for other effects:

Ernest Dowson

The long, long winter weather,
These many years and days,
Since she, and Death, together,
Left me the wearier ways:
And now, these tardy bays!

At times Dowson's poetry resembles the extremely individual manner of Hardy's, and this, so far as dates at least go, may be counted a contemporary bond.

More important for the way poetry has developed since, are Dowson's experiments and achievements in rhythm. In this he stands beside Mr Yeats. In the 'Trembling of the Veil' Mr Yeats calls 'Innisfree' the first poem he had written 'with anything in its rhythm of my own music....I had begun to loosen rhythm as an escape from rhetoric'. This loosening of rhythm has been found important by later poets, Mr Eliot using late Elizabethan blank verse as a further solvent. Dowson's loosening was mainly carried out in the alexandrine, which in previous English verse had been either the hexameter or the six-iambic-footed line, the alexandrine, which Pope compared to a wounded snake. Dowson gave the English alexandrine the flexibility of the French alexandrine: e.g.

And I was desolate and sick of an old passion.

He even began to loosen syntax, but not sufficiently to make him more than a first straw in the rising wind. (The torrents of the same wind which were raised by Hopkins were still howling in the sound-proof drawer of Bridges.) The loosening of rhythm connects Dowson with Mr Eliot, some of whose many roots may be found gripping Dowson's best poem, 'Non sum qualis eram bonae sub regno Cynarae'. It seems less than fantastic to note, among more elusive communications, that the repeated 'Falls the shadow' of the 'Hollow Men' seems to derive partly from this poem:

Last night, ah, yesternight, betwixt her lips and mine
There fell thy shadow, Cynara! thy breath was shed....
But when the feast is finished and the lamps expire,
Then falls thy shadow, Cynara! the night is thine....

Ernest Dowson

And a favourite phrase of Dowson's is 'the hollow land'. It comes three times, and twice with the symbolic deepening of initial capital letters.[1]

1 Mr Eliot in a letter to the 'Times Literary Supplement' of 10 Jan. 1935 confirmed the first of these guesses: 'The derivation [suggested] had not occurred to my mind, but I believe it to be correct, because the lines [quoted] have always run in my head, and because I regard Dowson as a poet whose technical innovations have been underestimated'; but not the second: 'I do not think that I got the title "The Hollow Men" from Dowson. There is a romance of William Morris called "The Hollow Land". There is also a poem of Mr. Kipling called "The Broken Men". I combined the two.' Perhaps we might go on to connect Morris and Dowson.

1934

XVIII. THE PUBLICATION OF HOUSMAN'S COMIC POEMS

MOST readers of the Bibliography in Mr A. S. F. Gow's 'A. E. Housman' have been puzzled by the appearance there of a volume of poems intermediary between 'Last Poems' and 'More Poems'. Mr Gow's unexpected item reads as follows:

Three Poems: The Parallelogram, The Amphisbaena, The Crocodile (reprinted from the Union Magazine)	Privately printed in the Department of English at University College, London, 1935.

This article is intended as an elucidation by the means of narrative and bibliographical expansion. It is unfortunate that the elucidation cannot be complete without the intrusion of personal experience which would otherwise be impertinent.

I

It is one of my duties in the Department of English Language and Literature at University College, London, to supply bibliographical students with copy and instructions for the setting up, printing, and making of small books. In selecting copy one naturally aims at something which, as well as its intrinsic merit, has some local appropriateness. For this reason I soon began to covet the four comic poems which Housman had supplied to the College magazines during his tenure of the chair of Latin and which had not been reprinted. I was to spend part of the Christmas vacation of 1934–5 in Cambridge and recognized early the temptation to call on Housman for his permission. I was later assured by more circumspect friends that the scheme which I formed was bold, but the only person I consulted before the event was Professor R. W. Chambers, who had been Librarian of University College and Lecturer in the English Department during Housman's professorship. The attention of Chambers became intense as soon as I mentioned my plan. He encouraged me to try.

The Publication of Housman's Comic Poems

He acknowledged that he himself dare not: 'Housman', he said, 'can suffer young fools gladly, but will not suffer old fools with equal gladness.' The truth of his epigram has since been strikingly confirmed in general by Mr Gow and exemplified in particular by Mr Houston Martin in the 'Yale Review', Winter 1937. Mr Gow writes:

...now and again an undergraduate, who knew enough of him to desire further knowledge and not enough to be aware of the presumption, would call on him uninvited. On these occasions Housman would display an affability on which those who knew him better would not have counted.[1]

About five in the afternoon of 5 January 1935, I walked from King's towards Trinity. On an evening in the Christmas vacation Cambridge is like a village, deserted, silent, lit in pale patches, and the scene and the person walking recalled the more-than-Virgilian fearfulness of Housman's poem about Hell Gate:

> But the city, dusk and mute
> Slept, and there was no pursuit.

The porter at Trinity, however, seemed almost glad to see me, and took me seriously. 'Yes, sir, Professor Housman is in his rooms. It should be all right. He will just about have finished his tea.' He offered to notify Housman of my wish to see him and soon returned to guide me into the heavy quadrangle of determined sham-Gothic in which Housman had his rooms. Significant at any time, it seemed doubly significant then that Housman should deliberately prefer a grim gaol for his seclusion. But preoccupations became less gloomy when, in the anteroom from which his rooms branched, I noted a brown-enamel kettle still steaming on a gas ring. And almost all the remaining apprehension disappeared when Housman met me. He had risen to greet me from an office chair at a capacious office desk on the left of the fire where in green-shaded light he was engaged in writing on foolscap. He was wearing carpet slippers (green, I believe,

1 p. 44, and see the whole passage.

with a floral pattern). They seemed newish but of a kind which I did not know were still made. His face seemed nervously intent on clearing my mind of nervousness and intenseness. It was slightly in pain, but its smile was that of one who would have smiled even more welcomingly if the constitution of its muscles had allowed him. His face had a bucolic brightness, like a crab-apple, and its patchy red seemed that of a man whose skin has gone hard and red with weather. (I have since learned that patchy red cheeks are a sign of age.) His eyes were quick and bright. His head, like that of an old man, seemed to be set lightly, even dancingly, on his neck as he approached me.

I told him that we in University College should like to print his four comic poems on our private press, adding that the edition would be limited to whatever number of copies he should decide. He said that he saw no reason to withhold his leave since he had given his brother permission to print some of his early verses in the autobiography that he was writing. He could not allow us to reprint all four poems. There was no justification for reviving his parody of Erasmus Darwin since 'The Loves of the Triangles' in the 'Anti-Jacobin' was better done. He had already, he said, refused permission for its reprinting to Mr E. V. Lucas and saw no reason to revise his judgement.[1] He stipulated one condition: that he should have proofs. He was polite enough to feed me with questions and I explained the part which the press played in the English course at University College. One thing is worth recording. I told him that I had recently noted as a 'curious coincidence' that one of the most notable stanza forms of 'The Shropshire Lad' was used also, though for other effects, by Dowson in his first volume, 'Verses'.[2] Both volumes were published in 1896. Did Housman know of an explanation? His reply was: 'Isn't the stanza used by some seventeenth-century poet?' I certainly had not come across it earlier than 1896 and have not since found any earlier example. Before I went, he hesitatingly

1 This earlier judgement is recorded by Gow, p. 22, note.
2 See p. 154 above.

made it clear that he did not know my status at University College, whether I was a student or member of the staff. I mentioned my professor, Chambers, and even recounted the epigram 'Housman can suffer young fools....' He was obviously pleased and alluded to Chambers's recent publication 'On the Continuity of English Prose'. But even here, as throughout my twenty minutes' conversation with him, his smile seemed a floating rather than anchored one.

2

Housman's contributions to the magazines of University College were five in number. No. 13 of vol. I of the 'University College Gazette' (25 Nov. 1897) contained the anonymous 'Fragment of a Greek Tragedy'. In vol. II, No. 21 (22 March 1899) came 'Extract from a Didactic Poem on Latin Grammar' to which was appended the footnote 'From a paper read by Professor Housman before the Literary Society entitled "Erasmus Darwin"'. This magazine was in quarto form and ran till 1904, when it was succeeded by the octavo 'U.C.L. Union Magazine'. Gerald Gould, then a student, was editing its first number and wanted something out of Housman. He wouldn't tackle Housman himself and asked Chambers to do so—Chambers was then a young teacher. Housman permitted 'The Parallelogram; or Infant Optimism' to be printed so long as his authorship remained unknown. After many years it came to be known, not through Chambers,[1] that Housman was the author of this and of the two subsequent poems, all three being intended to form a series. The poems are found as follows in the magazine:

(a) The Parallelogram; / or / *INFANT OPTIMISM*. Vol. I, No. 1, Christmas Term, 1904, pp. 21–2.
(b) The Amphisbaena, / or / *THE LIMITS OF HUMAN KNOW-LEDGE*. Vol. II, No. 1, June, 1906, p. 11.
(c) The Crocodile, / or / *PUBLIC DECENCY*. Vol. V, No. 1, March, 1911, p. 159.

1 This and the three preceding sentences were dictated to me by Professor Chambers.

The Publication of Housman's Comic Poems

3

The printing of 'Three Poems' took about six months, since our practice was to have relays of half a dozen students who worked in the press room officially for two hours in each of three weeks. We had the continuous help and supervision of Dr A. H. Smith, Reader in English, who had designed and built the press in the summer vacation of 1932 from the specification of Joseph Moxon in his 'Mechanick Exercises' (1683).[1] The first setting up of the type was of an inaccuracy unbelievable to any but amateur printers. It is possible, indeed, that the first pulls might have broadened Housman's professional knowledge of the possibilities of textual corruption, but only the revises were sent to him. His few corrections were written in with what I take to be the 'Ladies Pen' (probably medium size) made by Perry and Co. The following excerpts from Housman's letters to me outline the history of the edition:

I. ...23 Jan. 1935...My part in the reprint...is strictly permissive [*I had asked him if he would like to write a prefatory note*], and I express none of the preferences which you kindly suggest: I only want it to be as unassuming as possible. Six copies for me, since you are good enough to offer copies, will be ample, as no one outside my own family will be likely to want one. I naturally am quite willing that your assistants should have copies....

II. ...5 March 1935...I return the proofs, with such misprints as I have noticed corrected. As to 'changing any of the types' I am not competent to have an opinion, but I think that the 'or' in all three titles should be in capitals....

III. ...28 April 1935...I am content with your proposal for the title-page, and have no ideas of my own....

IV. ...20 May 1935...There seems to be nothing wrong with the proof which I return....

[*The foregoing letters were all addressed from Trinity College. No. V was addressed from a nursing home in Cambridge and was written in pencil.*]

1 The press, along with a great deal of University College, was destroyed by a land-mine and by incendiaries in September 1940.

The Publication of Housman's Comic Poems

V. ...24 June 1935...I believe I have not yet thanked you for the six copies of *Three Poems* which I have received from you since the doctor sent me here. I must therefore do so without delay, and add, though I am no judge, that they look very nice to me. I certainly shall not crave for any more....

VI. Trinity College, Cambridge, 17 July 1935....As I have been unwell lately, and part of the time in bed, my correspondence has been somewhat neglected, and I am apprehensive that I may have omitted to thank you for the six copies of *Parallelogram* etc. which you were kind enough to send me.

The typography, though I am not competent to judge it, seems to me agreeable [*the type used was 14 point Caslon Old Face*]. The third line on p. 8 ought to begin a new paragraph. This has probably gone wrong because the proofs were sent to me in two detached parts, and not simultaneously. [*Housman did not notice one other misprint*: 'advancing' (*p. 6, line 2*) *has a figure 1 instead of an i. In some copies a few letters in the bottom right-hand corner of p. 5 did not print because of the frisket's edging in between them and the paper. These letters, as in many of the books of the sixteenth and seventeenth centuries, were supplied by pen and ink.*]

I am much behoven to you and your associates for squandering your pains on producing what Martial I am afraid would call 'difficiles nugas' adding perhaps 'Stultus labor est ineptiarum'....[1]

Mr Gow tells me that, if his memory is correct, there were two or three copies of the book left in Housman's rooms at his death.

'Three Poems' was printed on two sheets, one placed inside the other. Its format is quarto and therefore there are 16 pages. The contents are as follows:

p. (i) *title page*:—THREE POEMS: / THE PARALLELOGRAM / THE AMPHISBAENA / THE CROCODILE / By A. E. HOUSMAN. / Privately Printed in the Department / of English at University College, / London. MCMXXXV.

p. [iii]: [*bibliographical note*]

pp. [1]–3: *The Parallelogram*

pp. [4]–6: *The Amphisbaena*

pp. [7]–9: *The Crocodile*

p. [11]: [*the device*]

1 These letters are published with the consent of Housman's trustees.

The book was issued with a blue stiff-paper cover on which we reprinted the title-page. Fifty copies were printed.

4

All three poems belong to the kind of verse of which Mrs Turner's moral stories and Mr Belloc's 'Bad Child's Book of Beasts' are respectively early and late nineteenth-century examples. Like most of their kind, they are written in tetrameter couplets, those of 'The Parallelogram' being arranged in quatrains.[1]

'The Parallelogram' takes as its material the moment when a child's mind is confronted either with the new world of geometry, or with a new item in that world of autonomous and seemingly alien abstractions. 'The Parallelogram' represents the possible meditations of a child, who is also a pious child, caught at the moment of meeting a parallelogram, and is an expansion in argumentative terms of its puzzleheadedness. But behind the poem is a wish to parody the smugness of eighteenth- and nineteenth-century children's hymns—the sub-title of the poem is 'Infant Optimism'.

The poem begins with a reasoned eulogy of 'Euclid, the intrepid Greek', a eulogy which ends lyrically:

> Oh, when I recollect how much
> Strange information, true or no,
> To that geometer we owe...
> My cheeks have often been bedewed
> With tears of thoughtful gratitude.

One 'cause of thankfulness' is for what the parallelogram might have been but is not. It is not, for instance, a terrifying monster: fortunately

> The hand of Providence confines
> Its form by parallel straight lines.

---

1 Housman forbade the republication of these poems in his will. The quotations from them in this article are made by permission of his trustees.

Being a plane, it does not harm you, or make noises at night. But there is no reason to covet its 'peaceful life', since it could not crawl away if placed in an unsuitable position, nor would it respond like plants to watering. The moral, therefore, is plain:

> Then morn and evening let me raise
> My little hands in duteous praise,
> Because a Christian child I am,
> And not a parallelogram.

'The Amphisbaena' seems to have been suggested by the phrasing of Dr Johnson's definition of this mythical beast. That definition Housman quotes as motto: 'a serpent supposed to have two heads, and by consequence to move with either end foremost.' Clearly as attractive a creature as any of those invented by the nursery poets:

> ...all who see it are perplexed
> And wonder what will happen next...
> Until it starts, you never know
> In which direction it will go,
> Nor can you even then maintain
> That it will not come back again.

But what distracts the author and

> bereaves of bliss
> [His] finite intellect is this:

which is back and which front? He rearranges the problem, but no answer offers itself.

> Philosophy, with head of snow,
> Confesses that it does not know;

nor is there any hope from Logic.

'The Crocodile' is mainly a narrative poem. The conduct of this beast does not appear to the poet as

> Consistent with sincerity.

164

The Publication of Housman's Comic Poems

On the banks of the Nile, infants 'run about with nothing on', the reason being that the London County Council is too far away. The crocodile simulates concern:

> 'Oh Infant! oh my country's shame!
> Suppose a European came!
> Picture his feelings, on his pure
> Personally conducted tour!
> The British Peer's averted look,
> The mantling blush of Messrs. Cook!
> Come, awful infant, come and be
> Dressed, if in nothing else, in me.'[1]

The child accepts the invitation, whereupon

> His mother, in the local dells,
> Deplores him with Egyptian yells.

The 'false, amphibious crocodile' also appears distressed, and the Nile consequently receives augmentation of its waters. Amidst the rising tide 'the floating fellaheen' inquire

> 'Is it that winds Etesian blow,
> Or melts on Ethiop hills the snow?'

and the Khedive and Sirdar note that

> 'There goes that crocodile again.'
> The copious tribute of its lids
> Submerges half the pyramids,
> And over all the Sphinx it flows,
> Except her non-existent nose.

The syntax of these poems, as in all successful poems of this kind, is that of simple prose. Long words of classical derivation add to the effect of closely confined dexterity: the best instance combines that effect with one of 'local colour'—the Egyptian yells of the mother in 'The Crocodile' are referred to again as 'hieroglyphic howls'. Sometimes the long words are 'unpoetical'. In the 'Personally conducted tour' they are those of modern ad-

1 In the printing, the first line of this paragraph should have been separated, as Housman noted, from the preceding one.

vertisement. The effect of that phrase is best analysed by reference to Coleridge's discovery that in poetry we are conscious of the words as words: we never noted the Latin pomp of its polysyllables till we came to roll them on the tongue within the limits of a tetrameter verse. In the contemptuous description, 'the false, amphibious crocodile', *amphibious* becomes a moral term of abuse. There are also other means of amusement. Housman introduces the elegant words and phrases of eighteenth-century poetry. There is 'mantling blush', 'watery plain', 'copious tribute', tears that 'bedew' the cheeks or 'augment' the Nile, and a 'faithful hound'. But some of the best effects are outside the form. 'Philosophy, with head of snow' is, for instance, excellently 'ambiguous'. And then there is the Miltonic expansion in the 'winds Etesian' and the 'Ethiop hills'.

These poems are not so fine as the 'Fragment of a Greek Tragedy' which received one of its earliest printings in the same college magazine. The parody of that poem was based on admiration for what was beyond the reach of parody. But, all the same, Housman would not have been himself if he had allowed these bagatelles to be published without first having made them as perfect as possible. It should not surprise one to find Housman writing these comic poems. Swift, another man of a severe and melancholy intellect,

> ...cr[ied] wisely, 'Vive la Bagatelle!'

1936

166

XIX. EPITHETS IN ENGLISH POETRY

WHEN one thinks of epithets one thinks of epithets alone or of epithets and their nouns together. One's units consist either of one or of two words: or, if the second kind of unit allots two or more epithets to its noun, it consists of three or more words. It is sometimes useful to take as unit the single epithet. This is especially so when the use of the epithet in itself forms a characteristic skill or failing in a poet. Certain poets seem to have a small fund of epithets from which they select to supply a comparatively large number of nouns. There is Victor Hugo with his eternal 'sombre', or Mr Humbert Wolfe with all his 'silvers' and 'cools'. Or, if Mr Wolfe is too easy prey, there is Miss Sitwell whose epithets come from a good but limited store. Homer and Virgil invite the application of the first kind of unit, the tradition of epic poetry requiring the continued use of allotted epithets ('wine-dark' sea, 'winged' words) almost as if the epithets were part of the nouns, as if the epithet and noun formed together another noun.

But this smaller unit is not much good when one considers Shakespeare, or rather it is useful for the early work of Shakespeare but not for the later. In the poems, of which 'Venus and Adonis' and 'Lucrece' are quite early work, Shakespeare does seem to be drawing from a fairly confined group of epithets: 'sweet', 'fair', 'golden', 'silver', etc. (It seems that when a poet confines himself to a few epithets, the precious metals, the colours of heraldry, are among them.) But even in his early poems and plays Shakespeare is beginning to use the epithet for conveying a larger significance than one mainly sensuous. Boasting of her subduing of Mars, Venus tells that:

> Ouer my Altars hath he hong his launce,
> His battred shield, his vncontrolled crest....

Epithets in English Poetry

Shakespeare is beginning to weight his epithets with an intellectual content very different from the sensuous or immediately perceptible abstract content of the epithets he drew from his stock of 'poetic' ones, of Spenserian ones. In his later work, epithet with every other element of his poetry suffers—to use the inevitable phrase—its sea-change. Like his nouns, like his verbs, the epithets sprout and spring with the promiscuous fountaining of wild things. Here the unit for understanding them is the double one of epithet and noun: or perhaps one ought to see Shakespeare's late sentences as indivisible, as splashes of meaning, rather than as meaning conformable to grammatical analysis. Certainly in the late work of Shakespeare the noun and adjective are indivisible: the noun requires its epithet in the same way that a face needs a nose, or a flower its particular smell.

I take Shakespeare as the example of those poets whose epithets and nouns instantaneously amalgamate into one. This is the test of the proper use of adjectives. Perhaps this unit is a development of the Homeric unit in which a chosen number of nouns-and-adjectives go together like man and wife, the difference being that each couple in modern poetry appears once only. As another example of this best use of the epithet I will take Spenser, since, as I have implied already by my use of 'Spenserian', most people would be inclined to group him with those poets (not the best) who draw eternally on a small group of epithets they consider suitable for poetry: look at Spenser, they say, and find *fair* women, *dainty* limbs, *cruel* fights, etc., by the score. Spenser, of course, does frequently see no reason why he shouldn't repeat his epithets —his eye, or rather his ear, is sometimes concerned for other ends. But it is quite as true to think of Spenser as the first of our poets to use the *mot juste* in descriptive passages, not because of searching for it but because of good luck. There are many examples of this in the 'Shepheardes Calender'. The two I quote are from the 'Faerie Queene'. The team of dolphins:

> As swift as swallowes, on the waues they went,
> That their broad flaggie finnes no fome did reare....

168

Epithets in English Poetry

And this of the angels leaving 'their silver bowers':

> How oft do they with golden pineons, cleaue
> The flitting skyes....

In other words, Spenser sometimes makes one treat his epithets as part of his nouns.

Epithets, even when of the kind which are fast to their nouns, should not need to be used too often. If a poet is charged with using too many epithets, he might reply: 'Yes, but they are all of your second kind. They are part of the noun. If they went, the noun wouldn't mean the right thing.' That might be true without being an excuse. If a poet has too many adjectives all apparently necessary, it means that he is not giving the other parts of his grammar enough to do. As it stands, his meaning will be changed for the worse by removing any of the adjectives. But the whole effect is not at its best. The improving of the whole effect will necessitate a different spacing of the meaning, perhaps a perceptible change in the meaning. But it may be worth the bother.

This is what Keats learned. In his early poems the epithet is frequently part of its noun. It is organic in the poem. The epithets couldn't be cleared away simply with blue pencil. The meaning, as well as the metre, would suffer. This means that Keats had not yet mastered the problem of the equable division of meaning throughout a line. He was making his epithets do too much, allowing his verbs and nouns to do too little. Indeed, he sometimes has to make up with the beauty of his adjectives for the bathos of his nouns. When the need to rime makes an unpleasant noun—i.e., a noun unpleasant in that particular context—unavoidable, Keats piles up his heavily beautiful adjectives in an attempt to forestall disaster:

> ...their full lips
> First touch'd; what amorous, and fondling nips
> They gave each other's cheeks....

(Keats seems to have been uneasy how exactly to word the failure of l. 2: the manuscript shows that he first wrote: 'What fondleing

169

[*sic*] and amorous nips. . . .') In the later work he knew better how to distribute his meaning more equally. But to the last he was a little too fond of his adjectives. In 'Endymion' he could write:

> . . . soon these limbs became
> Gaunt, wither'd, sapless, feeble, cramp'd, and lame.

The revised version of 'Hyperion' retained this from the first version:

> Through bow'rs of fragrant and enwreathed light
> And diamond-paved lustrous long arcades.

In the second line, though each epithet adds something new, the contribution of the second and third has been partly anticipated. And though one must allow him credit for the rightness of

> Where palsy shakes a few, sad, last grey hairs,

(where the effect is due to the number of common primitive qualities discovered harsh as salt in aged hair) it remains true that Keats was often too readily enchanted by dumped epithets. He was constitutionally incapable of attaining his richness in the way Shelley attained his in 'Music when soft voices die. . .', where there are two epithets to the eight lines. But the fine fragment of the 'Ode to Maia' shows that he was learning to control both the number and the temperature of his epithets.

1932

XX. QUOTATIONS

UNOBTRUSIVELY in the mind of anyone who is reading or conversing with a friend, a kind of ghostly commonplace book is being prepared. He may be paying only a surface attention to words, but a glancing phrase here and there is likely to print itself on the mental page, frequently with some reference to its chapter and verse. Aphoristic and proverbial sentences—the pulpit gestures of speech—will transcribe themselves in a copybook hand, far more decoratively and durably than subtler meaning. 'All the world's a stage' will write itself down currently on first meeting, while 'A fool, a fool, I met a fool i' the forest' may never become cerebral manuscript. 'A rolling stone' will settle itself squatly on the page and perhaps a sorry quip from pantomime, or a letter ending from Stevenson like 'With my hand on my heart'. There will not be much discrimination. The elfish pen will write or will not write. It will painstakingly enter a vapid 'saying of the week' and never budge to chronicle a thing for all time. And a profound sentence—a *sententia*—will occupy no more space than the trivial one lying next to it. It will be written, perhaps, in blacker, more enduring ink, or perhaps in water. How many pages will be completed, how soon the earlier pages will wear to dust, how many and what coloured inks will get employed—all these and minor speculations are matter for heads vanished with the seventeenth century—for a Sir Thomas Browne whose spidery consideration travelled even finer cobwebs.

Along the margins of completed pages, as one may figure it, a pencil is running, up and down, asterisking this item, then suddenly skipping pages and pages and underlining that. As life presents itself, the pages of the commonplace book will flutter and slide open, revealing a disjointed commentary. At any moment a phrase may start out, apposite as an oracle. One's tongue will then launch the timely words into air and ears. Or the pen in the quick bodily hand will transcribe it on material pages. A quotation will have been made. But, conversely, the tongue may stumble. Perhaps the pen will hover in irremembrance. The words in the mind may have faded almost out. The reference to their source may have rubbed away, too. One may merely feel that there was once a propitious thing lettered out there. If this last has happened, the quotation may never be found again, never be reinscribed. But if the indications of chapter and verse are not too far decayed, the lapsed fragment may be readily reinstated in a reference library. If only the gist of the words remains, then the owner of the mouldering commonplace book, painfully ready with a pen new-dipped, has three courses open to him. He may leave the space bare for ever; he may renew the transient script, and renew it in indelible capitals, by enquiring of learned friends: or he may print an S.O.S. letter in a literary weekly or Sunday paper.

2

Quotation of one sort or another forms the staple of much conversation and writing. In talking among themselves, people quote their private commonplace books endlessly. They quote the authors they have read and transcribed from. They quote their other friends. They quote their own previous selves. And since quotation marks cannot be indicated in speech, the fine words of another are vocally indistinguishable from their own newest re-marks. The chancel rails are gone. The quoted and the original fall identically into the one seemingly homogeneous mosaic. Very honest or timid persons introduce a quotation by some such placers as 'in the words of X', or 'as Y so eminently remarked'. And there is at least one man recorded who preferred not even to quote his earlier self without quotation marks and formal docket-ings—the Cambridge don who, when asked for his views on any-thing, would say 'I have dealt with that topic in my *Collected Essays*, volume III, pages 219 *et seqq*'. Less fastidious people, however, quote and invent in the same proprietary tone, wildly hoping for the best. Even if a friend recognizes one of your quotations, there will be many his own commonplace book has no record of. And even for the one from his own book he may have taken the quotation marks as having been almost audible. But, as Bacon might have counselled, do not quote your earlier good things too frequently because such a citation if noted is fatal. Beware of the disgrace that befell the old self-quoter in 'The Vicar of Wakefield'. After one such detection heavily inked inverted commas spring up like pricked dog's ears around almost any decent thing you say.

3

In written speech quotation marks are there or they are not there. Their omission may be dishonest, imposing, gracious. If all the possible quotation marks were supplied in most newspaper prose, the columns would appear doubly flyblown. One feels that the typewriters of reporter-journalists have been so strictly drilled in their clichés that the keys would function automatically if the appropriate sergeant-major command could be hit on. No one very much minds these counter-like quotations, even when they are mixed in metaphor. They all make for the necessary impersonality of news. 'A point has arisen', 'hope was entertained', 'fully choral'—all these quotations do not talk to us as a novel talks to us. They ring small electric bells in our brains and their meaning is registered passively and instantaneously. We should feel ourselves intolerably overstrained if some morning our 'Daily Paper' appeared fresh from the pen of Mrs Virginia Woolf or Mr H. M. Tomlinson. The shock would disable a man for the day's routine. He would get through about a tenth part of the contents in the time he usually takes to read the whole. He would want to underline this remark, celebrate that turned phrase with more than a moment's afterthought. But a newspaper exists to be read without friction, to be skimmed effortlessly by everyman. The rails have to be oiled so beautifully that the mind may receive what sense there is without knowing that it is receiving it. The smoothly clicking stereotypes provide the mind with an Eastern horizontality of repose which is all the more repose because hammocked within the bodily joltings of tube and bus.

4

No one doubts that these unticketed stereotypes are quotations from the 'Daily Paper' of yesterday which in its now forgotten turn quoted its predecessor. And no one doubts the historical origins of those innumerable two-or-three-word phrases of Shakespeare and the longer aphorisms of Pope which lie like flakes of faded silver-gilt over our speech. 'Thereby hangs a tale', 'yeoman service', 'to err is human'—these, outside this sentence, would need no inverted commas. They are now as impersonal as dropped coins or trouser buttons. And, since we avoid mounting these phrases on inverted commas, we might also avoid the exaggerated honesty which insists on mutilating a quotation in full public gaze. A writer finds he wants to make a quotation. But, as it stands, the grammar of the quotation is at variance with the grammar of his own sentence. He may adapt the setting, which is the neatest way. Or if that course is too troublesome (and it often is) he may hack and trim the quotation. But let him do it humanely. To take a random unhappy example: a sentence from an introduction to some translated dialogues of Plato reads:

'What, then, are we to think of these dialogues, and especially of the *Symposium* and the *Phædrus*, which seem so obviously to be devoted to the praise of inspiration and to breathe the spirit expressed in—

the Poets,....
...men endowed with highest gifts,
The vision and the faculty divine?'

One can see what has happened. The quotation was fixed on early during the shaping of that sentence. Every word of the quotation was looked on as holy. Any omission made had to be compensated for in a full toll of dots. The result is a sentence disastrously malformed. Its architecture would have stood less totteringly if the writer had mingled his own words and Wordsworth's and built freely and indiscriminately, preserving intact perhaps the last line which is the only one worth preserving without its first context. By itself that line would have made a pleasant antique frieze across the façade of a firm sentence. And for all the literal conscientiousness of the quoter—his dash, his ', . . ./ . . .'—the niggling logic breaks down. Why print the query following 'divine' in the same type as the quotation? The query does not belong to the quotation. It belongs to the sentence. To be logical, the query should have been in the larger type. Moreover, logically, it should have been set up at the beginning of the line following the quotation. If one is to quote poetry, first let it be good poetry, and secondly let it grow naturally as a leaf from the stem of the sentence.

And, further, why trouble to dog-ear a quotation familiar to everyone likely to read an introduction to Plato-in-English? Why not treat the fragment of Wordsworth as one treats a fragment of Shakespeare or Pope? Why not fling the vision and the faculty divine naked among ragamuffins like yeoman service and to err is human? Why insist that you are quoting when everybody knows it? One is weary of meeting Keats's magic casements crudely voluted with quotation marks. If one must quote them, let them be built cleanly into the new wall and do not trouble to stick a bill explaining. There is more faculty divine in a quotation made in a way which credits the reader with some intelligence.

5

The poets themselves have taught us not to be overparticular about our use of inverted commas. The Elizabethan and Jacobean poet frequently insulated by means of quotation marks what he felt to be a quotable line, a line with a leaden touch of proverb in it. But he did not trouble to wave the little black flags when he was tangling another author in his own web of words. He made his quotations either unconsciously or as a tribute. When Shakespeare was versifying a length of Plutarch-North he pushed blotlessly ahead. He left it for his editors to rail off the words of Plutarch if it suited them. Poets of all times have quoted. They have quoted phrases, ideas, rhythms, innocently enough. Their mental commonplace books, rubricated, ribboned, well thumbed, chronicle most of the poetry of the world. Arabesqued among all this beauty of other men trail the inkings of their own poetry, already composed and done with, or perhaps still to assemble into a poem. Which is the word of this poet, that poet, and which his own becomes indeterminate sometimes. For him the divisions of *meum* and *tuum* dissolve away. Milton, in the eighth book of 'Paradise Lost', has the line:

> And feel that I am happier then I know.

And Wordsworth closes the 'After-thought' appended to his sonnets on the River Duddon with:

> We feel that we are greater than we know.

He was quoting a cadence rather than an idea. He was quoting probably without knowing it. At another time his commonplace entry remained clear enough to make his quotation seem a quotation. But even here the reference has worn dim. In 'Tintern Abbey' he included a line not wholly his own and appended the note:

> This line has a close resemblance to an admirable line of Young's, the exact expression of which I do not recollect.

It is to some such process as this, which, for once, Wordsworth acknowledges, that one owes the long roll of echoes from poet to poet. Homer swells behind lines and passages of Virgil. Chaucer can write the lovely line

> That al the orient laugheth of the lighte,

perhaps never dreaming that he is almost literally translating Dante. Milton's poetry echoes and even quotes preceding poetry so frequently that reading him is almost like answering a series of gobbet questions in an exam. His commonplace books lay richly open in his mind. He did not of course quote literally. But more than any other poet, except of course Pope, he quoted consciously. His supremest effects are not always pure Milton. They are Milton's English words sung into a mind which at a touch has swarmed full of other older poetry. When in one famous fantasia of similes Milton mentions 'that Pigmean race' and

> ...Faerie Elves,
> Whose midnight Revels, by a Forrest side
> Or Fountain some belated Peasant sees,
> Or dreams he sees, while over head the Moon
> Sits Arbitress, and neerer to the Earth
> Wheels her pale course,

one's mind at the same time is reading Homer and Virgil, peering at older poetry through a glass darkly—through a glass innumerable indeed of stains and splendid dyes. 'Sees or dreams he sees....' And so one goes through Milton hearing, or is it dreaming that one hears? the voice of Greek, Latin and older English poets chiming like boys and men into the counterpoint. Mark Pattison said, 'An appreciation of Milton is the last reward of consummated scholarship'—a starched saying but one that for most of us is unfortunately true. Only Milton could appreciate Milton comprehensively and with minutest delicacy. And the more closely our commonplace books tally with his, the farther his utterance will range and rove in our minds, the longer the echoes that it will strike from the scooped stone. One cannot hope to catch the full tone of his quotations until one's mind is built like his of the old and newer marbles of past poetry.

The same kind of quotation at a more wadeable depth may be noted in most of our poets. It is shown lucidly in Clare's 'Autumn'. As Mr Blunden has pointed out, the poem recalls Collins's 'Ode to Evening', almost, I would say, with an unfortunate completeness. The outward stanza is the same, the atmosphere the same in effect, and some of Clare's phrases are Collins's pure and simple. The poem is almost blushingly derivative as well as being a good indication of the integrity of Clare's own genius.

6

One finds the same kind of homage by quotation in the prose of the early nineteenth century—and principally in the prose of Hazlitt. Unlike Lamb, Hazlitt did not compile any anthology of 'beauties' from the works of bygone forgotten authors. But he did the next best thing. He quoted past literature with brazen thoroughness. His mind was like an old library with its books all open in the shelves, their pages flapping noisily because of the open window and showering out phrases like warm spring rain. The phrases showered on to him. He did not pry in this and that likely book finding them. As they dropped on to his page so they stayed. He did not trouble to verify all that was falling so vividly. Meticulously regarded, his quotations are often incorrect. He would not have cared very much. The thing for him was the sweep and spirit of the quotations. Hazlitt's quotations are not there to show how learned he was. They are flying advertisements of the neglected glory of past letters.

To snub such enthusiasm seems uncalled for. And yet Hazlitt is the loudest example of how not to quote. Take his best-known essay, 'On going a Journey'. It opens:

> One of the pleasantest things in the world is going a journey; but I like to go by myself. I can enjoy society in a room; but out of doors, nature is company enough for me. I am then never less alone than when alone.
> The fields his study, nature was his book.

Here the first quotation escapes quotation marks. The Senecan proverb about being least alone when most alone was used by Cowley in its Latin form to open his essay 'Of Solitude'. That quotation has been adapted, has become parcel of Hazlitt's prose. But the second quotation, the line of verse, is uncalled for. It is brought in before the good chatter of the 'letterpress' has really got going. And its content is trivial. To be given a snippet of verse while the prose is still engaged in shaping itself on the tongue unsettles one at a stroke. Why, we ask, interrupt admirable original prose (slightly tinctured with half-quotation) by rhythms that are heterogeneous and by matter which has nothing to commend it? By all means quote a thing which the world since Pope despairs of improving on. But do not cite any old indifferent thing simply because you once chanced on it in a wormy second-hand folio, especially when you yourself could manipulate it much more happily into words. One would like to have said to Hazlitt: Digest past literature, let it steal like juices through your veins: do not revolve it in the maw as an ape doth nuts. And one would have liked to show him the quality of some modern quotations—perhaps by handing him a page here and there from the lectures of 'Q'. But to his contemporaries each quotation must have tasted like a spoonful of old wine from bottles open to anybody. 'O taste and see' is his continual invitation.

Like Hazlitt, C. E. Montague overdoes quotation. No man has kept Shakespeare's fine phrases more serviceably handy in his memory. But Montague could manage English handsomely on his own account. Montague-cum-Shakespeare was an unnecessary intertangle of verbal genius. An erudition which is amorous like Montague's, but lighter and more catholic, quivers in the newspaper prose of Mr Humbert Wolfe. Almost every sentence he writes as journalist runs with freely spilled quotation. It is a mistake to quote and allude too frequently in this manner. Mr Wolfe's passages are quite purple enough without the splashed claret. I have said 'allude'. Mr Wolfe uses few quotation marks since his citations chime accurately in everyone's memory. His quotation is allusion and often cleverly twisted allusion. The twist, however, though sometimes a contortion, not infrequently says much in little space. It drags a lighted context with it, and an atmosphere which modifies the setting unexpectedly. Marlowe is the master here. No half-application has more whole significance than his Faustus cry of

O lente, lente currite noctis equi.

7

Quotation by one art of the same art is the rule. Words are quoted by words. Occasionally music quotes music—for example, Schumann's many citations of the Marseillaise, Bach's calm super-imposition of the chorale 'O Lamm Gottes' upon the multi-tudinous counterpoint opening the 'St Matthew Passion'. Painting quotes painting—for example, Vermeer's frequent quo-tation of chairs, curtains, dresses and people from his own earlier canvasses. Much more uncommon is interartistic quotation. Butler printed four lines of Händel's harpsichord music instead of attempting to sound verbally the music of the Erewhonian statues. T. E. Brown concludes a poem by writing down the last phrase of the chorale 'O Haupt voll Blut und Wunden'. The same venture has been taken in jazz. The music will cease and there is a soft American voice talking alone: speaking perhaps Vachel Lindsay's 'Daniel Jazz':

> And she was a golden lily in the dew.
> And she was as sweet as an apple on the tree,
> And she was as fine as a melon in the corn-field,
> Gliding and lovely as a ship on the sea,
> Gliding and lovely as a ship on the sea.

Then jazz thumps in again, bespattering the Solomon-like loveli-ness of those lines. Fielding comes near quoting pictorial art. In 'Tom Jones', he uses some such formula as this when introducing a woman:

> The lady, no more than her lover, was remarkable for beauty. I would attempt to draw her picture, but that is done already by a more able artist, Mr Hogarth himself, to whom she sat many years ago, and hath been lately exhibited by that gentleman in his print of a winter's morning, of which she was no improper emblem, and may be seen walking (for walk she doth in the print) to Covent Garden church, with a starved foot-boy behind carrying her prayer-book.

Quotations

This is as far as interartistic quotation should go. Actually to make the quotation, to stop the words and start musical sound, or *vice versa*, is to require too sudden a readjustment in the mind of the reader or listener. The two effects—verbal, musical—remain physically incongruous.

1930

XXI. THE ANCIENT MODERN

Ther nys no newe gyse, that it nas old.

I

ISLANDED in 1930 with a much predicted but still undivulged future and a past invisibly accumulated, we realize our insulation acutely. The present, even as we think of it, has passed: is past. *Temps perdu* has sucked another drop into its Ocean. That Ocean to most eyes presents a grey receding surface, wrinkled perhaps into individuality over scattered patches, here and there mustering a 'hither-and-thithering', or even sometimes a blunt wave, and perhaps once in a while supporting something thought to be rather like a cockboat. But it is hard to think of lost time as composed of small rounded particles, of hours, of seconds individual and once precious. While they are being lived through, minutes may slide along a string of pure boredom; or the string may be pure ecstasy. Most of them anyhow are consciously spent. They play familiarly with our most private emotions. They fatigue, delight, sooth, distress, spurn. But to conceive even the ephemeral space of our own life as an accumulation of such sentient moments is beyond the power of a human mind. Time and space are two things at which the fretful human imagination boggles in complete helplessness. Time appears to have no very efficient memory. His face in Dürer's famous engraving is half hog, half imbecile; the squinting eyes sprawl like ineffectual suckers of an octopus. It is to the perplexed brute mind behind the squint that we entrust the tale of our allotted minutes. What were a million individual drops, clear or mudded microcosms, merge indistinguishably and are lost in his memory. They are swallowed into the misted and silent Ocean of the past.

Historians and readers of old literature manage to make out the marbling on waves even far out from the brink of the present.

The Ancient Modern

They may even descry diminutive white horses and feel themselves equal to dubbing this one Dobbin, that Bayard, another
Bucephalus. They make it their business to sit like Canute, ever
pushing back their armchair from the encroaching lap of the tide.
(I am not thinking of those scholars whom the tide immerses
without their knowledge, who themselves become cold fish before their date.) These new Canutes screw their eyes into a further
penetration of vision. And one of the amusements of their far
watch is the noting of a distant pattern of foam, a remote flicking
tail or swirl of current, when they have already noted the identical
pattern and disturbance here at their feet. The waves gurgling and
bashing about their chair are suddenly matched with vivid
accuracy by waves far out. Reading their old things, it suddenly
seems that they are reading something written last week. Looking
at old pictures, they find themselves staring at a canvas that seems
still wet from the drama of a modern brush. Playing their old
music, a harmony shouts at them 1920 or 1930. One of the
excitements of dabbling in the past is that momentary sense that
we are actually dabbling in the present.

2

Since the past we dabble in is mainly human past, and since the
elements of human nature have remained almost static throughout
word-recorded time, any ancient observation of men is likely to
have modern reference. The story of the prodigal son, for instance, reaches that purity of simple human meaning which makes
it the parable of the Prodigal Son. Andromache and Hector
saying their farewell are given such fundamental significance that
they remain valid to-day. The account of Daphnis and Chloe's
sitting on the cliffs and listening to the boatmen's chant is in most
particulars as true for 1930 at Beachy Head as it was for the fifth
century on Lesbos. Chaucer's lines describing the Man of Law:

> No-wher so bisy a man as he ther nas,
> And yet he semed bisier than he was,

apply to the profession as neatly now as in the spring of 1387. Langland tells us that chapmen put better things in the window than they have in the shop. And so on, obviously. These records have lived simply because they make lasting universal reference to Man. They move us as profoundly, as pleasurably, as they moved ancient Greeks, early Christians and mediaevals.

But there is a rarer and more cheerful pleasure to be got out of the literature of the past. While living through the present we tend to think a great deal of it assembled out of uniquely modern elements. Unconsciously we accept our twentieth-century things as the last word, hitherto unspoken, and moreover the wittiest, freshest, most sophisticated word. Another quite novel fringe has been trimmed along the old Ocean. Man, we know, is the same in essential spirit now as in Homer's day. And yet, in other important particulars, he seems so agreeably, so ingeniously different. His dress, his manners, his daily environment, the level and colouring of his mentality—all these are changed. Poor Shakespeare—to fish up a fairly recent body from the brine—would stare incredulously blank if confronted with the latest in men. He would scarcely recognize the species. The stockbroker, say, in bowler and spats would seem parcel of Othello's experience rather than of his own

> . . . travels' history
> . . . of the Cannibals that each other eat,
> The Anthropophagi, and men whose heads
> Do grow beneath their shoulders.

And yet Shakespeare has the knack of startling us by the gilded modernity of a phrase or observation. We wince a little, feeling our skin brushed by something we thought of as having safely suffered its sea-change.

3

Everyone, though informally, will have culled his own anthology of the ancient modern. Almost any old book he picks up will open his eyes to the tradition behind his newly invented context,

The Ancient Modern

the bedded age below the glittering surface. What strikes one person, however, as incongruous commentary in antiquity appears to another as expected. Education, accidental environment, the wits of one's friends will have developed a mind into individual homesteads, pastures, backwoods, creeks, and just exactly what old serpents and ignorant beasts inhabit the map is more or less accidental. The following pages will not interest those whose knowledge of antiquity and of the more recent past was from childhood more complete than their knowledge of the world in our own time. They are written for those who have lived first as moderns and then as scholars. And probably for young people—such as beamed with astonishment when they found their sister's newly bobbed hair and newly tailored dress brilliantly copied in the margin of a mediaeval manuscript. But even the crabbed scholar who inhabits the past more familiarly than the present cannot fail to have had the normal pleasure in an inverted form. He will have noted with dry and cynical emotion how his contemporaries are but ignorantly mimicking Greeks, mediaevals, Christians of all time. And even he can remember his guffaw at encountering the tiniest, most mushroom-looking villages firmly seated among the statistics of Doomsday Book.

It is details like that of Norman bobbed hair which strike one most forcibly, details of manners and customs. Our newspapers, perhaps, foster the readiness with which we accept the manners and fashions around us as being the inalienable quota of originality that we make a free present of to history. Since their paragraphs and illustrations were typed, photographed, set up an hour or two ago, they pass as additions to knowledge rather than as repetitions of knowledge. The armchair that we are continually pushing back from the lip of the tide is often a basket one, and it is Mr Minty, we know, whom we have to thank for basket chairs. But no: the article is mentioned casually in a poem of Donne's. Funereally horn-rimmed spectacles—those at least one would date as novelties a few years old. And yet El Greco's portrait of Cardinal Guerana exhibits a nose saddled identically with our own; and,

185

185

moreover, a pair of school-ma'am pincenez droop from the nasal bridge of the donkey who is shown playing the organ in an engraving of the early sixteenth-century school of the Lower Rhine. Pepys speaks of a silver pen 'to carry inke in, which is very necessary'. The Quennells in their 'History of Everyday Things in England' have traced the primitive and successive forms of many deceptively modern details of common life. Excavated cities reveal slick Selfridgean civilization. An Athenian relief, discovered in 1922, shows a game of hockey in progress. Submarines and aeroplanes are well on their way by the time of the fourteenth-century romance of King Alexander. Museums abound in modern commodities dim with the dust of centuries. The recent idea of a children's museum is meant to call attention to the course of such traditions. A great deal of the sly charm of past diaries, letters, periodicals springs from the straightforward way they introduce us to our own diaries, letters and periodicals. They show us our own environment in embryo, and sometimes in full swing. The bobbed style of hair is now slipping into the past. A transitional fashion obtains. But the past, at least once, and probably frequently, has been there before us. Fielding, introducing Sophia Western, writes:

Her hair, which was black, was so luxuriant, that it reached her middle, before she cut it to comply with the modern fashion; and it was now curled so gracefully in her neck, that few could believe it to be her own.

Montaigne collects instances of folk who, like modern undergraduates,[1] never wear hats, using no 'other bonnet abroad than in the warm house'. In 'Troilus and Cressida' comes the game 'I spy. You spy! What do you spy?' In 1423 we find the Brewers' Company letting their hall out to 'the Footballplayers', presumably for a celebration.[2] Umbrellas are mentioned in Drayton's 'Muses Elizium' (1631).

1 The fashion has now spread well beyond the universities, like the fashion for 'Oxford bags'—G.T. 1941.
2 'London English', ed. Chambers and Daunt (1931), p. 148.

The Ancient Modern

The preceding desultory sentences properly represent the way things haphazardly flash out of the sea.

4

Our slang and vivid colloquialisms have roots deeper and darker than any sea-dingle. The Anglo-Saxon Chronicle under the year 1140 mentions a darkness on 20 March at noon and adds that people 'lighted candles to eat by'. Yorkshire-men, reading 'Sir Gawayne and the Green Knight', meet 'it is nobbut an old cave'. In the York miracle play of 'The Harrowing of Hell' Satan greets Christ with the expression:

> Thy father knew I well by sight.

Professor Abercrombie writes as follows in his 'Theory of Poetry':

...colloquialisms are not so perishable as is sometimes supposed. *Let on*, in the sense of *blab* or *boast*, seems the very phrase for poetry, in the forthright strength of its expressiveness. Is it only an evanescent modernism? It seems too good for that; and in fact the very phrase occurs, with wonderful effect, in poetry written centuries ago. A torturer in the Wakefield crucifixion play says of Christ:

> 'Lo, he *lets on* he could no ill;'

that is, he boasted he was incapable of evil. Instances just as remarkable could be multiplied.

Chaucer has the line:

> Til crowes feet be growe under your eye.[1]

In the 'Merchant of Venice' we read:

> What's here? the portrait of a blinking idiot.

The phrase 'anything for a quiet life' is centuries old: a play of 1621, attributed to Webster, bears it as title. One of the Verneys in the seventeenth century writes: 'I shall chear up when you com'.

---

[1] This is the first recorded instance of the expression but Chaucer's manner of using it suggests that he is not inventing it for the occasion.

187

The Ancient Modern

Pope has '...singing, laughing, ogling, and all that'. Defoe is a master of modern slang: things may be called 'frightful', even 'really frightful'; and in 'Roxana' we read, 'Well, Amy talked big...'. Swift ironically commends the use of expressions such as 'it is a little more-ish'. A character of Goldsmith will refer to things as 'cute'. And could one wish for a more Shavian remark on the heavenly overstatement of modern conversation than this from 'Tom Jones'?—

Jones now declared that they must certainly have lost their way, but this the guide insisted upon was impossible; a word which, in common conversation, is often used to signify not only improbable, but often what is really very likely, and, sometimes, what hath certainly happened; an hyperbolic violence like that which is so frequently offered to the words infinite and eternal; by the former of which it is usual to express a distance of half a yard, and by the latter, a duration of five minutes.

Apart from the pointing, the word 'hath' and the balanced close, this is prose which might have been written yesterday, and by Shaw. We are inured to finding passages of pure Shaw in the works of Butler, passages which have not only his style and theme behind them, but the very mind. To find the same style, the same mind and frequently similar themes a century earlier in Fielding's delightful multitudinous talks on novel writing and general topics is more softly startling.

One imagines the loudest touring American to be post-war. Noisy Americans travelled before, of course, but not, one would have imagined, with quite that verbal brutality thick as rouge on their lips. But a torrent of Western lingo was poured into the soft-conched ear of Shelley—of all people. Trelawny recounts how he took Shelley over an American clipper. Her mate described an adjacent Greek vessel as 'Crank as an eggshell, too many sticks and top hamper, she looks like a bundle of chips going to hell to be burnt'. Trelawny continues:

The Yankee would not let us go until we had drunk, under the star-spangled banner, to the memory of Washington, and the prosperity of the American commonwealth.

The Ancient Modern

'As a warrior and statesman', said Shelley, 'he was righteous in all he did, unlike all who lived before or since; he never used his power but for the benefit of his fellow creatures...' [Shelley quoted or extemporized some verses applicable to Washington].

'Stranger,' said the Yankee, 'truer words were never spoken; there is dry rot in all the main timbers of the Old World, and none of you will do any good till you are docked, refitted, and annexed to the New. You must log that song you sang; there ain't many Britishers that will say as much of the man that whipped them; so just set these lines down in the log, or it won't go for nothing.'

5

The profoundest shock which the twentieth-century mind has received in the way of the old new is probably the one so exquisitely dealt by Mr Arthur Waley in his successive translations of 'ancient Chinese and Japanese classics. There in the East a thousand years ago and more was a civilization vividly modern, *mutatis mutandis*, in spirit, in outlook, in values. (The same quality has led us back to Restoration comedy under the winning guidance of Mr Bonamy Dobrée.) It is incredible that Chinese poets were writing like this at a time when our own literature was just raising a primitive head from the mud:

> Families, when a child is born,
> Want it to be intelligent.
> I, through intelligence
> Having wrecked my whole life,
> Only hope the baby will prove
> Ignorant and stupid.
> Then he will crown a tranquil life
> By becoming a Cabinet Minister.

'The Pillow Book of Sei Shonagon' reads for pages like 'Gentlemen Prefer Blondes'. 'The Tale of Genji', written by Lady Murasaki in the eleventh century, never dips far from the choicest spirit of the twentieth. One quotation must suffice: the cult of the colour scheme in dress was Parisian centuries before that epithet can have acquired any sophistication:

The Ancient Modern

After much debating, the presents were distributed as follows: to Murasaki herself, a kirtle yellow without and flowered within, lightly diapered with the red plum-blossom crest—a marvel of modern dyeing. To the Akashi child, a long close-fitting dress, white without, yellow within, the whole seen through an outer facing of shimmering red gauze. To the Lady from the Village of Falling Flowers he gave a light blue robe with a pattern of sea-shells woven into it. Lovely though the dress was as an example of complicated weaving, it would have been too light in tone had it not been covered with a somewhat heavy russet floss.

Such a book as the 'Tsure-zure Gusa', the miscellany of a Japanese priest of the thirteenth century, is packed with placid criticism of modern life. The following section 'Against Pedantry' might refer to the villa titles of our suburbs, and the exotic film names (Gloria, Marlene) of the new generation:

When naming monasteries, nay, when giving names to many other things also, the men of old took little thought, but freely gave names just as they happened to come. Nowadays, however, we find men pondering over the question anxiously and trying to display their own erudition, which is indeed a great pity. In naming people also it is quite useless to employ characters with which one is not familiar. But in all matters, alas! men of shallow intellect ever seek after oddities and love the abnormal.

6

The more old music one plays the more frequently one encounters contemporary idiom. The modes, newly excavated folksong and plainsong stump and hobble behind much contemporary English music. Herbert Howells has recently applied modern idiom to the Elizabethan forms—pavane, ground, galliard—but there was much of it there already. The variations on 'Carman's Whistle', on 'Woods so Wild', Bull's experiments in modulation, to say nothing of Byrd's amazing liturgical music, all these might persuade us that the centuries have somehow got mixed up.

Bach, Mozart and Beethoven seem compendia of almost everything in music that has happened since. The 'Anhang' of Bach (secreted at the end of a volume in Peter's edition) would of itself explain Brahms. The 'Chromatic Fantasia and Fugue' imply the splendid mannerisms of César Franck. And further, the most modern 'scrunches' of discord, like those bold ones of Purcell, give the daub of realism to his sequences which the modern mind hails like a discoverer. The late work of Beethoven, especially the last quartets, is at least penultimate to the most modern. In the first variation of the adagio of the E flat quartet, as in the slow movement of Mozart's G minor quintet, pure jazz works and waxes in marvellously constricted abandon. Scarlatti rings with modern accents and stark modern harmonies. Couperin, beloved of Ravel, has bars and lines of pure Ravel. The reason for all this, of course, is that the moderns have deliberately schooled themselves in the old. Most of us, however, encounter the modern first and the ancient second, and the later encounter shocks accordingly.

It is the same with pictorial and plastic art. Cave paintings exhibit the vivid formal contortions beloved of our time. Ancient Egyptian faces stare down from Eric Gill's stone figures, mediaeval human angles pattern his sculptured bodies. Graeco-Roman art seems newly done. The ink and wash sketches of Rembrandt filch the last touch from the brush of the impressionists. 'But we thought...' we mutter slowly, and eye the bottom so neatly knocked out of our cleverness.

7

There are, however, crumbs of consolation. We have considered ourselves as the enskyed ultimate leaf, 'the last of its clan, that dances as often as dance it can', the last remaining leaf, red and giddy. And in reality we are no more than the top leaf of a lofty and very leafy tree that is already preparing newer twigs to push beyond our topmost pirouette. Still we *are* the top leaf, and shall go on being it for a while. We are modern. And old things may have been the top leaf in their own time, pre-eminent, red and giddy. But not quite so tall in pre-eminence, not red with precisely our total kind of red, not identically giddy. In the examples transcribed above, there has always been a flaw, an old decayed fly in ointment that surprised us with its freshness. Pepys didn't know the word 'fountain-pen' nor the fifteenth-century brewers the word 'footballers'. Pepys's ink-bearing pen was silver not vulcanite. Fielding used the word 'hath'. In an age of wigs he gave Sophia Western such lovely hair that 'few could believe it to be her own'. An edge has chipped off the tablets of old Nile. Rembrandt's impressionist sketches treat of objects since treacherously dated. There is always some cankered touch to give the show away. And, turning to our really modern things, we may say: Not the first things of their kind perhaps, but integral, flawless, still with a human warmth about them, the latest chronologically at least, ours.

1930

XXII. THINGS IN HEAVEN

I

IT is a great feat of the human imagination to figure a race on
Mars, and a greater to figure a member of it on a visit to the earth.
It would be a greater feat still if the imagined Martian appeared
less like one of ourselves. But common utility discourages the
imagination from going all out. The end for which we image
the far-fetched specimen at all is a human end. We image it for
the homely purposes of a tale or an argument. We may find the
creature a picturesque mouthpiece for fresh, astonished, impartial
criticism of earthly things as they are. Goldsmith, for the same
purpose, manufactured his Chinaman, and Montesquieu his two
Persian travellers. We do not visualize the planetary type for the
fun of it, or in pure scientifical seriousness, as Sir Thomas Browne
would have done. In consequence of which, the imagination is
not given unrestrained freedom. It can construct its Martian as
fantastically as it likes, always provided that the experience of
everyman remains its material. If the imagination worked in godlike abandon, the resultant Martian might emerge as anything.
It might emerge, for example, as the pure form which Picasso
achieved for the patterning of his rug, after laying in trance the
human and earthly of his mind. But even if we endowed this
shape, this visual Idea, with life and said 'Here is the visitor from
Mars', we should not be able to make any argumentative or
artistic use of the thing. And so for convenience the 'it' becomes
a 'he'. The warm words *he, him, his* raise its value for the human
mind a hundredfold. Even if we succeeded in describing verbally
the animate form of Picasso's formal mingle of lines, we could
find it no place in an extravaganza or satire. The thing would be
too alien to bear. The human members of the scheme would die
of fright, or of some malignant planetary smell, as certainly as if

they were taken out of the air. Even Lear or Carroll could have found it nothing to do. When the human imagination has *carte blanche*, that is, when its images cannot be disproved, those images generally, naturally, almost inevitably, form themselves out of human and earthly elements. We have found no use for a new heaven and a new earth that are unlike anything we have come across during our time on earth. Unless our visionaries behold things recognizably assembled out of the semi-chaos of everyman's experience, we follow their eyes in vain.

2

The human imagination has conceived heaven. Over long ages and for different races it has conceived it in many forms. All those forms have been materially imaged. Heaven has always been full of things. Sometimes the things have been simply earthly things transplanted, sometimes they have been earthly things curiously overhauled. Heaven, the scene or place of some future life, was an idea that had to stand much handling. It had to strike men as real. Heaven could be hoped for, and so had to be desirable. While men were still on earth they had to feel that its comforts were worth ensuring. Again, heaven had to be describable in words, the commonest of human media. And since man has only made words for what his sense can reach and his mind easily compass, heaven had to be patterned firmly out of sensuous images and such simple virtues as majesty, power, loveliness, love, which mean something to everyman.

If the conception of heaven had waited until the other great imaginative media had been perfected, it might have escaped the materiality of verbal images. Palestrina might then have been its Christian inceptor in sound. The images of music had been unrepresentational almost from the start and in the counterpoint of Palestrina they achieved a spiritual perfection. But the plastic arts have dealt in concrete images until quite recently and time has not yet brought on the man equal to conceiving heaven in purely abstract relationship of line and mass. Michelangelo produced anthropomorphic celestials. And the idea behind Picasso's rug was not meant to be heavenly.

The idea of heaven was humanly necessary, then, before man had power to keep it, as it were, unspotted from the world. The Egyptian, the Assyrian, the Greek, the Roman, the Christian races have all pictured their heavens as simulacra of what was best, rarest, most desirable in the world. The builder or maker might be God but with a divine adaptability he had limited himself to the materials he drew upon for the creation of the world. Nirvana, Abraham's bosom, Elysium, the Islands of the Blest, the Heaven of 'Revelation', 'Paradiso'—all were compounded poetically out of stuff sensuously significant. Mr Davies has recently hit this off in a lyric which opens,

> That paradise the Arab dreams,
> Is far less sand and more fresh streams.
> The only heaven the Indian knows,
> Is hunting deer and buffaloes.

And in his 'Intercepted Letters', Moore has the couplet,

> A Persian's Heaven is eas'ly made:
> 'Tis but black eyes and lemonade.

The horses and head-feathers of the Indian, the prune-eyed virgins promised in the Koran, the guardian dog Cerberus, the wrestling matches, the innumerable presence of near constellations, the singing 'with undiscording voice', the harps massy with gold— tactile and visile images stand solidly in heaven.

3

In any history of things in heaven, St John must be prominently placed. Wherever Christianity has gone, the basic Johannine conception of heaven has gone too. That heaven was the work of an imagination molten with mystic ecstacy and longing. Moreover, it was the work of a poet whose mind was jewel-burdened like a queen's. John writes, and the fragments of acknowledged sublimity which lie scattered over the earth and the tracts of man's mind rain like shooting stars into a compact image of glory. Every ounce of gold, every jewel, every crystal in the world rockets up as we read and fits into the golden honeycomb, dustless and without a scratch.

...a throne was set in heaven, and one sat on the throne.

And he that sat was to look upon like a jasper and a sardine stone: and there was a rainbow round about the throne, in sight like unto an emerald.

And round about the throne were four and twenty seats: and upon the seats I saw four and twenty elders sitting, clothed in white raiment; and they had on their heads crowns of gold....

And before the throne there was a sea of glass like unto crystal: and in the midst of the throne, and round about the throne, were four beasts full of eyes before and behind....

'Eye hath not seen, nor ear heard....' But in a vision things must strike the mind clearly and be recognizable. And so similes chime through 'Revelation' incessantly. They hang heaven with gold chains about the feet of earth. Fantastic as the vision becomes, the jigsaw elements in it are known to any child. The locust, devised in heaven, is an unbelievable creature, but every atom of him is already familiar to us in some place or another:

And the shapes of the locusts were like unto horses prepared unto battle; and on their heads were as it were crowns like gold, and their faces were as the faces of men.

And they had hair as the hair of women, and their teeth were as the teeth of lions....

And they had tails like unto scorpions, and they had stings in their tails: and their power was to hurt men five months.

Centuries later, Dürer was able to translate 'Revelation' into pictorial shapes.

Christian theologians and poets with John's white light in their eyes did not look much further for their heaven. But mediaeval theology developed a system of eight sub-heavens which formed a kind of pyramid and crescendo of holiness. Dionysius Areopagiticus formulated this system with the cleanest precision and Dante flooded it with his light and solemn music. But for the

Things in Heaven

ninth heaven John's suffices. Dante, Milton, Bunyan all accept heaven as readily as though it were demonstrable as a burning cumulus cloud at sunset. Milton encounters great difficulties since his theme requires archangels among its active characters and celestial wars among its episodes. What with armour weighty and yet imponderable, and dynamite dug out of the floor of heaven, and archangels' blushing, and angels who though vulnerable are immortal, Milton's singing robes swing a little foolishly. His explanation is ingenious, but naïve:

> What if Earth
> Be but the shaddow of Heav'n, and things therein
> Each to other like, more then on earth in thought?

Hamlet's is a humbler mind. For him it is all an 'undiscovered country'.

4

Perhaps the next step I record is partly due to the protestant theologians themselves. Holding the grace to mould their own beliefs, they speculated a little freshly. Sir Thomas Browne, for instance, spiritualizes the whole conception:

Briefly, therefore, where the Soul hath the full measure and complement of happiness; where the boundless appetite of that spirit remains compleatly satisfied, that it can neither desire addition nor alteration; that, I think, is truly Heaven: and this can onely be in the injoyment of that essence, whose infinite goodness is able to terminate the desires of itself, and the unsatiable wishes of ours: wherever God will thus manifest Himself, there is Heaven, though within the circle of this sensible world.

Things in Browne's heaven are, then, purely casual, and the passport of death is no longer necessary. This idea of a purely mental experience of heaven, irrespective of place, does not widely spread, though there is Milton's

> The mind is its own place, and in it self
> Can make a Heav'n of Hell, a Hell of Heav'n.

But Milton is suspect as saying anything that came conveniently on this difficult theme.

Things in Heaven

Although the idea that heaven was some kind of place remained unshaken, what kind of place it was prompted speculation outside theology, the speculation of earthy minds. Charles Lamb in his most overwhelming essay speculated de profundis. 'New Year's Eve', published in the 'London Magazine' of January 1821, complains and questions with the misery of a child left alone on a dark moor. The thought of death, the immediate gate into the next world, wrings him till he screams:

> Some have wooed death—but out upon thee, I say, thou foul ugly phantom! I detest, abhor, execrate, and (with Friar John) give thee to six-score thousand devils, as in no instance to be excused or tolerated, but shunned as a universal viper; to be branded, proscribed, and spoken evil of! In no way can I be brought to digest thee, thou thin, melancholy *Privation*, or more frightful and confounding *Positive*!

There is Lamb's incurable fancy lurking in the expression of all this, but the agony of mind is real agony and strange matter for a magazine. Since an after life is possible, Lamb hopes for the best. For him, Francis Thompson's scheme—the ladder pitched between heaven and Charing Cross—would have sufficed, provided that he could have perambulated for ever at the London end of it. A new state of being 'staggers' him, and he asks passionately,

> Sun, and sky, and breeze, and solitary walks, and summer holidays, and the greenness of fields, and the delicious juices of meats and fishes, and society, and the cheerful glass, and candle-light, and fire-side conversations, and innocent vanities, and jests, and *irony itself*—do these things go out with life?

Leigh Hunt caught up the idea suggested by Lamb and toyed with it exquisitely in another magazine seven years later. 'An Earth upon Heaven' is a cheery pagan essay, as Lamb's had been a tortured pagan essay.

'People are accused of having earthly notions of heaven', he writes, and continues, 'As it is difficult to have any other, we may be pardoned for thinking that we could spend a very pretty thousand years in dining and getting acquainted with all the good fellows on record'. And Hunt enthuses at the thought of entertaining Fielding, Berkeley '(an angel in wig and lawn sleeves!)', and Shakespeare. St John, it appears, has received a hearty dig in the ribs, the high lighted structures of Dante and Bunyan are dripping away like candles. Hunt laments that all the great poets have been content to adopt a standard heaven, instead of inventing riotously on their own. Then he, for his part, points a light fantastic toe and is off. John's reverend vision, he hopes, was one of a *final* perfection, comfortably distant in time. Other earthier states lie between:

Nothing shall persuade us, for the present, that Paradise Mount, in any pretty village in England, has not another Paradise Mount to correspond in some less perishing region; that is to say, provided anybody has set his heart upon it:—and that we shall not all be dining, and drinking tea, and complaining of the weather (we mean, for its not being perfectly blissful) three hundred years hence, in some snug interlunar spot, or perhaps in the moon itself, seeing that it is our next visible neighbour, and shrewdly suspected of being hill and dale.

(The first heaven of the mediaevalists was on the moon, so Hunt's fancy is not the waif he thought it.) His pointed toe leads him briskly. In the heaven he descries one will have one's best friend, a mistress (not an illegal term, since 'upon the best authority' people are 'neither married nor given in marriage'), books, 'tea beyond anything Chinese' mingled with cow's milk ('One's landscapes cannot do without cows').[1] And 'the weather will be extremely fine, but not without such varieties as shall hinder it from being tiresome. April will dress the whole country in diamonds; and there will be enough cold in winter to make a fire pleasant of an evening. The fire will be made of sweet-smelling turf and sunbeams; but it will have a look of coal.' Just

[1] A hit at the landscape painters and at Gilpin who had treated of the matter in 'Observations, Relative Chiefly to Picturesque Beauty' (1786), II, 258 ff.:

'Cattle are so large, that when they ornament a fore-ground, a few are sufficient. Two will hardly combine. Three make a good group....He who studies landscape, will find himself very deficient, if he hath not paid great attention to the choice, and combination, both of animal and human figures.'

as surely as Hunt's heaven has the look of some hamlet in an English county.

So in the nineteenth century the sublime conception of heaven was no longer felt to be binding. Man might gape at sublimity, but he could not feel comfortable in it. The old idea of heaven as choral and electric was stuffed under the sofa. The white and gold *décor* of Paradise seemed too chilly to these amused iconoclasts, as a modern bathroom seems to ourselves on a winter afternoon. The astral continual singing struck them frigidly beside the merry courantes and *alla Turcas* on their pianos. Even the harps were too unwieldy, like golden horsecollars, and who could be sure that breezy arpeggios were allowed? The pearly gates became the charge of a quipping Peter familiar as an inn-keeper, and hundreds of draughty stories made the saint and his institution look ridiculous. St John's vision had become a dream.

The sublime idea, however, continues to have power—immense, hysterical power—in religious teaching. But being taken up by the Salvation Army, it fell into unconscious parody, and especially when it reached the misty heads of the Christy Minstrels. In the deciduous leaves of a thousand songs, heaven and its laundered angels receive the souls of the humble and good —mothers, village maidens faded in decline, home-sick, glee-chanting heroes of the battlefield. Heaven becomes the theme of tear-voiced street singers. In one of these laments, a beggar 'old and grey' has just enough breath to squeeze out the following phrases:

> And I wonder, *oh* I wonder
> Will the angels, *'way* up yonder—
> Will the angels *play their harps* for me!

I italicize the words that receive on their baying vowels an additional pathos as the tune hovers and slides over them.

Things in Heaven

5

As far as modern letters are concerned, heaven begins from emptiness and is furnished exactly as the writer fancies. It floats, indeed, as free and variable as the fairyland of children's books. But just because heaven is a swept room, empty even of echoes, it matters enormously what new furniture the author selects for it. Like a millionaire in a toyshop, he can choose anything, everything. And we watch him narrowly to see exactly what things he decides to lift up into that waiting void. Anything he selects immediately becomes significant. As, touch by touch, the celestial scene embodies, things become symbols and the story a parable—a parable inverted, a heavenly story with an earthly meaning.

Take three modern tales of heaven. The author of 'The Celestial Omnibus' has two other heavenly stories not quite so well known—'Mr Andrews' and 'Co-ordination'. The parabolic element, the 'philosophy', in both of them is so pronounced as to find almost aphoristic expression. In 'Mr Andrews', an account of a respectable Englishman's taste of heaven, scattered sentences read dogmatically: for instance, in heaven 'no aspiration of humanity was unfulfilled', and 'in that place their expectations were fulfilled, but not their hopes'. And after Andrews and his chance Turkish companion have decided to leave heaven, both alike being dissatisfied at finding everything more or less as they imagined it, the story concludes,

As soon as they passed the gate, they felt again the pressure of the world soul. For a moment they stood hand in hand resisting it. Then they suffered it to break in upon them, and they, and all the experience they had gained, and all the love and wisdom they had generated, passed into it, and made it better.

In 'Co-ordination' an archangel trumpet-tongued speaks the philosophy. The story, itself co-ordinated exactly and brilliantly as the facets on a crystal, shifts its scene between a girls' school and two official quarters in heaven. Miss Haddon has been teaching

201

couples of girls to execute a duet version of Beethoven's 'Eroica' symphony. Strange things ensue, co-ordinating beyond her ken:

Meanwhile, high up in heaven Beethoven sat, and all around him, ranged on smaller clouds, sat his clerks. Each made entries in a ledger, and he whose ledger was entitled '*Eroica* Symphony: arranged for four hands, by Carl Müller,' was making the following entries:—'3.45, Mildred and Ellen; conductor, Miss Haddon. 4.0, Rose and Enid; conductor, Miss Haddon....'

The deaf Beethoven, approving, decrees 'that Miss Haddon and her orchestra and all in their house shall this very evening hear a perfect performance of my A minor quartette'. Napoleon, similarly employed in his nebular office, approves of the report on another section of the school's napoleonic activities, and decrees 'that they and all their house shall participate to-morrow morning in the victory of Austerlitz'. But (to pull out only one strand of the story) these alarming orders remain, it appears, totally unfulfilled. When, however, Mephistopheles rehearses to Raphael this new and crowning charge against the Judgement Seat, the archangel points out with epic courtesy that the two worlds *have* co-ordinated. 'They have co-ordinated through the central sources of Melody and Victory'. For in the course of the story, Melody had sounded with significance—the girls had heard a 'most spiffing' cavalry band, and Miss Haddon and the Principal a shell cocked to their ears—and Victory had been experienced, since Miss Haddon, on the sudden receipt of a legacy, had been able to resign her tiresome post with a gesture that only a school treat could celebrate.

Finally, one may think of Mr Coppard's 'Clorinda Walks in Heaven', the most intangible of stories. The prose evaporates as one passes over it. The parable behind the veil of words is itself no more than a fume slightly sweet, slightly acrid. The parable takes as its images a group of heavenly men, 'lightly clad in beautiful loose tunics of peacock and cinnamon' (all of whom have been Clorinda's husbands in previous lives) and a strange coloured scarf into which 'all her past had become knit...into a

Things in Heaven

compact pattern of beauty and ugliness of which she was entirely aware, all the multiplicity being immediately resolved'. In the end she asks a foolish question about Weston-super-Mare and the scarf is twitched off her shoulders. Then Mr Coppard muffles and curtains, his voice mumbles unintelligible as music:

It cannot now be told to what remoteness she had come, or on what roads her undirected feet had travelled there, but certain it is that in that moment she was gone.... Why, where or how cannot be established: whether she was swung in a blast of annihilation into the uttermost gulfs, or withdrawn for her beauty into that mysterious Nox; into some passionate communion with the eternal husbands, or into some eternal combat with their passionate other wives... from our scrutiny at least, she passed for ever.

An exquisite feat of words. But unsatisfactory. Word by word our mind has rarefied, emptied, and at the end to replenish it we have to turn from that 'blast of annihilation' and 'that mysterious Nox' to a tale of earth—perhaps to 'The Hurly-Burly' of the same volume. If heaven is not to overtax us it must have definite strokes, it must have things and mundane ideas, such as Mr Forster had in 'Co-ordination'. Let our authors return to something like the Islands of the Blest for their heavens, islands perhaps a little off the mappamundi, but solid and lovely for all that as the island of Prospero. Or, better still, let them neglect the place altogether, especially if their parables are not deliberate and tangible as those by which Jesus enlightened the idea of the kingdom of heaven. For we cannot now believe in the new heavens as Dante and Bunyan believed in their old ones.

1930

APPENDIX I

WINDOWS IN SHAKESPEARE

THE facts which explain Shakespeare's use of the window-eyelid image have been overlooked by most of his editors and even by the 'O.E.D.' They are not, however, inaccessible, being contained in two notes in 'Notes and Queries', 1876, and in a note by the late W. J. Lawrence first published in 'The Irish Statesman' and included in his volume of essays 'Shakespeare's Workshop' (1928). In neither is the full evidence set out, and it is therefore presented here.

It is first necessary to make it clear that *window* is used, in five places in Shakespeare, as an image for eyelid, and secondly to show why this image should be a possible and even an obvious one to an Elizabethan writer. The following are the instances in Shakespeare (references to the Oxford text):

(1) Her two blue windows faintly she up-heaveth
                    ('Venus and Adonis', 482)

(2)   thy eyes' windows fall
    Like death
                    ('Romeo and Juliet', IV, i, 100)

(3) Ere I let fall the windows of mine eyes
                    ('Richard III', v, iii, 117)

(4) Downy windows, close
                    ('Antony and Cleopatra', v, ii, 318)

(5)   the enclosed lights, now canopied
    Under these windows, white and azure lac't
                    ('Cymbeline', II, ii, 22)

When these passages are read together, no doubt should remain. These windows belong to, but are not, eyes; they shut out light; they are blue when the eyes themselves are grey. Venus has, of course, the conventionally grey eyes of the mediaeval romance heroine (see l. 140), and the blue, as with Imogen, is that of the

204

Appendix I

veins. The meaning 'eyelid' was not doubted by Schmidt (in whose 'Shakespeare-Lexicon' (1902) all five passages are cited), by Onions ('Shakespeare Glossary' (1919), in which the first four are cited), or indeed by 'O.E.D.' (though here only (1) and (3) are cited); but in none of these is there a hint of any reason for the image. The commentators, with one exception, are still less helpful. In the Arden editions, (2) and (3) have no notes at all, and the others only scanty ones; and in the Variorum, (3) alone has a really adequate note. Take, for example, (1). C. K. Pooler (Arden edition) still considers 'eyes' as a possible meaning; H. E. Rollins (the most recent volume in the Variorum edition, 1938) gives an inconclusive summary of earlier opinions and has no cross-reference to the grey eyes of l. 140; in his note to that line he seems to accept the idea that there is not necessarily an inconsistency since *blue* and *grey* could signify the same colour. Rollins does, however, give the pertinacious reader a partial clue to the truth by adding a bare reference to B. Nicholson's note in 'Notes and Queries', 1876, pp. 462 f.

The Variorum note on (3) (H. H. Furness, Jr., 1908) is, however, sensible and illuminating, and here alone among editorial notes are quoted two other important and relevant lines in which *windows* is used literally to mean something solid:

(6) Shuts up his windows, locks fair daylight out
                ('Romeo and Juliet', I, i, 144)

(7) Pluck down forms, windows, anything
                ('Julius Cæsar', III, ii, 264; the con-
                text shows that the *windows* are to
                serve as weapons, shields or firewood)

This editor alone thinks it necessary to suggest some reason why a word usually connoting transparency should be used to suggest opaqueness. This is precisely the deficiency of the 'O.E.D.' on this point. The following is the only relevant information given under *windows*:

4. *fig.* Applied to the senses or organs of sense, esp. the eyes, regarded as inlets or outlets to or from the mind or soul (also *transf.* in Shaks., applied to the eyelids).

Appendix I

The transference from an inlet or outlet to that which blocks the inlet or outlet seems an odd one.

The other annotated editions of Shakespeare that I have consulted are still more reticent. The ordinary reader seems to have only two sources of helpful information: the Variorum note to 'Richard III', and, indirectly, the reference to 'Notes and Queries' in the Variorum note to 'Venus and Adonis'. This reference is incomplete and does not mention the first of the two notes, which is by Charles Sweet (pp. 364–5). There, at last, seventy-five years ago, we find somebody asking the pertinent question 'But why should *window* signify an eyelid?' The answer is simply that *window* could mean shutter. The only alternative (suggested by Vaughan, 'New Readings' (1888), cited in 'Richard III') is that of a window itself opaque, a window, for instance, of horn; this alternative is, I think, eliminated by the remark in Harrison's 'Description of England' (1577), II, ch. 12, that 'horne is now quite laid downe' because 'glasse is come to be so plentifull'.

The correct meaning, shutter, is first suggested by Charles Sweet in 1876. He bases his argument on the evidence of a fifteenth-century chronicle in which it is recorded that 'fenestres' were used as shields, and from the parallel with Latin in which *fenestra* could mean a shutter. The second note in 'Notes and Queries' collects all the relevant Shakespeare quotations and adds valuable further evidence from earlier dictionaries, of which these two, from Cotgrave, seem conclusive:

> Contre-fenestre, a wooden window (on the outside of a glasen one).
> ...Volet...a shut or woolen window to shut over a glasse one.

W. J. Lawrence (who had not seen the notes in 'Notes and Queries') wrongly takes *window* as meaning shutter only when applied to shops; but he is clear about the Shakespeare passages (1) and (5), and gives a new instance of the image of window-shutting used to imply absence of light from Marlowe ('Tamburlaine', Part I, v, 1). Professor F. P. Wilson has kindly pointed out

Appendix I

to me a passage in Dekker's 'Seven Deadlie Sinnes' in which the same sense is literally used (Percy reprints, 1922, p. 30). The 'O.E.D.' incidentally supplies further evidence under *shop window*. Taking '*to open* or *shut* (one's) *shop-windows*' simply as a figure of speech meaning 'to begin or close the business of the day', the editors quote from an ordinance of 1646–7:

the shopp windowes of all persons that trade in this Town whoe are not sworn burgesses shalbee forthwith shutt upp.

We know that the Elizabethans had shutters for houses as well as shops; yet the word *shutter* in this sense is not recorded before 1683, and the word *window-board* not before 1628 ('O.E.D.'). They called their shutters *shut windows* or *wooden windows*, or, more briefly, *windows*. Perhaps Shakespeare ought strictly to have distinguished between glass window and wooden window, but he counted on the context to make it clear which he meant. He did not expect to be so carelessly read as to have eyelids taken for eyes, nor, what is nearly as bad, to have a recurrent image so understood as to make nonsense.

KATHLEEN TILLOTSON

APPENDIX II
ADDITIONAL NOTES

P. 3. Chaucer's attitude towards his rascals is not unlike Pope's towards Belinda ('Rape of the Lock', ii, 17 f.) though there is a difference in degree:

> If to her share some Female Errors fall,
> Look on her Face, and you'll forget 'em all.

P. 6. With the remark that the Elizabethans required that function should show spirit, compare Coleridge on Shakespeare's wit ('Shakespearian Criticism', ed. T. Raysor, 1930, ii, 124): 'The wit of Shakespeare is, as it were, like the flourishing of a man's stick, when he is walking, in the full flow of animal spirits: it is a sort of exuberance of hilarity which disburdens, and it resembles a conductor, to distribute a portion of our gladness to the surrounding air.'

Pp. 46–7. Since we now know that 'The Alchemist' was acted by September 1610, the simplest explanation of Ananias's arithmetic would be that he counted the year as beginning in January.

Pp. 70 ff. The remarks on the orange sky need to be modified so as to allow for an earlier orange sky than Shelley's: one of the excerpts from 'The Prelude' that were published separately includes the line:

> The orange sky of evening died away.

('Influence of Natural Objects...', published 1809, l. 46: 'Prelude', 1850, i, 445.)

Pp. 71–2. Cowper, perhaps subconsciously, echoes Pope's passage in 'The Task':

> ...The sheep-fold here
> Pours out its fleecy tenants o'er the glebe.
> At first, progressive as a stream, they seek
> The middle field; but, scatter'd by degrees,
> Each to his choice, soon whiten all the land.

208

Appendix II

('Poems', ed. 1798, ii, 11.) One may note two things: (1) the accuracy of Pope's description is firmly attested when a poet who is acknowledged to be an accurate 'nature-poet' echoes it, and echoes not simply details but substance; and (2) there is none of the Virgilian connotation preserved in Cowper's *whiten*. Virgil was no longer the power he had been (see p. 73 above), and Cowper is found reading Pope without fully appreciating his intentions. It is a tribute to the complex force of Pope's *whitening* that it can stand even when the stronger half of its meaning is gone.

P. 96. Professor Pinto, writing in 'English' (vol. ii, no. 7, 1938, p. 48), pointed out that I had overlooked Dryden's development of the word *dissolved* in his 'State of Innocence':

> Seraph and cherub, careless of their charge,
> And wanton, in full ease now live at large:
> Unguarded leave the passes of the sky,
> And all dissolved in hallelujahs lie.

(Ker's text, Dryden's 'Essays', 1926, i, 188.) Pope learns many of his comic tricks from Dryden.

P. 102. The prayer in Book v of 'Paradise Lost' was accounted one of Milton's greatest passages: see 'The Critical Works of John Dennis', ed. E. N. Hooker, i (1939), 513.

P. 128. I find another gratuitous red right arm in Dennis's prose translation of Horace's 'fulminantis magna Jovis manus' by 'the Red Right Hand of Thundring Jove' ('The Critical Works of John Dennis', ed. E. N. Hooker, i (1939), 219). The phrase is used later by Mason ('Poems', ed. 1764, p. 159):

> ...Heav'n is just!
> And, when the measure of his crimes is full,
> Will bare its red right arm, and launce its lightnings.

P. 135. The total of the sum is not correct. I cannot check the figures from my copy of the magazine since the incendiary bombs recorded on p. 161 destroyed it. My notes suggest that the error is the New Lady's.

Appendix II

Pp. 154–5, 159. Professor R. M. Hewitt has pointed out to me Christina Rossetti's use of similar stanza forms: e.g., in 'One Sea-Side Grave':

> Cold as the cold Decembers,
> Past as the days that set,
> While only one remembers
> And all the rest forget,—
> But one remembers yet.

P. 164. The moral of 'The Parallelogram' recalls Mr Chadband's remarks on the 'human boy' in 'Bleak House', ch. xix.

Pp. 174–5. The original text of the passage quoted from the introduction to Plato employs two sizes of type, the verse being printed in the smaller. This distinction has not been preserved here.

INDEX

Index

Index

Index

Index